The Disorder of Law

The Disorder of Law

A Critique of Legal Theory

CHARLES SAMPFORD

Basil Blackwell

British Library Cataloguing in Publication Data

Sampford, C.J.G. (Charles J.G.)
The disorder of law: a critique of legal theory.
1. Law. Theories
I. Title
340'.1
ISBN 0–631–15495–7

Library of Congress Cataloging in Publication Data

Sampford, C.J.G. (Charles J.G.)
The disorder of law.

Bibliography: p.
Includes index.
1. Sociological jurisprudence.   2. Legal positivism.
I. Title.
K370.S26   1989   340'.115   88-19331
ISBN 0-631-15495-7

Typeset in 10 on 12 pt Times
by Graphicraft Typesetters Ltd., Hong Kong
Printed in Great Britain by T.J. Press (Padstow) Ltd., Padstow, Cornwall

Contents

List of Figures

Acknowledgements

The ideas behind this book and the theories contained therein have been intermittently developed over thirteen years and through undergraduate essays, a doctoral thesis and drafts of this book. In that time I have accumulated many debts to those who stimulated and criticized those ideas and who helped me bring these projects to completion.

In Melbourne University, Petro Georgiou and Mark Weinberg encouraged me to develop my thoughts and pursue them in Oxford.

In Oxford my supervisor was Colin Tapper, who provided unstinting help and encouragement. In addition to suggesting new areas of reading and stimulating and directing my thoughts, he read and made detailed and illuminating comments on the various drafts of the thesis. He was also generous in his hospitality and made me and my wife feel welcome from our first day in Oxford.

While writing the 'book of the thesis', William Twining provided invaluable help and support. He read and debated the thesis and indicated how to convey the same ideas (as modified by debate) to the wider audience of a book. At Blackwell, Tony Sweeney provided a much appreciated balance of perspective, encouragement, guidance and understanding.

I would also like to acknowledge the debts I owe to Denis Galligan, David Wood, David Nelken, Susan Dodds, Richard Tur, John Bell, Donna Greschner, Steve Perry, Norman O'Brien, Mark Duckworth, Jane O'Shannassey, Penelope Cottier and John Glover, who read all or part of the earlier drafts and for the helpful comments and criticisms they made. Naturally enough no responsibility for the residual faults can be laid at their doors but the faults would certainly have been more numerous without their help. Thanks are also due to Helen Doungas, Anne Graham, Dorothy Hatton, Julie Jago, Carol Lawry, Kerri Abbot and Elizabeth Dodson who did the word-processing.

I would also like to thank Christopher Paul Sampford, who showed tolerance and understanding beyond the call of a three-year-old's duty and accepted the suspension of paternal duties over the last year. I hope he will not be too disappointed that the result has a lot more words and far fewer pictures than his other books.

But the greatest thanks of all must go to my wife Jenny, who put her own career in neutral so that I could study in Oxford, provided me with the support and strength I needed to finish first the thesis and then this book and provided constant editorial assistance in the form of transcribing from my virtually illegible scrawl, proof-reading, and drawing most of the diagrams from my wobbly originals.

1

Introduction

1.1 The Orthodoxy of Law-as-System

The idea that law forms a system would at first sight appear to be universally endorsed by those who write about and practise law. Most speak easily of the *legal system* and would never query the conjunction of the two notions. Indeed it is common to use the terms 'law' and 'legal system' interchangeably. Yet this very readiness of use and interchangeability highlights the weakness rather than the strength of general beliefs about law's systematic quality. For most lawyers, and even some legal theorists, 'law' and 'legal system' are just synonymous terms that can be plugged into the same sentences and used in the same situations, perhaps in successive sentences to avoid monotony. For them, 'legal system' usually conveys no more meaning than 'law'. It is a collective term for an aggregation of legal phenomena, used without considering whether there is any systematic relationship between them.

The belief that the law forms a legal system is only given real content and prominence by jurisprudential theory. So, unsurprisingly, it is to jurisprudential theory that we must turn in order to find any theoretical justification for the widespread view of law as a system. Certainly such theoretical justifications are not in short supply. Most writers use the word 'system' freely and describe law in what can clearly be recognized as systematic terms (see chapter 1.3). Indeed most theories of law are centred on one of three kinds of legal system (source-based, content-based or function-based).

Although there is almost universal agreement that law forms a system, the kind of system it forms is hotly debated. Each major school of jurisprudential thought offers a different theory of legal system, usually incompatible with other theories, which are vigorously criticized by their proponents. Indeed there appears to be a shifting majority against each and every type of system. In denying, as this book does, that there is system in law, it is merely joining the majority against each individual theory. Its departure is that it does not attempt to provide *another* systematic theory to fill the gap left by the rejection of the others. It suggests instead that law is best seen as not systematic at all. It suggests that much of what is wrong with modern legal theory, and many of the problems it creates for legal theory, legal practice, legal sociology and legal language, lie in its overly systematic portrayal of law and that much could be rectified by its removal. Where most theorists see the key to understanding law in the legal system they outline, this book sees the key in the appreciation that law is not systematic in each of the ways it is usually systematized and that the various kinds of nonsystemness are interrelated.

Some might seek to rule this departure out of order because they regard system as a necessary or defining feature of law (e.g. Kelsen, 1970, p. 47; Raz, 1970, p. 1). For many theorists, legal or otherwise, the creation of systems is synonymous with 'theory' itself (e.g. Singh, 1986, p. 55; Eisenstadt and Halle, 1985, pp. 5, 17) and essential for any kind of explanation, understanding or interpretation. Even among the minority of jurisprudential writers who deny that there is system in law, this view is common and leads to the rejection of legal theory, or at least theory broad enough to encompass the law of a society. As the purpose of this book is to consider whether it is useful and appropriate to see law as systematic or not, systemness cannot be accepted as part of the definition of law, theory or explanation, and the question must be treated as at least arguable. Most theorists will accept this, following Kamenka's dictum that 'definitions are neither true nor false, but more or less useful' (Kamenka, 1966, p. 135). Certainly, if this book succeeds in describing something that would be clearly recognizable as law, it may reject, as not linguistically useful, a definition of law that regards law as necessarily systematic. If it succeeds in convincing the reader that no system can be found within what we regard as law, definitional insistence that law is systematic would lead to the conclusion that we have no law.

Nevertheless, though not accepting the proposition that law forms a system as definitionally true, this book does acknowledge, in Quinian vein, that for many legal theorists it is one of their most entrenched organizing beliefs about law (Quine and Ullian, 1970). As such it is very hard to dislodge, because there is a tendency, when confronted with difficulties (or 'recalcitrant experiences') to reject or modify other beliefs first, allowing almost indefinite retention of the belief that law is systematic. Thus it is common to find theorists taking more and more unrealistic positions ignoring or denying the existence of various aspects of law or trying to call them irrelevant in order to protect their beliefs in law's systemness. For example, Stone acknowledges the contrary evidence, notes what he calls the 'teeming disorder' and the 'hurly burly of legal norms' and goes on to say, 'that merely shows just what sort of order it is' (Stone, 1968, p. 26). Alternatively, theorists will engage in a partial retreat, accepting some of the criticisms as limiting the scope of the legal system and giving it somewhat fuzzy edges but still seeing the key to their theories in terms of a systematic account of some of the key elements of law.

Each of the systems theories can be seen as encapsulating one or more valuable insights about law, insights which explain their continued support. But because they hold just as strongly their belief in law's systemness, systems theorists are forced to abandon the insights of other theorists, and sometimes even to blur or distort their own. These other theorists reject the theories which ignore their pet insights. But because they adhere to the orthodoxy of law's systemness they create new theories of legal system incorporating their own insight; and, to protect it, they must in turn reject the insights that the other theorists have had. Perhaps it is not too great an exaggeration to say that the disagreements between systems theorists are due to their *common* belief in legal systems and that this leads them into arguments about what is sufficiently unimportant to be thrown out in order to protect that belief. Their common belief is their common error which leads to a common criticism – the distortion they must apply to law to make it fit the system.

In the face of such an entrenched belief, all that can be done is to make life as difficult as possible for the believer in legal systems by providing as many recalcitrant experiences as possible to dislodge that belief. This can be done by the multiple difficulties that legal system theories face, exploring some of the reasons for this, and providing a nonsystematic alternative theory of law to show that such theories are possible.

1.2 Outline of the Argument

Chapter 2 clarifies the enterprise of finding and challenging the systematic theories of law by looking at how legal theory constructs legal systems – as good answers to the questions *it* poses about the phenomena of law or from specific points of view. Chapters 3 to 5 examine the three kinds of system found in modern legal theory. Chapter 3 looks at the largely source-based systems found in legal positivism, chapter 4 at the predominantly content-based theory of Ronald Dworkin, and chapter 5 at the predominantly functionalist legal systems found among the more 'sociological' theories.

Each of these three 'critical' chapters will concentrate on one recent and prominent example of the relevant systems theory and compare it to other examples. The major theory will be chosen for its prominence and currency rather than its age or purity (features which may prevent it from being taken seriously). It will show how the insights of the theory are welded onto a distinctive theory of legal system and how the system conforms to the general characteristics outlined in chapter 2, and it will demonstrate that this systematization produces many of the greatest problems that those theories face. Some of these problems are 'internal' to the theory in the sense that they prevent the system working in its own terms or that they distort the theory's insights and reduce its value to those for whom it was created. Some of these problems are 'external' in the sense that they ignore the insights of other theorists, reduce its value to the 'social observer' (see chapter 2.4) trying to understand law, make assumptions that cannot be sustained or reduce the legal system to an insignificant portion of legal phenomena. Some of these problems are notorious, some are raised here for the first time. However, these 'critical' chapters emphasize their common source – the attempted systematization of nonsystematic phenomena.

Each critical chapter will consider how subsequent theory has responded to such problems – by partial retreat, by restricting the scope of the legal system or by reducing its systemness. It will be argued that, by adhering to 'system', later theorists have failed to avoid the key problems of the main theory. However, they still rely on the relevant theory of legal system to provide the essence of their theory of law. This process underlines the disordered nature of law both directly, by tacitly conceding that legal phenomena are less ordered, and indirectly, by showing that the trend is towards increasingly disordered theories of law and that the problems are still related to the retention of some of the systematic views of the theories from which they back away.

Chapter 6 considers some of the reasons for this general failure of legal systems theory. These include the infinite variability of individuals and the social relationships between them, the limited sharing and limited effectiveness of norms, the imperfect reasoning of human beings which, rather than immobilizing them into irrational actors, allows them to act in a world of insufficient reasons, the irreducible complexity of social life and the difficulty caused by conflicting attempts at more limited ordering. This chapter also considers and rejects some of the reasons for the continued popularity of systems theories. Finally, it argues that it is only by turning to theories of legal and social disorder that it is possible to explain the phenomena and fulfil the functions claimed for legal systems theory.

The centrepiece of such an argument, of course, lies in the provision of such an alternative. This alternative is necessary, first, to show that such theories are possible, thereby establishing competition between systematic and nonsystematic theories of law, and secondly, to show that, in such competitions, nonsystematic theories are preferable. Chapters 7 and 8 attempt to do this and hence show that theories of legal disorder are possible and preferable to theories of legal system. Quite naturally these chapters also present the author's preferred theory of legal disorder and the author's preferred alternative in the competition among potential nonsystematic theories.

Chapter 7 sees society inevitably lacking in system and chapter 8 sees law as part of such a society and describable in the same nonsystematic terms. This theory is built upon those features of law and society which made their systematization impossible. But it can also include the insights of the various systems theories without the distortions their systematization imposed on them and without the rejection of those insights that do not fit into the systems of others. Thus it can include both the insights which led to the construction of legal systems theories and the insights which led to their destruction – able to coexist again after the excision of the requirement that law be systematic. In brief outline the theory sees both law and society as composed of almost infinitely variable individuals and the consequently variable relationships between them. It depicts law as part of a society that is composed of individuals and the social relations between them. Those social relations include relations of power (which include 'authority'), unintended effects and value–effects (which include phenomena some would call 'norms'). Institutions are formed from the unpatterned sets of relations found between those in closer, more frequent or more intense interaction with each other than with outsiders. The nature of these social relations and the way they interact and merge is such that they generate disordered conflict within and between institutions. This explains why those sets of relations are unpatterned and why theories that insist on finding either intra- or inter-institutional structures among those relations are rejected in chapter 6. This combination of conflict within and conflict between institutions, in which the former mutes the latter, also explains why disorder is compatible with relative social peace. Law is depicted as an important part of this scene, comprising some of the institutions which are integral and subject to that conflict. Indeed much of the conflict is channelled through legal institutions.

Chapter 9 will consider some of the possible implications such a nonsystematic theory of law would have for those who have close contact with legal institutions – the profession, the judiciary, academics and citizens.

1.3 Why the Question is Important

Understanding anything with which we come in contact is always worthwhile to some degree, especially when that contact is as intense and continuous as that with law. It helps to satisfy our natural curiosity about our environment, and to predict the law's effects on us. But it is doubly important because our contact with the law is not merely passive – we interact with it in that we are not only affected by law but seek actively to change or preserve it. If our contact were merely passive then some reliable method of predicting its 'behaviour' would be sufficient, though not as satisfying as a theory which explained why it so behaved. But to alter or preserve something successfully it is much more important to understand its nature, what sort of beast it is and how it works. Our approach to both changing and defending law as a whole will be affected by whether we regard law as systematic or not. Whether one seeks to preserve, alter or destroy law, the orthodox view that law forms a system is comforting. Many who might be called 'conservatives' believe there is a 'legal system' which protects in a co-ordinated way, those things that they most value in a community. Many 'radicals' largely agree, dissenting only on what values really are protected or whether the values protected should be endorsed. They take comfort from seeing one enemy to strike at, one entity to replace. As Wallace puts it, both agree that violation of any law 'starts to unravel an intricate functional fabric' (1978). This is the fear of the one and the hope of the other. Somewhere in between is the liberal reformer, who hopes that, by capturing the centre of the system, he can modify the goals or values which it furthers or protects. But if there is no legal 'system', there is cold comfort for all. For the conservative, if law is not systematic, it may not comprehensively embody any values, his or others'. The hope of the radical, that pulling the right string will unravel the intricate functional fabric, is dashed. He must instead begin the laborious task of changing society piece by piece. The hope of the liberal, to modify the system piecemeal by controlling or influencing the centre, is seen to be inadequate because law is not so much the centre as an important set of institutions in the mêlée. This book argues that the intractability of our society and its law to either reform or revolution is precisely due to its lack of systematic organization, so that when the revolutionary strikes or the reformer moves there is no one system to attack, no one key institution to change. Lack of change is the result of social and legal *dis*order producing social and legal inertia rather than, as is more usually supposed, social and legal order providing social and legal stability. Awareness of this may necessitate fundamentally different strategy and tactics for all participants in the political fray.

Although few of us spend our time grappling with problems of socio-legal change, most of our activities touch upon, and are touched by, law. Legal theorists are particularly concerned with the activities of judging, legislating, advising and advocacy. In addition, the activities of bureaucrats, police, criminals and business executives are particularly affected by parts of the law. But most are usually concerned with a small part of the law – lawyers specialize, criminals specialize, executives are affected by corporate and consumer law, police with the criminal law, bureaucrats with the act(s) they administer. Even judges specialize, sitting in divisions and finding certain cases constitutionally, statutorily or practically barred from their jurisdiction. At any one time, they are usually concerned with even narrower areas of law in the cases they argue and laws they break, skirt, enforce and interpret respectively. In dealing with these limited areas of law, most have learned particular ways of doing their jobs, which include the methods for dealing with (and, to some extent, the attitudes towards) the law as it touches them. This allows them to do their jobs 'unperturbed by doubts and disputations' about law and whether it is systematically organized (Stone, 1968, p. 162). Yet an appreciation of law in general, and especially whether law is systematic, and therefore whether their activities are a part of a larger system, is important. It can influence their attitudes to law, the way it affects them and the way they try to affect or use it. Those at the centre of the previously imagined system, legislators and judges, may have to reconsider their sense of self-importance and realize that further action beyond mere decision-making is necessary to transform their pronouncements into law. Those at the periphery may realize their effectively greater autonomy and with it their increased opportunities (and, perhaps, responsibility?). Judges may see themselves making individual decisions rather than welding a logical masterpiece. Lawyers may delve more confidently into the labyrinth, looking for those parts of the legal morass that can help their clients. Citizens will see the law as neither an ass nor a liberal pearl but as the actions of many individual officials, and concern themselves with those actions that affect them.

Thus the question of whether law is systematic is important not only so that we can understand and appreciate an important human phenomenon, but also in the practice of activities that affect and are affected by law.

PART I

Three Kinds of Legal System

2
Law, Legal Theory and Legal System

2.1 Introduction

As the previous chapter outlined, this book seeks to challenge the orthodox view that law is, in some or other sense, a system and to claim that
much that is wrong with contemporary legal theory is due to its assumptions of system and could be cured by the removal of that assumption.
However, before setting out to attack current legal theory and create an
alternative, some understanding of the use of terms such as 'law', 'legal
theory' and 'system' is necessary.

2.2. Law and Legal Theory

The difficulties with the word 'law' are hardly new to jurisprudence. Law
encompasses many activities and aspects of social life. Its use reflects
this, cropping up in a fascinating variety of 'language-games' (a Wittgen-
steinian concept which places the use of words in the context of human
interaction and social life in general: a 'language-game' involves the use
of a word and the activities by the speaker and others that accompany
it). In each of these, 'law' is a descriptive word used to refer to some
perceived feature or features of social life in which the language-game
occurs. (These features may involve people, objects, actions, ideas in the
social environment of the language-game participants.) Such language-
games range from a child asking her father why he stopped at the traffic
light and being told that it is 'the law', to language-games played out in
legislative chambers, police stations, solicitors' offices, courts and seminar
rooms. The features that are picked out by its use vary correspondingly –
no one feature or set of features will always be present. Indeed a feature
may seem central in one use yet its opposite central in another (sanctions
may be central to the use of the word 'law' among criminals yet freely

entered agreements may be central in treaty-based international law). No particular set of features will be jointly sufficient but the word frequently will be used where several features are present. Thus there will be a good deal of continuity, a continuity which explains our preparedness to use the same word. Gasking used the term 'cluster concepts' for such words (1960) and Wittgenstein has coined the term 'family likeness' to capture the sense in which the uses of such words are similar (1958, p. 23). A long, but still not exhaustive, list of features associated with law in its many uses might be: written; socially relevant; created by a public body; backed by coercion; enforced by courts and police; possessing moral force; obeyed or used by most of the people most of the time; expressible in the form of a rule; in accord with the content of natural law and the values of members of the society that spawned it; general, promulgated, non-retroactive, clear, non-contradictory, not requiring impossible action and infrequently changed. 'Law', as used in different language-games, will refer to some (rarely, if ever, all) of these features and the language-game that involves *argument* over the use of the word will be most prevalent where someone is trying to use 'law' to refer to only a small number of them.

Thus in one sense 'law' is a set of the features of social life which in various combinations are called 'law' by members of the society in question. For other societies the list of features is added to and subtracted from so that the uses of the word law *between* societies bear the same family likeness as the uses of the word *within* societies.

Jurisprudence (or 'legal philosophy' or 'legal theory') is that subject which poses fundamental and (preferably?) intractable questions about these features of social life we call law, questions such as: What is law? What is the nature of legal rules? How do judges decide cases? Is there a generalized obligation to obey the law? What is justice? How is law related to broader social phenomena such as culture, ideology, power and economic activity? Do different kinds of society have different kinds of law? Could there be a society without law? Among these, the most fundamental, persistent and intractable is the question 'What is law?' However, such questions are not asked in a vacuum. Such questions are always asked for some purpose, by or on behalf of such person, from a particular point of view.

As noted previously, each language-game picks out only some of the features that law exhibits. This is because in each language-game, and in the more general activity of which that language-game forms a part, only certain features of the law come into contact with, and are significant for, the word-user. Indeed, it is this activity, in which the theorist or his audience is engaged, that, being touched by law, leads to and gives practical impetus to a desire to understand law and ask questions about it.

The answer to the question 'What is law?' becomes a set of features of social life used to describe law that is claimed to be most useful to someone in the performance of a certain activity. The question that this thesis poses about whether or not law is systematic becomes: 'Is it more helpful to a person in the pursuit of that activity to see the elements of law so picked out as, in some sense, systematically ordered?' The contention of this book becomes that much of what is wrong with legal theory is that too many of its answers see law as a system and that the solution lies in a nonsystematic theory of legal disorder.

But before we can commence arguing for that contention we must first consider what might be meant by 'system' and the points of view from which the contention might be made.

2.3 System

Despite the orthodoxy of the view that law forms a system, what is meant by 'system' in the various theories is not always either clear or uniform. Most theorists are reasonably certain about the theory they are advocating and that what they are advocating constitutes a system. But they rarely indicate which of their theoretical claims are in their view necessary to establish law's systematic quality and which claims go further to provide a more detailed description or fulfil other purposes. The general assumption of system means that effort is directed to telling us what *sort* of a system law is claimed to be rather than what claims would be necessary to establish any kind of system at all.

Under these circumstances it is useful to consider general views about the nature of systems found in definitions, explications and ideal types propounded in 'general systems theory'. This is a body of theoretical and philosophical thought which attempts to discover what is common to the use of the term 'system' in the many and varied disciplines in which it is found. Its adherents want to find common features in the river systems of geography, the digestive systems of mammalian biology, the solar systems of astrophysics, the atomic systems of nuclear physics, the economic and political systems of the social sciences, the weapons systems of modern war and, especially, the computer systems of the new technologies and the production and management systems of large companies (e.g. Laszlo, 1972; Emery, 1981). In so doing they hope to find out what it is about those systems that is 'systematic'. Having done so, systems theory hopes to hone the concept, and to develop a common vocabulary and expository technique so that systems thinking can be more fruitfully used in existing areas and made useful for new ones. Some hope to go further to establish a new 'paradigm' for all knowledge (von Bertallanfy, 1972). Whatever its ambitions, general systems theory is based on belief that certain properties are common to many or all of the systems found in the real world. They also believe that those common properties and the most useful concept of system can best be created free from the biases and distortions that may be found in systems concepts developed in relation to particular disciplines.

The reason for delving into general systems theory is to provide a focus for our consideration of various theories of legal system. It is not the purpose of this section to adopt a restrictive definition of 'system'. There is no point in idle controversy over whether a theorist has wrongly appropriated the term 'system' to his conception of organization. Even if such debates could be won, the consequence of defeat for the theorist would mean that his conception would merely have to be given a new name. Such statements will be challenged on the basis not of the terms used in describing law as a system, but of how closely the description corresponds with reality, and how useful such a statement is in understanding law.

Most conceptions of system found in general systems theory display a core of features common to most uses of the word. These are highlighted in Dewey's explication of the term and echoed in other discussions of systems in general. 'The term system is employed to designate a whole from the standpoint of the methodic connection and arrangements of its constituent members' (1901). Here Dewey sees a system as a *whole*, whose wholeness is peculiarly tied to the *interrelations* between its parts. 'It differs from such terms as aggregate, collection and inventory, in expressly conveying the way inherent bonds bind together ... the parts of the whole [and] it differs from such terms as organism, totality and whole in expressly connoting that the parts are interdependent.' The same point is made by Angell, who speaks of the 'parts of a social system fitting together to form a whole' (Angell, 1968), and Johnson, for whom a system is 'a group of interdependent variables which are arranged to form a whole' (1966, p. 40; see also Laszlo, 1972, p. 36).

We see then that the system requires a *wholeness* factor, something which allows us to see the system as a unity (or 'entity': Buckley, 1967, p. 41). Thus a river system may be seen as a whole because it drains a certain area of land, a digestive system is a whole because it performs the function after which it is named, and the little system within an atom is a whole because it is a unit which combines with other similar units to form molecules. But it must also have *parts* or *elements*, for a system comprising an undivided whole would be unintelligible and a system without any components would be redundant (Angyal, 1981, p. 31; Jordan, 1981, p. 24). These elements must have some independent existence, or at least some way of being considered independently. Otherwise they would not constitute elements but merely parts of something else. One could not consider a quarter of a helium nucleus as part of a sub-atomic system but one could when it is understood as a proton or neutron.

These elements must be related to each other in some way – otherwise they would be, as Dewey puts it, a mere 'aggregate, collection or inventory' (1901). The same point is implicit in Emery and Trist's definition of a system as a set of *interrelated* elements (1981, p. 322) and in Laszlo's view that what you add to the elements to get a whole is the ordered relations between them (1972, p. 36). For example, the elements of a river or digestive system are related in the way their contents and the elements of our sub-atomic system are related by electromagnetism and sub-nuclear forces. When Dewey requires that the inherent bonds be 'orderly' and Laszlo describes the above-mentioned addition as 'ordered relations' they are referring to a final requirement of a system on which almost all system theorists insist – *structure* (Laszlo, 1972, p. 101; Buckley, 1967, ch. 2; Selznick, 1981, p. 302; Angyal, 1981, p. 27). This is found in the way the rivers of a river system all join together to flow into the sea at a specific point. It is found in the essentially linear pathway of food remains through the organs of a digestive system and it is found in the way sub-atomic particles of the atomic system are structured into a nucleus and surrounding electron clouds.

Two ideas are involved in this requirement of structure. Firstly the relations must form a *network* by which every element is ultimately linked directly or indirectly to every other (Ackoff and Emery, 1981, p. 30; Feiblemann and Friend, 1981, p. 42). The second is that the network must conform to some pattern or order (Laszlo, 1972, p. 101), a merely random set of interlocking relationships being insufficient to provide structure for a system. Compare the marks on ice left by a few independent novice skaters and those left by a champion figure-skater. Both involve a network of lines which all link up, but only the latter has the pattern to be structured. Others express this second idea as a requirement that a system's relations be 'organized' (Laszlo, 1972, p. 42; Fitzgerald, 1975). This conveys the same notion, some pattern, order or sense that has been brought to what would otherwise be a random formless set of relations. If it goes further it does so in connoting that the pattern or order has been purposively constructed or is the kind that might have resulted from such purposive construction. However, such connotations are not required by the concept of structure adopted here. Note that sometimes a third idea is implied in structures – that of 'stability' in the network of relationships. However, there are many systems in which this stability appears to be lacking. Indeed in several the system itself supposedly changes those relations in response to the environment. Consequently many writers do not mention stability (e.g. Dewey, 1901) and many writers reject it as a requirement of system (e.g. Laszlo, 1972, p. 108). It is not required here. Indeed it is a major claim of this book that 'stability' is better accounted for by a nonsystematic theory than by a systematic one.

Naturally enough, other definitions of 'system' include many other features. For an extreme example, von Bertallanfy (1972) includes 'hierarchic structure, teleology, differentiation, steady state character and goal directness'. Others restrict the types of wholes, structures and especially relations that can be found in systems. Such definitions restrict their usefulness as a general concept of system for different applications. They are better seen as partial descriptions of the type of system the writers have in mind for their own application. If the reader should insist on such a full-blown definition of system it merely provides more hurdles for the systems theorists to clear and makes it easier for the author to contend that they have failed to do so.

So here we have a general view of systems and their characteristics. They are *wholes*, they have *elements* and those elements have *relations* which form a *structure*.

This view of system is the one adopted here. As we have seen, this view accords with most general definitions of 'system'. It is consistent with, though rather more specific than, general conceptions of legal system (Cotterrell, 1984, p. 74; Jenkins, 1980, p. 20). More importantly, we will find that it is echoed in almost all the theorists considered in the next three chapters. Their descriptions of legal systems explicitly or implicitly include reference to these features and frequently highlight their importance.

Source-based systems have legal rules or norms for elements. These are related by relations of authority or validity to higher rules. These relations are classically formed into a pyramidal and hierarchical structure with one ultimate rule, 'basic norm' or 'legal science fiat' at the top. The wholeness factor is provided by the structure itself and by its function of providing the authoritative basis for all law in a community.

Content systems may also have rules or norms as elements, although the most prominent content theorist gives a special place to principles and decisions. The relations are relations of justification. A lower rule is justified by a higher principle, in that the lower is derived from or at least consistent with the higher, rather than on the positivist basis that it is authorized. The structure is more complex, a 'truncated pyramid lattice', in which there are several levels of principles each of which collectively justifies the level of rules or principles below. The wholeness factor is found in the coherence and consistency of the principles and its ability to provide answers (even a 'single right answer') to legal questions. In

Dworkin the wholeness factor is found in the role the system plays as a moral theory that publicly justifies the traditional role of an ideal judge.

Functionalist systems have actions or roles (expected or required actions) as elements. The relations are the social relations between actors by which the action of one causes, influences or is expected to lead to the action of others. The structure is provided by the way these relations link individual actors or roles into institutions which perform particular functions and by the way the joint performance of these functions by those institutions allows law to perform its overall function. Wholeness is provided throughout by the functions performed.

For most theories this general conception acts as a focus for considering their claimed systematic qualities. It indicates what we should be looking for (indeed, without outside criteria we would not know which part of a theory, which claimed that law was systematic, we should look at). It allows a uniform type of exposition. Each theory can be expounded in a form which tells us what that theory has to say about the type of system law is claimed to be. By expounding the theory in this form we are getting an answer to our question – what justification can be found in jurisprudential theory for seeing law as a legal system? This allows us to discuss theories where the theorist has not clearly outlined just what it is about his theory of law that is systematic. It also means that, even where the theorists themselves are not primarily concerned with describing law in systematic terms, their theories can still help us to answer our question. Once they are expounded in this form they can squarely be seen as offering what are, in the terms of this book, systematic theories of law. They are theories which provide content and substance to the general supposition that law forms a system, and hence theories which need to be considered in determining whether law can usefully be seen as systematic.

Thus it is not necessary that the theorists themselves emphasize law's systematic character or that its systematic character is important for them, or even that they perceive their own theories in systematic terms. It is sufficient that their theories can be interpreted as systematic theories and/or that they contain the ingredients for constructing systematic theories which provide potential answers to our question.[1]

Where theorists such as Dworkin switch from systematic to non-systematic explanations, this book, of course, commends the latter and criticizes the former. Supporters of those theories may suggest that I am over-emphasizing the systematic aspects in the theories considered. They could say that this book offers an overly systematic reading of other theorists in order to make room for its own theory. In fact readers are encouraged to adopt nonsystematic readings of other theories – the overall aim of the critical chapters is to seek out possible systems theories and show their failings. Where a theorist can be read in one of two ways, it will be argued that the systematic reading weakens the theory and pre-judices its insights; a nonsystematic reading preserves more and can play a part in building up a nonsystematic theory of law. Such nonsystematic theories of law could form a part of my own theory or could themselves be built into rival theories of legal disorder, a rivalry which I argue should be the basis of legal theory. Such a nonsystematic theory could be developed itself into a full-blown nonsystematic theory of law, again adding to the rivalry.

The final and most important advantage of this method of exposition is that it facilitates comparison between the different systems theories on offer. We can compare the types of elements, relations, structures and wholeness they contain. Indeed we shall see how these variations account for many of the differences between the legal systems theories considered. We can also see some of the ways a theory may fail in that it may be difficult to establish the existence of the postulated elements, relations, etc., in the law of modern western nations. Indeed, some of the variations between the theories can be explained on the basis that one school criticizes the usefulness of the type of elements, relations, etc., postulated by another school and substitutes another. A simple example would be the realists' criticism of formalist elements (rules) which led them to substitute different elements (actions, predictions, psychological states, etc.) in their own theories.

Although most writers who use the term 'legal system' include these four features in their theory, some require less of a system. Luckily such cases are rare among legal theorists (apart from those who merely use the term 'legal system' as a synonym for 'law', conveying no extra meaning). More often, a description is proposed that includes all four features but on closer inspection we can only find three or less in law. In such cases the view of system offered here acts as a yardstick, not to rule out the weaker system, but to question whether, if law conforms to this weaker system, it is descriptively useful to call such law a system or to highlight its lack of systematic qualities by not so calling it. Even if the reader does accept a lesser view of system, discussing the proposed system in terms of these four features has at least helped illuminate the *kind* of system law is said to be.

Note on the Use of the Word 'Systematic'

In this book the adjective 'systematic' is merely used as a shorthand to indicate that what it refers to can be described in terms of a system. A systematic theory is one that attempts such a description. The only issue which needs to be clarified is that the word 'systematic' refers to a property of the thing described rather than a common property of its constituent parts. This is like saying that a 'large' regiment is taken to mean a regiment with many men (a property of the regiment) rather than one formed from big men (a property of the elements of the regiment). Thus, when this book questions whether law is best seen as 'systematic', it is merely restating the query raised in chapter 1.1 – i.e. is there an adequate theory of law which, by describing law in terms of a legal system, justifies the widespread tendency to equate the two?

2.4 Point of View

There remains the question of the 'point of view' (Hart, 1961) or 'standpoint' (Twining and Miers, 1982) from which law's systematic quality is to be debated. As Twining emphasizes, the answers to many questions, indeed the point of the questions themselves, can depend on the spatiotemporal position, the activity and often the interests and values of the questioner. For each theory discussed, the point of view adopted by the relevant theorist(s) will be elaborated. Each theory will be found to suffer severe problems from that chosen point of view. However, the theories will primarily be discussed from the standpoint of a 'social observer', someone involved in the activity of describing and understanding law as a part of society. This corresponds to a type of 'external' point of view noted, but passed over, by Hart (1961, p. 86). This views the behaviour of the people engaged in the many activities involved in, and touched by, law. It takes note of the external manifestations of their behaviour as well as their internal attitudes towards it. These attitudes are not adopted by the social observer – that would be to take Hart's internal point of view. Nor is law described as it appears to someone who has those attitudes – the 'detached' internal point of view of Harris and Raz (and, for the most part, Hart). These attitudes are merely regarded as relevant psychological facts, important in explaining and predicting behaviour, but with no special place in its description.

This is a departure from the strong jurisprudential tradition of adopting a purely 'legal' point of view, delimited by a distinctive 'legal' activity, in order to describe or understand law. There are several reasons for this departure. First, there are so many activities within law – those of judges, barristers, policemen, bureaucrats, legislators, etc. This is not merely an idle catalogue of legal specialties. These activities lead participants into contact with different areas of law (chapter 1.3), and to label different aspects of law 'significant' – thereby generating different conceptions of law. The judge comes in contact only with certain areas of the law and only when there is a dispute or an alleged breach of a criminal provision.

The judge's activity might be described as applying the law to the resolution of disputes that come before him, drawing for his decision on the legal materials presented. To him law might appear as a large number of binding norms of varying strength. A barrister's contact with the law is limited by the sort of practice he has and the sort of disputes in which those who can afford his fee are involved. His own activity could be described as finding, formulating and enunciating arguments advantageous to his clients' interest which can be put in a court of law. For him, the law might be seen as a storehouse of debating points, or as the personnel before whom he argues them. The solicitor's contact with law is limited by similar factors. The activity of most solicitors deals not with disputes, but with the arrangement of clients' affairs. For a solicitor, the law may be seen as certain words and officials and his activity as taking advantage of the opportunities provided (e.g. in contracts and companies), and avoiding the pitfalls (e.g. liability to tax) associated with those words and officials. One could continue, but the message is clear. These legal activities lead their participants into contact with different areas of the law and to have different views of it – sufficiently different to qualify as the basis for different points of view.

These several activities within law mean that law cannot be adequately understood from the point of view of any one of them. Just as the attitudes of judges are important in comprehending the activity of judging, so the attitudes of barristers are important in understanding the activity of the Bar. Thus to understand law which includes both activities and the interaction between them, it is not sufficient to adopt the attitudes of either. As we shall see in chapter 8, interaction between those with different points of view is one of the hallmarks of law. No less is required by law's claim to govern all. This 'asymmetric' interaction cannot possibly be understood adequately from either point of view – only a social observer can do that.

Not only are there many activities within law, but those activities are controversial. There are rival descriptions of them adopted and used by various participants on the basis of their varying interests and values.

Some would describe a solicitor's activity as advising clients on the law rather than helping them around it. This dispute is so fundamental as to amount to a quite different point of view with a different image of law. The former description of a solicitor's activity and point of view sees law as something having normative force, the latter almost the opposite – seeing law as something without value but rather an obstacle to be avoided if possible in the pursuit of the client's ends.

The nature of judicial activity is particularly controversial. Some theorists see judges choosing the decision they personally feel to be the best among those arguable under existing precedent; others see judges choosing the decision that is entailed by the 'best' justification of past decisions. The former involves a view of law as a partly incomplete and inconsistent mass of sources, the latter as something amenable to rational reconstruction.

So even if we were to choose one of the above activities as *the* legal one, we would still be unable to answer questions about law until we had entered and resolved for ourselves the argument over the correct description of that activity, the appropriate goals for that activity and hence what parts of law are relevant and significant in our descriptions of it. It is contended that theorists can only resolve this question about the appropriate description of an activity within law by having fixed in their minds a clear image of *law*, the very thing the adoption of the legal point of view was designed to provide. Thus the task of picturing law and concluding whether it is systematic or not must be regarded as logically prior to the adoption of a legal point of view.

Indeed, the social observer's point of view is important for all legal theories, even those theories which take more limited viewpoints. We will find and frequently criticize the assumptions, conclusions or theories from the social observer's point of view. These are necessary to establish the place, significance or the activity whose point of view is taken. Thus even vigorous theories self-consciously constructed from a 'legal scientist's point of view' claim that 'legal science' is part of the shared understanding of judges and other lawyers (Harris, 1979). Without that or some similar claim, the whole theory would be rather pointless.

The social observer's point of view is important for law students. Practising law takes many forms. Because of the diversity of careers open to lawyers, the development by students of a broad view of law as a part of society rather than merely a professional speciality is surely important. If they are not going to take one of the professional careers available to them, such a viewpoint may help them understand what law is and therefore what it is that they are skilled in, what their skills in fact *are* and how those skills may be put to use outside law. If, like most, they are going to enter one of the branches of the profession, they will benefit from such a view by understanding the institution they are entering and have a conception of its place within society and the place that their sort of job has within it. Furthermore, by putting the activity they are about to pursue in a social context, they may not only better be able to choose which branch of the law to enter but much more importantly be able to resolve for themselves the disputes about the nature and goals of their activities. By having an appreciation of law from this social-observer point of view, they are able to form their own points of view *as* barristers, solicitors, etc. Thus, taking the social-observer standpoint is not so much an alternative to taking that of a barrister or solicitor, but an essential prerequisite for the formation of such a viewpoint. Practising lawyers have this same need to reappraise their view of law occasionally by taking a social-observer point of view to reappraise law. Lecturers have a special reason for adopting this approach from time to time – if their students are to learn it, they will have to teach it.

There are two further reasons for both lawyers and law students to adopt, for a time, just such a point of view. First, by seeing their own activity in a broader social context, they will suffer less from the insularity and ignorance of the consequences of their actions – faults for which the profession is so often criticized. Secondly, a point of view which gives lawyers an understanding of the law as part of society will provide them with a better chance of understanding and interpreting legal change, thereby appreciating the trend and even foreseeing individual changes in specific legal rules.

Of course, once students, practitioners, judges, academics, etc., have formed their view of law from a social observer's point of view, they may choose to construct theories about how they should go about their activities and create internal, participant points of view. Some indication of what such theories would be like is given in the final chapter.

This discussion of the social observer's point of view has so far avoided the value element of standpoint. Social-observer points of view are not exceptions, they are affected by their occupants' values. Certainly, the values of this writer will probably differ from those of other legal academics and have an effect on what is said from the writer's social-observer point of view. However, the conclusions reached from a social-observer standpoint informed by one set of values include many that would be reached by such a point of view informed by other values. In Twining's terms, they are more 'transferable' (Twining and Miers, 1982). Indeed the transferability of some of the conclusions reached in chapters 7 and 8 have led some to puzzle over whether it is extreme left, extreme right or somewhere in between. As already indicated, the view of law as non-systematic would lead conservatives, liberals and radicals to change their activity (although in different ways). This should not surprise. A statement that there has been a coup may be thoroughly value-laden in cause, content, delivery and implication. But the message is transferable in the sense that it can be adopted by and acted upon by fascists or democrats.

A statement that the elephants are coming may be similarly value-laden but is equally transferable to conservationists, hikers, hunters and film crews. This book's message may be less urgent but its consequences are as profound for the way we think about, and act towards, law.

Notes

1 This is similar to the interpretive technique used by Dworkin to derive answers
to his question 'How should judges decide disputes?' from theories which did
not address the question. However, it is perhaps less cavalier than Dworkin's
approach because the systematic character of the theories considered is important to, and is emphasized by, most of the theorists themselves. This fact is
partly indicated by their frequent use of the term and, more importantly, by the
large proportion of their writings that can be encompassed within their theories
as recast in terms of the elements, relations, structure and wholeness of what is
or becomes 'their' system.

3

Positivist Theories of Legal System

3.1 Legal Positivism

Legal positivism provides the natural starting point for discussing theories of legal system. Not only do those who call themselves 'positivists' use the term 'system' more liberally than most other theorists, but law's systematic character is, for many of them, the most central feature of their image of law. Unsurprisingly, they have some of the most precisely conceived images of legal system in jurisprudence.

The same precision cannot be found in defining positivism itself. It was born out of natural law theories by emphasizing the role of human institutions in determining the law. As this emphasis grew, in line with the actual increase in power of those institutions, positivists started to regard themselves as distinct from the natural lawyers in that they saw law as a human and social phenomenon rather than a divine, metaphysical or natural one. This characteristic has endured from Bentham, who insisted that law was the command of a political sovereign (rather than God, nature or reason), to Raz, whose 'social thesis' considers the identification of law a 'matter of social fact' (1979, p. 37).

The social facts earlier positivists had in mind were activities of certain legislative institutions which were taken to be the sole sources of law and whose output constituted the law. Later positivists extended the range of social facts that could be sources, using adjudicative institutions as a yardstick of the source and content of law. Other 'social facts' were all but excluded. As new theories suggested that law was a function of social practices (Ehrlich), interests (Jhering, Pound, Stone), productive forces (Marx) and judicial psychology (Frank, Olivecrona), these social facts were added to the list of exclusions. Kelsen's (1970) list of exclusions was more comprehensive than those found in most insurance contracts. He excluded all that psychology, sociology, ethics and political theory had to offer. But virtually all modern positivists, and certainly those considered here, construct their theories of law from a very small number of social facts. This has an important consequence for the type of system the positivists see in law. It is a self-contained system in which the elements, relations and structure are described independently of outside social forces. Its systemness is *internal* rather than derived from its position in, and relation to, the outside world (cf. sociological systems, chapter 5.2).

Positivist systems share other characteristics. The *elements* now tend to be rules or norms rather than actions or events. In early theories they were the commands of a real person, later they became institutionalized, depersonalized, 'depsychologized' and finally were not described as commands at all. But the rules, norms and reasons that took their place retained some of the characteristics of a command in being verbal and in having a certain 'bindingness', the nature of which is a continuing puzzle to which positivists offer a variety of solutions.

The *relations* between the elements are usually held to be 'legal' rather than 'causal'. They are related either by the meaning of the words in the norms or rules, or by the authority one confers on another. The *structures* have tended to be pyramidal with one key norm or rule at the top linked to other rules. *Wholeness* is usually provided either by that structure or by the key norm or rule itself.

Positivist systems are built on insights about the importance of sources and the part they play in lawyers' (practical) reasons and the largely content-independent form of those reasons, the importance of rules and, especially in Hart, the variety of rules (including the fascinating concept of 'social rules') and the insights into law gained from comparing it to a simpler imagined past.

This chapter will deal most extensively with Hart's theory. His is not the most systematic positivist theory but, as the most influential modern positivist, his is the one that most commands attention and requires rebuttal. We will see that many of the major problems, whether internal to the theory or external to the social observer, arise from the over-systematization of the above-mentioned insights and the ignoring of other theorists' insights. We will consider three lines of retreat taken, whether consciously or otherwise, by Raz, Harris and MacCormick/Weinberger. Raz makes the system more complicated by doing away with its simple hierarchical structure. MacCormick downplays the importance of apex rules and concentrates on the ontological status of lower-level rules. Harris's neo-Kelsenian theory retreats into a restrictively defined point of view of a 'legal scientist' (Harris's theory is examined in preference to Kelsen's because, with Harris's update, it makes a more difficult target and it shows that a return to Kelsenian purity does not solve the problems of Hart's positivism). These retreats try to deal with some of the problems with Hart's theory, but do not escape the central problems caused by the attempt systematically to structure legal rules according to their source. Some of the retreats involve significant improvements in the positivist insights (including Raz's view of the normative elements of his system as 'practical reasons') but at the cost of making them less systematizable. Other retreats are very specifically and self-consciously in the direction of more limited systems (Harris) or less systematic ones (Raz). But the fact that this gives them relatively greater plausibility points clearly to the conclusion which this chapter reaches – that although lawyers use statements of legal rules and source-based reasoning, these rules, sources and reasons are not systematically ordered, and it is misleading to see them as such.

3.2 Hart's Theory

For Hart, 'the union of primary and secondary rules is at the centre of a legal system' (1961, p. 96). Primary rules are rules that impose duties on human beings to act or not to act. They are found in all forms of law, but by themselves they do not constitute a system, merely 'primitive law'. Legal systems need the addition of secondary rules. The exact distinction between the two types of rules is uncertain, as Hart offers several distinctions (MacCormick, 1981, p. 103). Nevertheless, secondary rules can all be said to be 'rules about rules' and specifically include three identifiable types: rules that establish exactly which rules are valid (rules of *recognition*), how and by whom they can be changed (rules of *change*) and how and by whom they can be enforced (rules of *adjudication*). Hart sees the addition of these rules as remedying certain 'defects' in primitive law – rules of recognition reduce uncertainty, rules of change make laws less rigid and rules of adjudication provide more efficient and centralized enforcement. But they also turn what would otherwise be a set of rules into a system by providing for *relations* between secondary rules and the primary rules they regulate (e.g. between the rule of recognition and the rules 'recognized'). The rules of recognition also enable a hierarchical *structure* to be formed with the ultimate rule of recognition at the top and the constitution, statutes and by-laws at successively lower levels and provide a criterion by which the system can be viewed as a *whole*.

The point of view from which this system is supposed to exist is never clearly specified. Hart's reference to the book as an 'essay in descriptive sociology' and his description of social rules would seem to indicate a social-observer point of view. But he also says that law should be seen 'essentially from the internal point of view' (1961, p. 96). As he makes statements from both internal and external points of view, it cannot be either exclusively, but must in some way incorporate both. In fact, he starts by taking something very like the social observer's point of view in his discussion of social rules. But, as the book progresses, the balance changes. He makes fewer external observations of behaviour and more comments about the meaning of rules to judges from their internal point of view.

Harris sees Hart progressing through increasingly 'purer' internal viewpoints, so that by the time he comes to discuss the 'open texture' of rules he is treating them as Kelsenian 'pure norms' (1979, p. 62). Hart's point of view becomes the 'detached' internal one with just a little added sociological comment. Hart's system is thus described from that point of view and exists for those who share it. However, it is not clear that any such shift occurs. The emphasis on the internal point of view can be seen as no more than insistence on the importance of psychological facts about judges' beliefs and mental processes to exposition of Hart's legal system. As such, the social observer's point of view is retained throughout and it is only Hart's narrow behaviourist definition of the 'external point of view' which leads him to describe his own point of view as 'internal'. When Hart sets the 'minimum conditions' for the existence of a legal system (officials accept secondary rules and citizens comply with primary ones, p. 111) he certainly appears to be speaking from something very like the social observer's point of view. It is from that view that Hart's theory will be primarily questioned – though the problems for narrower points of view will not be ignored.

The next six sections will examine the elements, relations, structure and wholeness factor of Hart's system and the problems a social observer would have in accepting that they, and hence the legal system, exist as described in societies like ours. Many of these problems are due to the distortions involved in trying to fit Hart's insights into his system. A system needs pure norms rather than social rules, it needs a single rule of recognition which cannot be formulated or found among officials, it needs shared understandings and consensus about key rules, it needs an overemphasis on authority relations and it needs a degree of content independence that cannot be sustained. Finally, to make our law a system, what has to be added to Hart's concept of 'primitive law' is a set of dubious secondary rules rather than much less systematizable institutions and practices which in reality separate us from Hart's 'primitive law'. Even if the social observer accepted that a legal system as described by Hart existed within societies such as ours, it would play such a small part in law that the social observer would not be justified in calling law, in such societies, systematic. To the extent that Hart's system is seen from the internal point of view of officials, the problems with the rule of recognition and with the relativity and the content independence of legal rules remain. Thus even from the internal point of view Hart's theory of legal system cannot be accepted as a theory of law.

3.3 Primary Rules

Hart lists two kinds of rules, primary and secondary, both of which must
be present for there to be a legal system (1961, p. 111). He characterizes
primary rules as duty-imposing in the sense that they require persons
subject to the rule 'to do or abstain from certain actions' (1961, p. 78).
Problems with this formulation have been raised by several writers (e.g.
MacCormick, 1981). But any fuller picture of primary rules is clouded by
the fact that Hart offers two models for them.

The first model of a primary rule is contained in his celebrated notion
of a 'social rule', which exists if two sets of conditions are met. First,
there must be a regularity of behaviour within some social group, an
insistent general demand for conformity to it, and great social pressure
brought to bear on those who deviate (the 'external aspect'). Secondly,
the rule must be felt as an obligation by a large proportion of the members of the relevant social group. From an internal point of view, those
members feel that the rule ought to be obeyed and that it provides a
good reason for critical reaction and social pressure applied to those
whose behaviour does not conform to it (the 'internal aspect'). Hart
sees such rules as two things rolled into one. They are 'Janus-faced',
having both an internal and an external aspect visible from their respective points of view. It is a rule stating what ought to be done and it is
also a statement about the behaviour of members of the social group.
To Hart it is important that social rules are neither one nor the other but
both. He sees the feeling of obligation as the internal manifestation and
the relevant behaviour as the external manifestation of *the same thing*.

Hart has touched on an important phenomenon. But his insight into
it, and the concept of a social rule he uses to encapsulate it, are distorted because he has to find the kind of general rule that could fit into a
legal system. This causes many problems. Unfortunately for the positivist
emphasis on the internal, the greatest problems are provided by the
quality, content and specification of the internal aspect of social rules.
The first problem concerns the kind of internal attitude required. Many
people may be conscious of a rule and obey it for various reasons –
prudence, fear, desire for conformity, tradition, as well as a feeling of
obligation. All these involve an internal awareness and use of that awareness as a sufficient reason for action. Hart quite clearly excludes all
but the last from the required internal attitude. This is puzzling, for it
makes social rules both rarer and more difficult to discover. It also seems
to exclude a very important human phenomenon – the convergence of
behaviour by persons having different reasons for behaving similarly. If
there are to be many social rules the percentage of persons required to
hold the internal view must be reduced. The social observer will be sur-

prised that, of two rules, one which 10 per cent believe to be obligatory and which 90 per cent follow for other reasons, and another rule which 20 per cent believe to be obligatory and to which 80 per cent conform by accident, the latter would be more likely to count as a social rule for Hart.

The second problem concerns the enormous number of rules that could be felt internally which would forbid (or require as needs be) the action that is regularly avoided (or performed). This makes it highly unlikely that a majority will feel the same rule internally or that there will be correspondence in their internal beliefs. Suppose it is observed that most of a population abstain from killing one another and that the few who do are criticized and feel great social pressure (say in the form of a lynching party's noose). The whole population feels very strongly that it is obliged to refrain from such action. Here surely is a classic social rule. But what the members of the population feel will vary greatly. Many will hold beliefs that enjoin a much wider range of behaviour than killing human beings. Some may feel it wrong to harm any living creatures, others may feel it wrong to harm human beings physically, or to kill any living creatures, or any living creatures capable of feeling pain. Other members may hold beliefs that enjoin a narrower range of behaviour, such as killing members of their own race or social group, but have little contact with members of other social groups, and rarely in circumstances where they have any desire to kill (thus the narrowness of the felt obligation does not have any significant impact on the general conformity). It might be said that, from the wider principles believed by some, the narrower principle of not killing human beings might be deduced, and that therefore all agreed to this narrower principle. However, those with wider principles may find such a deduction repugnant because it weakens, for them, the overall force of the principle. In any case it is not the deduced principle but the wider one that is felt and followed. A related problem occurs when people hold wide principles but would in certain cases not adhere to them. They might believe that they would never kill, but would in fact in some circumstances kill foreigners though not fellow country-men. Some would make the distinction if they considered it carefully in advance. Others would vehemently deny that they would act against their 'principles' but would in fact change their minds about what the principle required if those circumstances actually arose. Most, however, are never called upon to make such fine distinctions about their beliefs, so their beliefs remain fairly general. The general prohibitions in their minds will not correspond to the more specific and precise rules, with all their inclusions and exceptions, found in the minds of those who made those distinctions.

The internal feelings of obligation, though very real to those who have them, may not even take the form of *rules*. They may merely take the form of standards (MacCormick, 1981, p. 40) or of images of behaviour that have strong positive or negative moral connotations. Though a lawyer might turn these images into rules, most citizens would not bother. Even if they do, their inexperience in creating such rules (and in considering a variety of cases to provide qualifications and exceptions to such rules) will mean they are likely to produce rules which do not correspond to their likely behaviour and feelings should those cases arise.

This variation in internally felt normative phenomena accords with reflective common sense, although fuller reasons for this will emerge from the theory of law and society outlined in chapters 7 and 8. Two that should be noted here are the indeterminacy of language, especially normative language, and the difficulties in its communication (chapter 7.3). Even under the most favourable circumstances, where one person is prepared to be taught rules of social behaviour by another, the rules the teacher understands and attempts to communicate may not correspond with the rules understood and adopted by the taught. And circumstances are not often so favourable.

There is a second, converse problem concerning the 'external aspect' of social rules. Just as the internal rule could be expressed in more or less extensive terms so could the externally observed behaviour. Narrower and broader formulations will fit any criteria Hart might set for the degree of externally observable compliance required for a social rule. Thus, as Hart appreciates, we cannot determine the formulation of the external rule by observing behaviour. If the internal rule could be adequately formulated, we could test compliance with the internally held rule but, as we have seen, the formulation of the internal aspect is variable and rubbery too. Or rather, it cannot work as long as we are looking at these as *social*, rather than individual, phenomena.

Because of the variety and singularity of the internal beliefs involved, a social rule cannot be the same *thing* with internal and external aspects. At best it is a social phenomenon marked by the *convergence* of internal normative feelings, matched by a convergence of externally observable behaviour through a combination of internal and external pressures outlined by Hart. These problems can easily be overlooked by a theorist postulating a social rule. If a rule is felt internally, the question may be asked whether this is part of a social rule. The theorist will look to the behaviour of others to see if it conforms to the rule. The similarity of behaviour will be investigated at the level of generality at which the researcher's own rule is pitched, thus missing the second problem. When the theorist discovers that others have normative beliefs about this behaviour it is easy to assume they will be the same as the theorist's. This assumption is aided by the difficulties in determining the internal views of others: (1) the difficulty in penetrating other minds and the difficulties of communication, previously cited as a cause of the variety of internally felt rules, also protect the observer from discovering it; (2) the variety of meanings normative language has for different persons means that a report of similar internal beliefs may conceal significant differences in normative feelings and in the actions they endorse or enjoin; and (3) the unformed nature of many people's beliefs might mean that they will, when queried, endorse a rule suggested by the researcher that corresponds only roughly to their normative beliefs. Even asking the subject to think about these beliefs and express them in words may change the relevant beliefs and thus not express the beliefs the researcher was studying.

These problems are particularly likely to be overlooked by a legal theorist trying to create a legal system. Social rules as described by Hart, singular phenomena with back-to-back internal and external aspects, could fit into a system. The convergence phenomenon, which is far more important and far more common, would not. Hart's partial insight into this phenomenon accounts for much of the popularity of his concept of social rules, with which he tries to encompass it. But its distortion into one which could become the basic element of a legal system accounts for many of its problems.

However, despite Hart's elaboration on the nature of social rules and the test for their existence, and despite the distortion he applies to the important phenomenon they seek to describe, they are not really a part of his legal system. Social rules are the component elements of primitive law. But when secondary rules are introduced to create a legal system they do more than *add* to the primary rules. Secondary rules also provide new existence criteria for primary rules – recognition by the rule of recognition or creation by those authorized to make new rules under rules of change. The rule of recognition will recognize rules that are not social rules, and rules of change will change legal rules at different times and in different directions from the evolution of social rules. Thus we have a new existence test – one of validity according to secondary rules – rather than the dual requirements of general compliance and internally felt obligations.

The validity test is apparent only from the internal point of view – given the acceptance of the authorizing rule, the obligatory nature of the rule authorized under it is accepted. But it is not like the internal test for social rules because it is not necessary that anyone *feels* obliged, merely that they *would* do so if they accepted the relevant secondary rule and were aware of the circumstances in which the relevant primary rule was created.

Hart could require that primary rules of a legal system satisfy the social rule test, the validity test, both tests or only one test. He could justify the necessity of both tests on the basis that laws are to be seen as social rules but the only social rules that will be considered part of the legal system are those valid under the rule of recognition. He could justify the sufficiency of any one test on the basis that laws are created *either* by popular practice or by decree from above. Hart, however, clearly chooses the validity test alone by counting as primary rules those that are not enforced, not followed, not widely known or not widely accepted (1961, p. 101). Neither externally observable consistencies of behaviour nor actual normative attitudes are necessary.

This choice of validity test alone certainly makes law appear more systematic. There are clear links between the rules of recognition and the rules they recognize, links which can be built into a structure. Any other choice would make law appear less systematic. If both tests had to be satisfied then some rules that are valid under the secondary rules would not be part of law, so the 'legal system' would include elements from outside law. If only one test had to be satisfied, then all the social rules that were not valid would be a part of law, but outside the legal system.

Although the choice is clearly convenient for a systems theorist, the price is high. It severely limits the applicability to modern law of Hart's valuable notion of a social rule. It is also very hard to justify. There are some rules invalid according to the rule of recognition, but nevertheless treated as valid by the courts. This is inevitable given the imperfect ability of human beings to apply their own rules, let alone the ability of different human beings to follow consistently the rules set by others. This will be aggravated by the rule of recognition's lack of clarity and its varying degrees of acceptance (*infra*). But sometimes rules are accepted and enforced *despite* their invalidity according to the rule of recognition. One example is provided by *McKellar's Case* ((1977) 12 ALR 129) in which the Australian High Court ruled that the 1918 Electoral Act and the elections held under it had been unconstitutional for decades because the constitution required the numbers in the Lower House to correspond more exactly to the populations of the States. If one treats the Australian rule of recognition as establishing the constitution as the paramount criterion of valid law, then the parliaments were not properly constituted and their enactments were invalid. Consequently, hundreds of Acts owed not their validity but their invalidity to the rule of recognition. Nevertheless, the court accepted the validity of laws passed by those parliaments. Some might say that a new rule of recognition has emerged, and with it a new system. But most would probably accept that this indicates that validity according to secondary rules is neither necessary nor sufficient for the existence of primary legal rules. Clearly other potentially overriding factors are at work and Hart's test of validity needs to be supplemented, modified or, to some extent, made defeasible. In this willingness to override the rule of recognition we get the first inkling of how limited judicial commitment is, not only to the rule of recognition, but to the whole project of systematizing law. Unsystematized 'common sense' or intuition takes precedence over the consequences of a theory-imposed system.

Using a single validity test means that the rules felt internally need no longer be matched to any corresponding external conduct, thus avoiding one of the problems of social rules. But it does not make these rules felt internally any less individual, so the validity that is claimed for a primary rule is a *set* of validities in the minds of those who accept the secondary rules and the justifications of the primary rule that flow from them. Furthermore, by making the existence of primary rules a matter of validity according to secondary rules, all the existence problems are shifted from individual primary rules to secondary rules, from the part of law with which we are all familiar, and whose existence we are least inclined to doubt, on to unfamiliar things. Ultimately the existence of all law is made dependent on the rule of recognition that no one had heard of until Hart 'discovered' it.

The adoption of a single validity test denies a role for external observation in determining the existence of individual legal rules. However, the external aspect does have a role in determining whether the legal system exists. One of the 'minimum conditions' for the existence of a legal system is that an (indeterminate) majority of people conform to an (again indeterminate) majority of valid primary rules (1961, p. 111). This immediately makes the test a more difficult one to apply. A compliance test for a single law is simply a question of how many people in a position to disobey the law nevertheless do obey it. But for a system of laws, account must be taken of laws which fall below that threshold of compliance. What weight are they to be given, and does more than sufficient compliance with one rule compensate for less than sufficient compliance with other rules? These are oft-noted problems for Austin's test of 'habitual obedience' (1954) and Kelsen's requirement that a legal system be 'by and large efficacious' (1970). They are no less pressing for Hart.

The compliance test is not only difficult to apply – there must also be considerable doubt that it applies to societies such as ours. Much action by enforcement officials is *ultra vires* or in breach of apparently valid legal rules which limit their behaviour (Chambliss and Siedman, 1971), and many laws are violated by citizens. Indeed the proliferation of law seems to be matched by a proliferation of disobedience as the capacity of institutions to create paper rules far outruns the capacity of citizens to comprehend, or institutions to enforce, those rules.

Where the test does apply, most, though not all, of the primary rules would be complied with by the bulk of the population. However, this does not make them social rules. Where the minimum conditions are satisfied, most primary rules will be of a different type – what might be called 'hybrid rules'. They have an external and an internal aspect. Externally, compliance can be observed. Internally, they are thought to be valid, but only by the small number who accept the relevant secondary rules and are also aware that the criteria, required by that rule for the creation of valid primary rules, have been met. But in contrast to social rules, those who comply need not have any internal feeling of obligation, nor need they even be aware of the rule. Perhaps many such hybrid rules are also social rules. Certainly Hart thinks that this is usual and that this strengthens law. Furthermore, if a legal system is seen as the addition of secondary rules to a set of social rules, then many of the social rules will be validated by the secondary rules. But as law becomes more complex and new rules are created under the relevant secondary rules, many primary rules will not be social rules and many social rules will not be primary rules.[1]

We can summarize by saying that there are three tests for legal rules: validity, compliance (or, as suggested, convergence of behaviour) and acceptance (convergence of normative orientation). The elements of Hart's legal system, his primary rules, need only pass the first test. However, the legal system will cease to exist unless most pass the second as well and are thus hybrid rules. Social rules pass the second and third tests. That is neither necessary nor sufficient for membership of Hart's legal system. But then systems cannot be built of such things!

3.4 Secondary Rules

Secondary rules are central to Hart's description of a legal system. Their presence is necessary both for the existence of a legal system at all and for the existence of primary rules. We know they are 'rules about rules' that fall into three types. But what sort of thing are they and how do we know they exist? Some see secondary rules as social rules for officials (e.g. Hacker, 1977, p. 22). However, secondary rules would appear either to fail the social-rule test or to be untestable. Social rules require externally observable consistencies of behaviour and criticisms levelled at those who breach them. Hart says these things are required for secondary rules to exist (1961, p. 113). But what behaviour do we expect to observe, and is there any behaviour that would count as a breach? Most secondary rules are power-conferring rules (conferring powers to legislate, change rules and adjudicate), and power-conferring rules cannot be breached. *Exceed-*

ing authority is not a breach of the norm conferring authority but of another norm requiring officials to limit themselves to that authority. Official adherence to the latter norm is made highly questionable by their constant attempts to expand their authority. Harris has tried to reformulate secondary rules as duty-imposing rules (1979, p. 92), but, as Raz notes, such reformulations do not reflect the way in which they are used and held (1970, p. 225). The last point is particularly damaging as it means that the reformulated rule fails the internal acceptance test. Finally, even if it were possible to breach these rules, could we point to any great social pressure, of which physical sanctions are a prominent and usual form, that is applied at their breach (Harris, 1979, p. 60)? Even limited pressure is unlikely as judges tend to *avoid* criticizing other judges. (This avoidance of criticizing other judges cannot itself count as a social rule, as general criticism of non-compliance would itself constitute general non-compliance and it is against barrister interests to do so.) Whether or not Hart thought secondary rules were normally social rules, his theory does not depend on it. The minimum conditions for the existence of a legal system include merely the internal acceptance of secondary rules by the officials. Thus if only the *minimum* conditions are met, secondary rules will be purely internal phenomena in the minds of officials and will lack the external aspect a social rule needs. However, the test of acceptance is much stronger than for social rules – acceptance by *all* officials as a common standard is required (Hart, 1961, p. 113). Thus the addition to social rules which converts primitive law into a legal system is a consensus among officials about secondary rules. Although these are internal phenomena which exist for the individual official by virtue of his beliefs, the minimum claim Hart makes for their existence is a claim about official consensus, a set of psychological facts for the social observer to test. If, for any society, the test cannot be met, then there is no legal system in that society.

There are several types of secondary rules, but the one to which Hart devotes most attention and the one that serves as a lynchpin for the whole system is the rule of recognition. Yet the attempt to demonstrate its existence runs into many problems typical of positivism.

The first problem is to know among which officials this consensus is required. If the answer to this question is given in legal terms the argument becomes circular. This would not distinguish the legal system from systems of rules used by private organizations (Hughes, 1960, p. 1029). It would also become impossible to distinguish between a group of what we would all consider judges and a sociologically insignificant group who postulate a set of rules which happen to be congruent with what people actually do (indeed, by choosing rules carefully the latter could meet

Hart's conditions for the existence of a legal system far better than any group more usually considered to be officials). Distinctions such as these will require a sociological definition of officials.

If 'officials' are to be defined in sociological terms there are many simple and satisfactory definitions – one is offered in chapter 7.9. But it will include the officials of many institutions – bureaucrats, judges, policemen, possibly even ticket inspectors. Finding a consensus about anything, let alone a rule of recognition, in this group would be impossible and Hart would not claim one. Although he talks of officials in general terms, he concentrates almost exclusively on the central officials of courts – judges. To define judges in sociological terms involves an understanding of courts and their relations with other institutions. In short, a sociological theory of law will have to be offered. *Pace* Mac-Cormick, who criticizes sociological approaches to law for using and depending on positivist notions of law (1977, p. 88), it is positivist notions that depend on sociological ones.

The next problem in alleging such a consensus is that although judges spend a great deal of time enunciating and elaborating most of the other rules, virtually none ever says anything about the rule of recognition. Indeed there is very little evidence that they even consider it. Hart acknowledges this: 'for the most part the rule of recognition is not stated'. But he claims that 'its existence is *shown* by the way in which particular rules are identified either by courts or by private persons' (1961, p. 98). It is strange that something unstated and not directly considered from the internal point of view should nevertheless be 'regarded from the internal point of view as a public common standard' (Hart, 1961, p. 112). One writer has queried how a rule of recognition, in default of formulation, can be said to be a rule or exist at all (King, 1963, p. 298). It is also puzzling that one who emphasizes the importance of the internal point of view should be content to infer it from externally observed action.

Even if officials can be said to accept the secondary rules, the fact that they are unstated will make it very hard to compare them, and could hide many real differences between the rules which judges would state if called upon to do so (Dworkin, 1986, p. 42). These likely differences are spotlighted by the problems involved in formulating a rule of recognition that really would pass the official consensus test. As Lukes points out, most formulations are likely to be unclear, controversial and non-uniform (1977, p. 92).

Lack of clarity and vagueness in formulation may lead to a rule of recognition with which most judges would agree – possibly the *only* one with which a significant number of judges would agree. Hart seems to accept this, saying that rules of recognition will be 'open textured' like other rules (1961, p. 144). Most rules can be like this without losing their character as rules. Lack of clarity in primary rules merely makes some of their applications uncertain. But it is a much more serious defect in a secondary rule, especially a rule of recognition. As a rule of recognition must act as a test for the existence of primary rules, any vagueness in it will lead to uncertainty about what are the primary rules, and it will fail to provide that test. Such a vague rule cannot be a rule of *recognition*, although it may be something else.

Lack of clarity threatens not the existence of the postulated rule, merely the claim that what exists is a rule of recognition. On the other hand, controversy threatens the postulated rule's very existence according to Hart's official consensus test. One of the major sources of controversy and unclarity is that judges regard law as having several sources – at least one legislature, several courts, regulations and decisions made by the executive, and, in some cases, custom. A rule of recognition will need to specify and rank these sources so as to deny validity to rules emanating from inferior sources that conflict with higher ones. It will also need to specify to whom and to what degree the various sources can delegate power to subsidiary sources. The ranking of sources and the powers of delegation may be controversial and subject to controversy between the institutions involved. There is no reason to assume that individual judges will all take the same side in such controversy, and in any case judges will try to avoid pronouncing on such conflicts and risking politicizing their role unless absolutely necessary. Examples can be found in the controversy among Australian judges over the ranking of the Privy Council and Australian High Court as sources and the difference between some Scots and English lawyers over the status of the Act of Union of 1707 (MacCormick, 1981, p. 111) and the difference between judges over whether, and the extent to which, courts have the power to invalidate subordinate legislation (especially on the ground of unreasonableness). A final example is provided by subordinate legislatures. Many grow in prestige and power until they are treated as separate sources regardless of the terms of their original creation. The resolution of conflicts between their rules and rules made by the founding source then becomes uncertain. Such cases are common in colonies in transition to full independence. But a similar process can occur when a unitary state creates regional assemblies. This has not happened for local government in the United Kingdom, but where the units relate to an area with geographical, historical, cultural or ethnic identity and the delegation of power is more significant, this growth of prestige and power to become an independent source capable of contradicting its maker is possible (e.g. Hungary within the Austro–Hungarian Empire). This multiplicity of sources of partially determinate ranking may seem strange to those who expect law to speak as if it had the single authoritative voice of a sovereign. But the way that sources grow up over time as relatively independent institutional attempts to resolve a variety of problems makes it unlikely that a simple rule will cover and order them all.

Even the presence of a written constitution does not usually solve this problem. Few constitutions specifically recognize the courts as a source of law and most throw up controversies over the relative weights of different sources. Consequently, a rule of recognition merely recognizing the constitution will be inadequate for its task of the recognition and ranking of legal sources. Even where there is no controversy, there may be no uniformity among officials because jurisdictional limitations vary the sources officials recognize (compare the sources of law and hence the rule of recognition for state and federal courts in the United States, specialist courts which administer particular acts, and the old courts of equity which ignored so many of the sources common to courts of common law).

The several sources for law lead to another problem. In order to take them and their ranking into account the rule of recognition will become very complicated. In order to perform its task of identifying what are legal rules, it will have to incorporate all of constitutional and administrative law. But long before you have got that far you will find the judges disagreeing. This should not surprise us for it reflects a general problem for all consensus theories – the postulated consensus is either too vague to be meaningful or too controversial to be consensual.

Some writers attempt to overcome these problems by saying that there are several rules of recognition, each covering a single source (e.g. Raz, 1979, p. 68). Other secondary rules can then sort out the conflict. This destroys Hart's pyramidal structure but, provided an alternative structure can be established to reunite the several rules of recognition and the primary rules valid under them, this is not itself fatal to the postulation of a legal system. However, this merely shifts the controversy from parts of the rule of recognition to individual secondary rules. So the rules of recognition are saved but only at the expense of the existence of the legal system, one of whose minimum conditions of existence has been breached by the controversy of these secondary rules. The rules of recognition are also changed because they no longer recognize legal rules, only rules which are contingently legal (depending on whether another source rule contradicts it and in whose favour the conflict-resolving secondary rule works). Alternatively we could merely acknowledge that different legal officials have different rules of recognition. However, this would mean that there are as many legal systems as there are officials with differing rules of recognition and there is literally a different 'law' for every one of them. Another approach is to lower the requirement of acceptance to mere *use* of the secondary rules as a standard. Hughes (1960) cites the case of the enforcement of an invader's rules by the magistrates of the conquered nation (e.g. occupied France). Harris (1979, p. 108) and Kelsen (1970, p. 218) both refer to the possibility of an anarchist or communist judge who might deny the legitimacy of the regime yet still enforce its rules.

Although these acceptance requirements are intended to protect positivist theory, they point to other possible weaknesses in the consensus over the rule of recognition. Among the institutions that are seen as sources for rules, some may be treated as legitimate and others merely acknowledged as 'powers-that-be' which must be reluctantly followed. This dichotomy would be found in the French magistrates example: they would regard the pre-occupation laws still in force as legitimately sourced and the decrees of the occupying power as not (German lawyers would see the former as authorized by a decree 'saving' existing laws, but the French lawyers would be more likely to consider them legitimate on their own and still legitimate in *spite of* the German decree saving them). But it may also be found in less extreme circumstances as when some Australian judges very reluctantly followed a Privy Council which they regarded as an anachronism lacking legitimate authority. Even where there is full acceptance of all the sources, it is highly likely that different judges will value some more than others out of differential respect for the institutions or their personnel, thereby altering the effective rankings and the rule of recognition for that judge.

So even if, contrary to the doubts raised earlier, rules of recognition are used by, and exist for, individual judges, these rules will vary. Consequently, it is not possible for the social observer to say that even the minimum conditions of existence (internal acceptance by officials) have been met in societies like ours. The key secondary rules have *not* been added to social rules and there is no legal system as outlined by Hart. As with the concept of primary rules, so it is with secondary rules. Hart's attempt to force law into a system has necessitated an unsatisfiable judicial-consensus test that creates severe problems for the theory. He has converted secondary rules from a useful insight about the use of meta-rules by judges into an untenable hypothesis that a single meta-rule is used by all judges to derive all legal rules.

3.5 Relations in Hart's System

The relations between the elements of Hart's system are incorporated in the secondary rules. Indeed, the whole point of those rules is to provide those relationships. A rule of recognition provides a relation between itself and the rules recognized, a rule of adjudication provides a relation between itself and the rules whose application and interpretation are adjudged, a rule of change provides a relation between itself and the rules that can be changed under it. The relations are purely internal (Hart, 1961, p. 99) – the acceptance of a secondary rule leads to the justification of another rule (e.g. the acceptance of the rule of recognition leads someone to regard a rule issued by one of the recognized sources as a primary rule valid from the internal point of view).

One major problem with these relations is their dependence on secondary rules. Just as the existence of secondary rules is doubtful, or at best confined to existence as a personal rule for individual officials, so it is for the relations in Hart's system.

However, even if the rule of recognition is established, this does not create relations between rules. A rule of recognition recognizes sources, not rules. These sources may well have an output of texts but the generation of rules out of those texts is not automatic and requires further processing. What is necessary is the exercise of a very important skill involving the interpretation of statutes and judgments and this must be done before any recognition and ranking of rules is possible. What judges and other lawyers use to produce statements of legal rules is not so much a rule of recognition as a 'skill of generation'.

Another major problem which will become increasingly evident to the social observer is that the limited form in which the relations between *rules* is described has to be based on an extremely limited conception of the relations between *persons*. Just as Hart so rightly criticized Austin for seeing the relations between legislature and judiciary in terms of orders backed by threats, so he can himself be criticized for conceiving them in terms of what might be called 'rules backed by commitments'. A good social observer should fall into neither trap. As we shall see in chapter 7.2, social relations between persons, including legal officials, can be conceived as present where one person (A) regularly affects the actions of another (B). Such relations are many and varied depending on whether or not the effect is intentional, how the effect is achieved and the kind of reason for action it gives B. Hart's relations involve only one kind of social relation (legitimate authority) where A affects B because B believes A has a right to make the statement and that B ought to respond to it in a certain way.

The relations between real persons are rarely limited to any one kind of relation because the reasons for action created by the statements of others are usually several. This is just as true of judicial response to legislation by parliaments as to our response to a policeman's request. The mix may be different but a mix there will be, and to describe them in terms of one component will be to miss the important aspects of law represented by the others. However, to create a source-based system of authority relations, it is necessary to do just that.

3.6 Structure and Wholeness in Hart's System

Hart's greatest problems concern the structure of his system. He says little on the subject, but appears to give law a clear pyramidal form. His is a structure of authorizing relations with the ultimate rule of recognition at the top descending via 'a very familiar chain of legal reasoning' through a statute, a statutory order, to an Oxfordshire County Council by-law (1961, p. 101). This clearly links various rules of recognition with the primary rules but does not incorporate other key elements of Hart's 'system' – rules of change and adjudication. Despite seeing the key to understanding law as the union of primary and secondary rules, his own structure does not provide that union; and his image of law lacks one of the four characteristics of a system.

Even this partial structure is endangered if, as argued above, there is more than one ultimate rule of recognition. That would produce not one but several structures descending pyramidally from those rules of recognition.

Another problem concerns the number of officials who do accept this *structure* of authority relations from an internal point of view. Few, if any, will actually, rather than hypothetically, accept the structure as a whole because few will have considered each step in the many chains of validity. The most that can be claimed is that those who accept the validity of the final legal rules (e.g. the Oxfordshire by-law) would, if queried, trace that validity back through the chain described by Hart. But this is extremely doubtful. As different officials go back through the justifications for the by-law, many differences will be revealed. Some may stop at the very first rule, giving a Platonic justification based on comparative values of state institutions and the individual (Lloyd, 1973 p. 53). Some may simply say 'all "laws" must be obeyed' and that that is sufficient justification. Many will keep going back through Hart's chain of authorizing relations until they find a rule which they feel personally to be valid, and to which they can say: 'I agree with that.' Others may break off Hart's path for idiosyncratic reasons (e.g. 'It happens to suit me.' 'Because I was brought up to obey officials of this kind,' 'The judge/minister/official is a good chap/is a member of my club/gaols dope-pushers,' 'Because the content of the relevant rule is in accord with natural law/Allah's will,' etc.). Schematically, the two views might be put in the forms shown in figure 3.1.

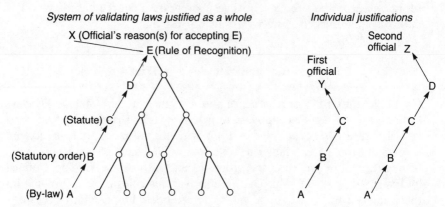

Figure 3.1 Two models for the acceptance of legal rules

Presumably Hart would limit this acceptance test to judicial officials just as he limits that for secondary rules. But even the paths by which judges justify legal rules will diverge. Variations in the secondary rules used will lead to variations in the authority relations and in the rules which judges reach along the path. There will also be a tendency to stop when they reach a 'subordinate' source which they regard as valid in its own right (e.g. when an Australian judge comes to the state legislature). Accordingly, the relations between the legal rules will be structured differently by different judges producing different systems of legal rules.

An even thornier problem is provided by the attitudes judges have to the *content* of laws. Few will accept, and fewer will enforce, *absolutely* any law valid under the secondary rules regardless of offence to moral sensibilities (Lukes, 1977, p. 93). Of course, the degree of tolerance is very great – the legal profession tends to produce, and governments tend to choose, those who agree with the bulk of a government's action and the rules used to justify it. But this tolerance is not unlimited. So even if we look only at judicial attitudes, a second test for legal rules has appeared. It may be a test that is rarely invoked – most governments would face a revolution from the populace before sufficiently offending the moral sensibilities of their judges, and therefore are rarely unlucky enough to suffer the latter. But it is a test nonetheless.

Yet there is another more common way in which content affects validity in the eyes of judges. Where they find a postulated rule more attractive in substance, judges will be less concerned to hunt for defects in the chain of validity that authorizes it. Effectively, if not consciously, judges use: (1) a prior substantive test that the rule be not outrageous to the

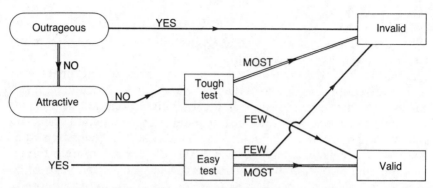

Figure 3.2 A model of mixed content/validity judicial reasoning

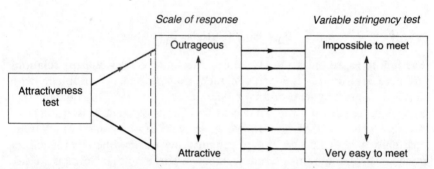

Figure 3.3 An alternative model of mixed content/validity judicial reasoning

relevant judge. A rule failing this test fails outright; (2) a second prior substantive test of attractiveness; (3) two authority tests – a stringent test (actively seeking out authorities to overrule it) applied where the rule fails the previous test and a more lenient test (defending the rule against attacks) where it passes. (See figure 3.2.)

These tests could alternatively be seen as: (1) a prior substantive test setting levels of attractiveness and outrage, and (2) a single authority test whose stringency is flexible, set by the substantive attraction of the rule itself, reaching impossible-to-meet levels where the rules go beyond the requisite level of outrage. (See figure 3.3.)

These content tests could not fit into Hart's structure of authorizing relations that supposedly determine validity. His system can be preserved only if these content tests are ignored.

Wholeness

What gives Hart's system its wholeness, its unity, is clearly the supposed structure and the rule of recognition at its apex. Therefore, if the rule of recognition fails, the 'system' lacks not only structure but anything to unify it. Even if the existence of the rule of recognition is admitted, it still cannot bear the burden of providing unity – first, because legal systems are likely to have several rules of recognition and, secondly, because no rule of recognition will bring under its umbrella all that judges regard as law in any one state. Finally, even if a rule of recognition were formulated that did recognize all the sources of law in such a state, it would be because we knew what the laws and the sources of law were, and formulated it accordingly. Thus the unity of law is a prerequisite for a rule of recognition, rather than a consequence of it. The basis of that unity must be sought elsewhere.

3.7 Practices, Officials, Institutions

The failure to establish the existence of secondary rules and the relations structure and unity dependent on them and the general problems with these concepts may lead observers and participants alike to conclude that there is no legal system as conceived by Hart and reject it as a theory of law. So what kind of law do we have without secondary rules? One possibility is Hart's description of primitive law (as modified by the earlier rejection of a common internal element in social rules). Perhaps we are closer to it than hitherto imagined – not least because it is obvious that our law suffers from many of its alleged defects. But we are not that close. One of Hart's most powerful contrasts is between modern law and his conception of a hypothetical primitive law. Clearly something has to be added to Hart's notion of primitive law to describe modern law adequately. To make law appear systematic Hart adds his elusive secondary rules. But the really important and plausible additions consist of officials, institutions and their practices, which cannot fit into Hart's system. Once again, an insight is all but lost because of the attempt to find system in it.

In real cases of 'primitive law' there will usually be some such added practices (S.F. Moore, 1978; Roberts, 1979; MacCormick, 1981) and, frequently, officials of a kind as well. Practices may involve the presentation of disputes to a certain person, a group of persons or the whole group at certain times or in certain ways. In the simplest case, a practice may involve the tendency to talk over alleged misbehaviour around the campfire before individuals take action, or an informalized practice of mockery or screamed abuse after dark in an attempt by an aggrieved person to shame his aggriever (Roberts, 1979, p. 61). In the simplest case, an official is merely someone who plays a bigger part when questions about social rules are considered. He may merely be a good talker or one who can mediate between the parties (Roberts, 1979, p. 72). Alternatively, his suggestions for solutions may carry weight because his counsel is considered wise (an 'opinion leader') or thought to have access to a special 'truth' (e.g. by sorcery), or other members are either dependent upon or used to receiving instructions from him, in the course of other social activities (especially production, without which there could be no community).

The addition of officials and practices would mark a very significant change for a Hartian primitive law. As well as the uncoordinated critical reaction and the haphazard violence inflicted by individuals against suspected offenders, there is someone who is expected to respond (an official) or a method by which the response of ordinary people is made (a practice). At the same time the critical reactions of others will *tend* to be smaller, partly because the official reaction is seen as more effective or more appropriate, partly just to save effort, and partly because some private critical reactions will *themselves* stimulate an official reaction.

The addition increases the scope and detail of the subjects that can be regulated. Even if the addition is simply the practice of discussing disputes around the campfire at night, many more matters can be dealt with than by haphazard private reaction. As the officials take on helpers and grow into institutions with ever expanding power, the growth quickens.

The addition also makes the reaction more predictable. This is not necessarily because there is more reliance on rules – indeed the fact that there is now an official to deal with a dispute reduces the need for a rule.[2] The predictability is merely based on the fact that it is known how and by whom the dispute will be dealt with. It is generally easier to predict a single person's behaviour, or the behaviour of a group participating in a known activity, than haphazard individual reactions.

Calling these practices 'additions' should not mask the fact that they fundamentally change the social rules. Initially, these rules involve a regularity of behaviour, observable critical reactions by many members of the community against nonconformists and a variety of internally felt rules or other moral connotations that support conformity. The addition of 'officials' means that the physically observable reactions of some members (those officials) become more common and those of the rest become rarer and weaker. This naturally shifts the attention of the social observer from the citizens in general to the officials in particular. The members of the community, official and otherwise, continue to hold a variety of internal views about the behaviour. However, as they become more powerful, officials can afford to be more at variance with their fellow citizens in the nature of the internal views they hold and the behaviour to which they react. At some point it might be better to think of the internal feelings and critical reactions of non-official citizens separately – perhaps as a residual 'primitive' or 'living' law – weaker than when there was no official reaction, but still there. However, most citizens will still think of official behaviour as enforcing social or communal rules (even though the variety of internal views meant they were never truly communal). Consequently, there is always the possibility of shock and surprise when the gap between official and citizen views and reactions is realized, providing a source of tension that is a permanent feature of non-primitive law.

Several writers criticize the absence of any account of legal institutions in Hart's account of law (e.g. Arnold, 1978). But Hart has not ignored the addition of institutions (or practices or officials). His error is in attempting to encapsulate their effect by stating the rules by which these institutions are supposed to operate – the rules of recognition, change and adjudication that give various institutions authority to legislate, enforce and interpret. The institutions and practices have been reduced to rules. This reduction is impossible and severely distorting despite the long pedigree of such views of institutions.[3] Institutions, legal and otherwise, are not mechanisms by which specified ends are pursued according to particular rules, but are filled with individual human beings who pursue different ends by different means and give different justifications (if any). These differences means that where officials do operate according to rules those rules vary, making them *individual* rather than *institutional* rules. Furthermore, there are distinct advantages for officials in avoiding even such individual rules. Leaving them unstated avoids controversy; and leaving them vague or unused provides valuable flexibility, whether in pursuing those officials' ideals and interests or merely in avoiding the conflict into which rigid applications of what they believed the rule to be could lead.

3.8   What About the Rest of 'Law'?

Criticism so far has been largely directed to the proposition that, especially from the point of view of the social observer, there can be no legal system as outlined by Hart. But even if all that Hart said was true and all judges did see, from their internal points of view, a set of primary and secondary rules united into a structure by the rule of recognition, the social observer would still be disinclined to see law as systematic.

The first problem is the exclusive emphasis placed on judges. Why should we be so concerned about *these* officials? Should we not enquire about other court officials, and whether they accept secondary rules, and whether a legal system could be said to exist from their internal points of view? Justices of the Peace are unlikely to know enough about constitutional and administrative law to construct rules of recognition for themselves. Even if they had the time and the requisite skills they would be unlikely to create the same ones as judges. Yet their place is pivotal, dealing with far more cases than judges, and, in some jurisdictions, dealing with those cases on their own. Another body with a key role to play in law is the jury, yet no one would suggest they would find system in law. For them the law is a set of bewildering propositions set before them by judges. If they did have a rule of recognition it would refer to a single source – the judge in their case.

But why not look at *non-court* officials and how law appears through the eyes of legislators, the executive and the police? Why confine these questions to *officials*? What about the views of the majority of the legal profession who do not have official posts and whose activities lead them to view the law in a different light – and what about the citizenry? Raz defends the emphasis on court officials by arguing that courts are the one institution always found in law and only found in law (1979, p. 111). But there is no doubt that in western countries courts are not the only institutions that must be added to primary rules to provide an understanding of law – a law that would look very different without legislatures, police forces and ministries. In western countries legislators come from different parties and the extent to which they share a 'unified and shared acceptance' of anything, let alone the niceties of rules of recognition, must be severely limited. Members of the bureaucracy are concerned with the legislation they administer. The law for them partly comprises rules they glean from an Act of Parliament and orders received from their superiors. The law for most policemen consists of criminal statutes (which they see as implying a duty to restrain or apprehend citizens who break them) plus court procedures and a set of instructions concerning police behaviour that make the above-mentioned duty more difficult to perform. To describe law from the standpoint of a policeman would be to picture not a system of rules like Hart's but *two* sets of rules in constant tension. Whatever view of law the police *should* hold, there is no doubt that the *actual* views held of it vary among them and are very different from those of judges.

Finally, there is the view of the citizen who will witness a selective set of actions of various officials of the legal institutions. Some of these will be seen in terms of rules to be followed. These may be accepted because of the value placed on the relevant institution, the substantive content of the law or the fact that it will be enforced anyway. But many official actions will be seen as merely actions of the powerful which have effects on the citizen and must be taken into account in planning how to act.

The second problem concerns how much of law is included within Hart's system. If the other parts of law are sufficiently significant, the social observer would have to say that, although there may be a legal system *within* law, *law* as a whole is not systematic. Some of these other parts of law have been noted by positivists (though not their consequences for positivist theory). Raz thinks a theory of adjudication has to be added to a theory of legal system to provide 'a conceptual foundation of our understanding of the law as a social institution of great importance to society' (1970, p. 209), and Harris adds a 'dynamic congeries of rules, principles, maxims, doctrines, morals, policies, delineations, classifications and so on, found as part of the tradition of a group of officials' (1979, p. 65). Even Hart sees that the union of primary and secondary rules is at the centre of, but *not the whole of*, law (1961, p. 96).

Other theorists would want to add even more to Hart's system in order to describe law. Honoré would add customary and conventional rules (1975, p. 163). Dworkin's 'principles' are unlikely to be captured by the rule of recognition because they are not derived from a source (1977, p. 39). Realists and their successors see the need to include the personal characteristics of judges, their political socialization (Nagel, 1979), their individual psychology (Frank, 1949), their values (Schubert, 1968a), the group dynamics of courts (Ulmer, 1965), and the ability of regular litigants to control the agenda of decision by settling cases that might involve unfortunate precedents (Galanter, 1974) that affect judicial decisions. Sociological theorists point to a variety of social forces that have a vital role in the generation and shaping of law. Pound (1954) and Stone (1966) have emphasized the part that major interest groups play in shaping the content of the law through their ability to organize themselves and exercise power over the appointment and actions of legislative and judicial officials. This affects not only the 'discretion' of legislative and judicial officials but also what decisions are in practice enforceable. Criminologists point to the importance of various 'sub-cultures' in affecting the administration of, and reaction to, law. Finally, the profound effect that the institutional nature of law has on its operation has led many sociological theorists to include facts about the workings of institutions in their description of law. The extent and nature of these other phenomena will be unravelled in later chapters. For the moment, all that is noted is their existence and that they involve far more personnel, and a greater variety of social relations between them, than Hart envisaged.

These phenomena may not fit into a system of primary and secondary rules. But they are familiar to even the casual observer of the institutions we call legal. Three responses are available to Hart: (1) to include these phenomena in law but to see them as minor parts of it, (2) to attempt to include them in his system (or an amended version of it), and (3) to exclude them from what the theory considers to be law. The first is hardly plausible. The second tends to turn the phenomena into Trojan horses able to destroy the structure and unity of the legal systems from within. Dworkin's principles as originally stated (1977, p. 14) were not so very different from legal rules (Tapper, 1971). But, as further explicated in 'Hard Cases' (1977, p. 81), their links with the judges' own moral judgments make them ineligible for membership in a system deriving its criteria of validity, its structure and its unity from a rule listing institutional sources of rules.

More often the attempt is made to exclude these phenomena from a narrowly defined conception of law. Social forces are acknowledged, but they are seen as having effects on law rather than as being a part of law. Even these are confined to strong social forces that affect which ultimate rule of recognition will be accepted by officials, and lesser social forces that may affect the content of laws created by those who are authorized by secondary rules to do so. But the role of outside forces in law is much stronger. They impose limitations and requirements far more exacting than any contained in the secondary rules of the system. Further, these limitations and requirements apply at all levels of the legal system, not just on the apex norms during revolutions. As a consequence, law cannot really be understood without them.

The exclusion of social forces from law has another effect. It reduces law from something central to the functioning of society to something merely peripheral (cf. Unger, 1976, p. 44) to it, to be found in the minds of judges rather than in the actions and thoughts of the bulk of the population and their officials. Because the elements have variable content and the structure of relations a variable pattern, legal systems can only be the product of, and exist in, a single legal mind. In a curious way, this seems to miss the social nature of law as a phenomenon resulting from, and existing through, many minds rather than one.

Hart provided a bold conception of law as a system which he hoped would be useful not only for lawyers but for sociologists as well. However, its sociological pretensions quickly evaporated and it did not even adequately cover or describe law from a more restricted point of view. The other three positivist theories considered start with more limited ambitions, two outlining less systematic theories and all clearly stating that they are describing law from an extremely limited viewpoint. This strengthens the apparent systemness of law from that point of view but, as we shall see, not sufficiently to prevent the return of all the same problems. Of course, from the social observer's viewpoint, the case is further weakened.

3.9 Harris

Harris's neo-Kelsenien 'pure norm' theory of the legal system portrays law as more systematic than does Hart's. His essential retreat is to claim that it only appears as such from the point of view of 'legal science' ('the activity attempting the systematic exposition of some *corpus* of legal materials as found in textbooks and treatises, in solicitors' advice, in counsels' opinion and commonly in the reported decisions of courts' (1979, p. 2). The limited nature of this point of view is stated categorically and it might appear to be limited only to those who agree with Harris that law is a system so that, if you do not believe law to be a system, you will cease the attempt at systematic exposition and cease the activity of legal science.

However, Harris has not retreated into such a tautologous fox-hole. He does not seek to protect his theory at the price of its relevance to those who operate in or observe legal institutions. He avoids this by claiming that his theory of legal system encapsulates the way legal science looks at law and is part of the 'shared understandings' of the officials of legal institutions (1979, pp. 14, 23).

Such a claim is important to, and challengeable from, the point of view of both legal scientist and social observer. We will see that Harris's pure-norm 'momentary legal system' contains all the ingredients of a systems theory but is unacceptable because it suffers from the same internal problems faced by Hart. We will then see the added complications provided by Harris's addition of a second 'system'. Finally, we will see how different the activities of judges and other practitioners are from 'legal science', rendering Harris's theory an inadequate description of law from the internal point of view of those engaged in the activity and of little use to a social observer who wishes to understand that activity.

Harris's Momentary System

The *elements* of Harris's system are legal rules. They take the form of 'pure norms') – abstract entities with an 'ought' or 'may' meaning content (1979, p. 34). They are imperatival in form and are either duty-imposing or duty-excepting (p. 93). Harris differs from Kelsen in that they are not seen as acts of will but rather have the same *form* and logical force as acts of will (p. 38). This *force* is provided not by the compulsion of the issuer of a command or the feeling of duty of the commanded, but by a 'legal' ought which legal science practice ascribes to the rules which are valid according to that same legal science practice.

For Harris the practices of legal science used for determining the validity of legal rules (with which come not only this legal ought but also membership of the set of elements of the legal system) are sufficiently rigorous to be formalized into four principles. The principle of *exclusion* 'presupposes a determinate number of independent legislative sources in any legal system' (p. 28). The principle of *subsumption* provides hierarchical connections between sources with delegated authority and the sources which delegated that authority. The principle of *non-contradiction* eliminates rules that conflict with other rules emanating from the same source (p. 11). The principle of *derogation* does much the same for rules emanating from different sources, rejecting any rule or any part of a rule that conflicts with a rule from a higher source. These principles are not empirical statements about what legal scientists do, but rather definitions of the activity of legal science (supposedly derived from the goals of the activities of legal science, p. 1). When examining the law of any social grouping, legal scientists will follow the principle of exclusion, will look for and state the list of sources and, following the principle of exclusion, will look for and state the list of sources and, following the principle of derogation, will look for a ranking of sources. If they do not, they are not legal scientists.

These principles, along with the ranked sources for any group, can be synthesized and stated in a standard form known as the 'basic legal science *fiat*':

> Legal duties exist only if imposed (and not excepted) by rules originating in the following sources: ... or by rules subsumable under such rules. Provided that any contradiction between rules originating in different sources shall be resolved according to the following ranking amongst the sources ... and provided that no other contradiction shall be admitted to exist. (p. 70).

This *fiat* is not a positive legal rule. It cannot be one for the same reason that Kelsen's basic norm could not. Positive legal rules only exist because they are valid according to the principles of legal science, so unless those principles can be self-validating they cannot be positive legal rules. Nor is the *fiat* something which exists by virtue of the actions or beliefs of any person or persons as in Hart. It merely exists because legal science presupposes it.

The *fiat* is something of an optional extra. Because of the complexity of the task, few, if any, legal scientists would actually make the synthesis and it is quite possible to operate the principles without it (p. 79). Nevertheless, Harris regards it as a useful way of highlighting and summarizing the central features of legal science. It also provides a single test

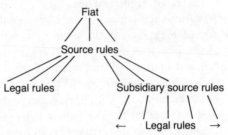

Figure 3.4   Harris's system

for determining the validity of norms, performing a similar function to Kelsen's basic norm and Hart's rule of recognition.

The four above-mentioned principles provide the legal *relations* that link them in a structure (p. 71). However, *pace* Harris, these principles are not so much concerned with relations between legal rules as with what *are* the legal rules, eliminating those that are not. They are directed towards creating a set of imperatival rules which do not contradict, rather than creating a structure into which those rules can fit. The first principle *excludes* all norms not originating in listed sources. The principles of derogation and noncontradiction eliminate some of the apparent rules originating in listed sources. The former eliminates contradictory rules from inferior sources. The latter principle is not so helpful – it merely tells us that one of two contradictory rules from equal sources is not law, but not which one. Indeed, only the principle of derogation removes contradictory rules in a *systematic* way. Even if the existence of the contradiction is seen as a relationship between the two rules, it is not a relation between two elements of the one legal system but between an element of the legal system and something outside it.

The only relations *between* rules are provided by the inclusive aspects of the principle of exclusion and the principle of subsumption. These provide the familiar positivist pyramidal *structure*. The principle of exclusion creates the first part of the legal science *fiat* which lists the sources. It also relates the rules originating in a source to a source rule (p. 79). The principle of subsumption permits some of the legal rules originating in legal sources to be source rules themselves, specifying other institutions as sources. These in turn are related to the legal rules they validate. Depending on the rules of subsumption that are followed, the pyramid so formed may have several steps and we could trace a path from *fiat* to Oxfordshire County Council by-law similar to that traced by Hart. (See figure 3.4.) The last step in each path relates the lowest legal sources to the legal rules directly emanating from them.

Harris's system highlights rather than resolves several difficulties that confronted Hart's. First, Harris acknowledges that courts sometimes accept or act on statutes, by-laws or court rulings that cannot be *subsumed* under the appropriate source rules. He says that such rules are nevertheless legal rules because the courts have authority other than by subsumption. He dubs these cases of 'forced subsumption'. But surely this highlights the fact that what makes it a legal rule is this 'other' authority of institutions, rather than the subsumptive system of authorizing relations which the legal scientist has built.

To perform its function, Hart's rule of recognition had to include all constitutional and administrative law. So would Harris's *fiat*. It has an initial beguiling simplicity only because the gaps have not been filled in – the few dots would stand for a myriad of details! Harris's approach makes the problem more obvious to those who try to use it. The list of sources recognized by an Australian legal scientist (assuming there are any) would be manageable though still running into dozens. But the *rankings* would be positively horrendous, taking into account federal, state and English courts. Furthermore, the complexities of exactly what powers maybe delegated mean that including the 'rules subsumable under such rules' is no simple matter. Needless to say, by the time the *fiat* had been finally read out there would be much controversy. If individual officials seek to resolve these controversies for themselves and do so, another of Hart's problems is reflected – different officials will have different *fiats* and have different legal systems. 'Legal science' does not find a legal system in law, at best it finds a gaggle of contradictory ones.

Two Systems

However, the momentary legal system is only one of two systems Harris's legal science sees in law. The nonmomentary legal system comprises the 'congeries of rules, principles, maxims', etc., that are used for the creation of new rules by the judiciary.

Harris says the 'nonmomentary system consists merely of a collectivity of verbal formulations' (1979, p. 121). It is hard to see this as a system at all. The nature and identity of the elements is both varying and unclear. There would appear to be very few relations between them – not even any to deal with contradictions between competing principles. Neither does there appear to be any structure or anything to unify the set of principles, etc., into a whole. This 'system' is an acknowledgment of the importance of content-based legal reasoning. But it merely acts as a dumping ground for many of those things, such as Dworkinian principles, which other writers have claimed to find in law, which Harris concedes are there and which even a legal scientist acknowledges, but which do not fit into his neo-Kelsenian system.

Harris's claims about a nonmomentary system show that, even for an individual legal scientist, law is at best two systems that are not consolidated into an overall system of law. If the nonmomentary 'congeries' are not regarded as forming a system, then law is at best only partly a system, with the rest a jumble. In either case, law *as a whole* is not systematic.

Harris's System and the Social Observer

But let us suppose that, when a legal scientist looks at law, he sees a momentary legal system and is satisfied it exists. Whether the *social observer* considers law to be systematic depends on Harris's claims about who practises legal science, what importance it has for how they act and how important their action is in law. But do judges and the other legal scientists listed by Harris practise legal science, do they follow those four principles and does the basic legal science *fiat* highlight their practices or distort them?

The first problem for Harris's claim is that the legal science described would be so clearly an *improvement* on what judges really do. Consequently, it tends to distort, rather than encapsulate, judicial practice. Judges do not reduce legal rules into duty-imposing and duty-excepting terms so that their contradictions can be exposed and eliminated. Judges not only leave rules in a variety of forms, conversion from which is difficult and controversial, they also embed them in long tracts of prose from which extrication in any form is difficult. Neither do judges have a ranking of sources that could be incorporated into a legal science *fiat*. Certainly some sources are regarded as higher than others, but there will often be several at the same level (e.g. supreme courts of Australian states). Furthermore, there are several criteria for adjudging one rule superior to another, including not only the seniority of its source but also how recently the rule was stated, whether it was *ratio* or *obiter* and how directly it bears on the current one. These cut across and partly negate any ranking on the basis of authority that judges may use.

As finding system in law is not what legal scientists *actually* do, it can at best be a *goal* of legal science rather than an achievement. System is not to be found in what judges do see in law but what they would like to see, and believe *could* be seen, if enough effort were put into it. Given the nature of the material sought to be systematized, that goal is rather quixotic. Although Harris's book clearly assumes it is possible, no one actually *has* filled in those blanks of a legal science *fiat* for the law of any nation. This is perhaps because to do so is to seek system in the legal meaning of an unsystematic set of actions within the institutions of law, to make systematic sense out of that which was done by a multitude of persons for a multitude of reasons, with the consequent myriad of varying and conflicting effects.

It is submitted that the goal of judges is not so wide (in fact, closer to their achievements). If they seek to create some system in law it is not in law as a whole but in some *part* of law. Indeed it is this more limited goal that Harris states is legal science's: 'attempting the systematic exposition of a *corpus* of legal materials' (p. 2). Judges seek to tidy up small portions of law and tend to keep those portions small for reasons considered in the next chapter. The systemization attempted is also more in terms of content than of the structure of authorizing relations. Even where such small bodies of legal rules are systematized, the uncoordinated nature of the effort means that it is unlikely that they could be formed into a larger system – especially as judges, in seeking not only to rationalize various rules from different sources but also to pick the substantively best, will tend to give slightly different weightings and rankings to the various sources in each of the areas they try to tidy up.

In any case, a rigid system of authority relations would tend to reduce their flexibility in achieving the systematization of content. This suggests that judicial failure to create such legal systems is due to more than judicial recognition of the time and difficulty involved. It is useful for a judge to have rules which give more authority to some sources than others, thereby justifying choice between rules. But a rigid ranking of sources would reduce a judge's flexibility and his ability to choose the sources from which rules of more appealing content can be found to originate. A set of overlapping and potentially contradictory methods of choosing between sources allows them to retain this flexibility, so it is hardly surprising that judges do not engage in the tidying-up operations necessary for the creation of a legal science *fiat*.

Yet this failure throws doubt on the judges' commitment to one of the four principles of legal science. The principle of derogation is supposed to resolve contradictions between pairs of norms, systematically and automatically, by invalidating the one from the inferior source. This is not possible without a ranking of sources.

With a weak principle of derogation, the job of excising contradictions is left to the rather more haphazard principle of noncontradiction (which tells us that one – but not which one – of a pair of contradicting norms from the same or equal sources is not law). Yet judicial commitment to this principle seems even more shaky. Judges undoubtedly see ensuring consistency as *part* of their role – but *only* a part, the importance of which varies from judge to judge (Paterson, 1982, p. 199). Their first concern is with settling the dispute in front of them. In fact they are *functus officio* when they have given their order though they will frequently give reasons, providing a guide for settling and/or prevention of similar disputes (although whom they are trying to guide is uncertain: Paterson, 1982, p. 30). They will frequently shy away from settling potential conflicts with other rules and the relatively inchoate structure of many of their pronouncements aids them in this: (1) they virtually never use language that is sufficiently formal properly to contradict anything; (2) where rules do appear to conflict they will normally attempt minor modifications to avoid the contradiction; (3) sometimes they ignore apparent contradictions and refuse to overrule either, thereby failing to use 'their' supposedly vital principle of noncontradiction. (Confining an old rule 'to its facts' does not remove contradictions between it and new rules; it merely indicates that the court does not think it necessary to overrule the old decision as those particular facts are unlikely to recur).

Even where judges do try to tackle contradictions they do not do it as believers in the principle of noncontradiction. Rather than saying that one of the contradictory 'rules' is *not* a rule of law, judges see *both* as rules because they have originated in legal sources and have a set of ways (themselves contradictory) of dealing with contradictions brought to their attention. This is borne out by the following tendencies. First, where a judge does find two rules in contradiction, *prior* to that ruling both rules had apparently had force, operating simultaneously. Naturally enough they had never both operated in the same case but they had both made effective and final distributions of property, determinations of freedom in criminal matters, etc. This highlights the way in which legal rules are operative (if at all). They will occupy the minds of some judges and affect the future of some citizens. It is this limited operation that makes contradictions in those rules so easy. One rule occupies the mind of one judge, the other the mind of another: one rule affects one citizen's fortunes, the other another's. A legal scientist would have to say that all the time only one had been really law. But without a principle of noncontradiction, he could say that two contradictory rules coexisted until a judge used one of the ways of resolving contradictions to remove one.

Judicial adherence to the other two principles of legal science is equally weak. Rather than operating a principle of exclusion, judges tend to have a rule of *inclusion*, a fairly definite but *nonexhaustive* list of sources. They do not wish to have specific limits placed on what they regard as a relevant source. They want to be able to cite something – like morality, 'policy', or 'judicial notice' – without having to decide whether they are treating it as a source or something far more vague. Subsumption is undermined because courts do not automatically accept delegated legislation. They impose limits on it via a large number of (reasonably flexible) rules: so what passes that set of rules is set up, at least temporarily, as another source. Thus the four principles do not encapsulate judicial practice but represent a formalized, over-consensualized distortion of them. Yet just such a distortion is necessary in order to found Harris's system.

Even if, contrary to all of the above, judges really did have a legal scientist's view of law, the social observer would ask how important this is in understanding the activities of judging. 'Finding' the law is only a part of those activities – filling gaps, deciding trouble-cases and, at lower levels, discovering facts and applying laws to them are also very important. The first two are explicitly acknowledged by Harris, but are compartmentalized into another, nonmomentary legal system. But this separation of the parts of judging is very difficult, if not impossible, and very few judges attempt to make it. Furthermore, judges are only one of the examples of legal scientists that Harris gives. The others are even less concerned with systematizing law. Although textbook writers may seek to systematize areas of the law, sometimes as great as whole subjects, they as often seek to expose its internal contradictions and tensions. Solicitors and counsel are as likely to muddy the law to protect their clients as they are to tidy it up.

Even if the judges, practitioners, etc., could and did create legal systems, there would be significant variations between them. Their legal science *fiats* would vary (reflecting the controversy of source-rankings and the variable commitment to the various principles). Thus the perception of law as systematic by various legal scientists would not make law appear systematic to a social observer who records the differences in the legal systems perceived. If law is seen as something encompassing the activities of multiple legal scientists, rather than confined to the actions of only one, then law is not systematic.

3.10 Raz

Raz's system is very similar to those of Hart and Harris. Norms are related by authority and other relations into a system supposedly used by judicial officials to understand law. The details will be provided in concentrating on the similarities to the other theories (which tend to throw up the same problems) and the differences (which fail to resolve them). It differs from Hart's theory largely because of its attempts to overcome Hart's problems. It differs from Harris's theory largely because of different approaches to the same problems.

In dealing with the problems inherent in Hart's mixed internal/external rules, Raz, like Harris, emphasizes the internal aspect. Indeed his major insight is his conception of the internal aspect of rules as practical reasons. In dealing with the uncertainty of Hart's point of view, he retreats into the internal 'legal' point of view of the practical reasoner. Raz's response to criticisms of pyramidal structures topped by apex norms is very different to Harris's (1979). Instead of redrawing the theory in more rigid terms and excluding all doubtful rules, he accepts some criticisms, rejecting hierarchical structure and a single rule of recognition. Consequently, his system is more open and flexible – and less systematic. In so doing he offers or acknowledges some important insights into law.

But he still calls it a system. Indeed, Raz is quite dogmatic about law's systematic quality. He regards it as a *'fact* that every law necessarily belongs to a legal system' and that law cannot be understood except through a theory of legal system (1970, p. 1). As is indicated by the use of the word 'necessarily', some of the argument is definitional. Law is found only where the process of social decision-making has been split into 'deliberative' and 'executive' stages and where those involved in the latter stage regard themselves as bound to apply the decisions reached in the former. The institutions of the deliberative stage are sources (1970, p. 137). Consequently, even when there is all the institutional paraphernalia of what we call 'law', if certain officials do not see themselves bound by sources then there is no law (1975, p. 137).

Despite the predominantly internal point of view and the occasional *a priori* argument, Raz does claim to be studying a social organization. He believes that the institutions we call 'legal' *are* split into ones with deliberative and executive functions, and that the view of one by the other is the key to understanding both. This view is clearly of relevance to the question posed by this chapter.

As we shall see, Raz's insight into rules as the reasons of legal actors is distorted by this insistence on finding or imposing on them what he calls a system and seeing their activities directed to that systematization. This destroys the usefulness of Raz's theory from both 'legal' and social-observer points of view. Neither would accept it as an accurate or adequate description of law. This is despite the retreats involved which may lead us to conclude that his theory does not depict a system. The problem is that he has not retreated far enough and the degree of systematization he attempts is the root of the problems his theory faces.

Elements

The elements of Raz's system include norms and nonnormative rules which are internally related to legal norms. Raz sees norms as practical *reasons*, those employed in 'practical reasoning' (the reasoning used to choose what action to perform). A practical reason is a relationship between a fact or belief and a person. Evidence of that fact, or adherence to that belief, is seen as a reason for or against performing an action. This is so because the reasoner holds a value that the action may help, directly or indirectly, to fulfil. Thus ultimately the relation is between facts, beliefs and values.

Raz distinguishes two 'orders' of practical reasons. 'First-order' reasons are direct reasons for action – facts or beliefs which affect the value placed on the act, or the probability and value of the expected consequences. Such reasons may conflict but some reasons have greater 'weight' than others. The conflict is resolved by a balancing of their respective weights. 'Second-order' reasons are reasons for acting on, or ignoring, certain first-order reasons – dubbed respectively 'positive' and 'negative' second-order reasons. Particularly important are the latter, which he also calls 'exclusionary reasons' (1975, p. 40). They do not have weight vis-à-vis first-order reasons but override first-order reasons within specified categories, regardless of the latter's weight. He notes two types of exclusionary reasons: 'rules of thumb' (including time-saving and error-reducing rules (1975, p. 59)), and rules made by those the actor regards as being in authority. The key elements of the legal system are exclusionary reasons of the second type. They exclude and replace all the other first-order reasons we may have for doing or avoiding an action (preferences, advice, values, fear, etc.), leaving only the dictates of authority as reasons. This gives them what he later called a 'peremptory' character.

Among these norms are 'duty-imposing rules' (1970, p. 224) or 'mandatory norms' (1975, p. 49). These offer both a first-order reason for doing the action mandated and a second-order reason for ignoring any reason for not doing it. Raz calls them 'protected reasons', (1979, p. 78) and, because the exclusion of other reasons is total, 'complete reasons' (1975, p. 79)

Other norms are nonmandatory and include power-conferring rules and permissions. (1975, p. 85). The former confer 'normative power' – the ability to alter norms, i.e. to change protected reasons (1979, p. 18). These are important *positive* second-order reasons which give us a reason to regard something else, the power-holder's action, as a reason for our own action.

Permissions are also exclusionary reasons, excluding reasons against the action contained in mandatory norms prohibiting it (e.g. a permission to kill in self-defence excludes the reasons against doing so provided by the norms proscribing murder). As such, there can only be permissions if there *are* such other reasons; if there are not, a permission could only be said to exist in a weak and, he claims, unnecessary sense (1975, p. 96).

The other elements of the legal system are not considered to be norms because they are neither exclusionary reasons nor, in a general sense, 'guides' to action, but they are still reasons. The only examples he has offered are rights (1970, p. 175), which he sees as reasons for courts to allow people to perform acts, reasons to stop others from hindering them (1970, p. 227), and perhaps reasons for providing assistance to the right-holders in performing these acts (if the right is a positive one).

In describing the elements of a legal system as reasons, Raz has opted for an extremely internal view, perhaps even more internal than he intended. Although reasons are described as relations between facts and persons, they are relations drawn by a practical reasoner between facts as perceived by *that* reasoner and the decision *that* reasoner is to make. They are part of the internal processes of the mind.

The internality of such elements is matched only by their individuality. Something is a reason because of the part it plays in a person's reasoning process. My reason is my reason, your reason is yours: however similar their content, they are separate phenomena. This isolation of the parts of legal systems as individual phenomena, and the consequence that systems built from them must also be individual phenomena, is common in positivist systems. This should be unsurprising – norms, and 'oughtness' in general, are irreducibly individual phenomena because, however general their application, their *locus* is in the individual. This is, first, because each individual possesses what might be called 'moral sovereignty' – the sole right to determine what is morally valid for that individual (even if everybody but individual A thinks A should not ø, but A still thinks he ought to ø, it is perfectly intelligible, indeed inescapable, that, for A, he ought to ø). Second, even if ought-ideas are communicated and are held in identical terms by different people, they have to pass through an 'interpersonal barrier' which splits them into separate individual phenomena. An ought-idea has to be formed into words, then speech acts, sensed by the second person and understood. Even if the communication is perfect, – i.e. if (1) the words used completely and accurately cover the first persons's ought-idea, (2) the second person understands those words perfectly, and (3) the ought-idea he forms corresponds exactly to the first person's ought-idea, – it will not be one idea that is shared but two identical ones, each held in an individual's mind separated by that gulf. Of course, in the world of interpersonal communications those 'ifs' are very potent: failure of expression is common, words have many shades of meaning and 'contested concepts' abound in normative discourse. Even if someone agrees with a suggested 'norm', this is merely a matter of finding a form of words that seems to approximate to that person's ideas. The difference in 'meaning' may only become apparent to us (and perhaps to him) when he comes to act upon it. 'May' is used because the multiplicity of norms that can justify an action means that action cannot clearly indicate the norms behind it.

Because of this individuality of reasons, it is very important to know exactly *whose* reasons they are supposed to be. On this Raz leaves us in no doubt. They are reasons regularly used by members of 'executive' institutions (1975, p. 142), i.e. by judges. These reasons are used in choosing what action (i.e. decision) to perform. But not all the reasons they use in coming to decisions count as legal reasons. Because the 'essential' (1970, p. 212) nature of law involves the binding of executive institutions by deliberative ones, legal rules are rules which originate in social sources and by which members of courts customarily regard themselves as being bound (1970, p. 214). Converting this into terms of reasons means that judges draw reasons for action from social facts about deliberative institutions (and other social sources, if any). These social facts may be about actions that were performed (e.g. the Queen signed an Act), or events that occurred (e.g. a majority vote was cast in a certain forum). *Reasons* were defined in general terms as relations between facts and persons, drawn by those persons. *Legal* reasons become relations between social facts and judges, drawn by judges. Just as in Hart, Raz's judges are looking at the social institutions of law. The only difference is that what they generate is described in terms of *reasons for action* rather than *rules*. This would not be an important difference if the method by which judges generate reasons is to generate rules first which are then treated as reasons – it would merely clarify the mechanism. But if, as argued earlier, judges reason only partially in terms of rules, the difference is an important one.

This view of law as reasons provides both existence and identity criteria for the parts of Raz's legal system. As reasons, they *exist* if they are used, i.e. they are somebody's reason. They are identified as legal if they are practised by the courts and are seen by them as originating in social sources. It also avoids some of the problems that had confounded other positivist theories of law. Command and will theories had difficulty in finding an intention or will in such complex sources as legislatures, let alone custom, but this is sidestepped neatly. There is no need to determine the actual intentions of the members of the legislature or to construct artificial ones – judges look at what has been done and draw reasons from it. Normative theories like Harris's face two more problems: (1) much of law is stated in nonnormative terms, especially power-conferring rules which did not seem to tell the power-holder to do anything at all; and (2) even when the law is put in normative terms, it is not directed at judges. But for Raz it does not matter what form of expression is used. If a legislature endorses a statement in the indicative mood, such as the example given by Honoré that 'a young person is one between fourteen and seventeen', then that is a reason for judges to treat people of that age differently (1977, p. 114). Power-conferring rules may not tell the power-holder what to do, but whatever is done provides a reason for judges in deciding what *they* should do. Finally, even if legislation is directed at others (e.g. speeding motorists) rather than judges, judges find reasons for their own actions in these directions (e.g. reasons for imposing sentences on motorists who have been speeding).

Raz's account of the elements of his legal system is constructed to meet some of the problems of positivist theory. In seeing them as reasons, he has achieved a major insight into the normative phenomena covered by traditional positivist systems. In pointing to, though not fully developing or necessarily realizing, the extreme internality and individuality of these normative phenomena, he has considerably deepened this insight. In seeing them as the reasons for action that judges and other legal actors derived from facts about social sources, he has refined positivist insights into the importance of those sources. I have only one quibble with this account of these phenomena. It is doubtful that judges' reasons and the relations they find between reasons take the *exclusionary* forms suggested by Raz. Raz makes some very important points. He notes several techniques that all of us have for sorting out which of the many available reasons to follow, and how we regard some rules and actions by others as reasons for ignoring some (or all) of the other reasons for an action. Yet the first-order reasons are not completely *excluded* from the calculation regardless of weight, but are rather *suppressed*. One of Raz's examples was the error-reducing rule that investment decisions should not be made when tired – but there may be an opportunity which presents itself that seems so clearly profitable and so urgent that the practical reasoner ignores that rule. The weight of the first-order reasons was so great that the second-order rule failed to suppress it. The same is true for authority. For various reasons we may obey the dictates of a particular authority, regardless of the values served by the prescribed action itself, and in most cases we do not consider the weight of the reasons against it. But it is in the nature of authority that we sometimes regard that which it prescribes as so senseless, or so ethically wrong, that we do not accept it. The second-order reasons are *suppressory* rather than exclusionary. Weight is relevant in that first-order reasons of a certain weight will fail to be suppressed by certain second-order reasons. Indeed such suppressory reasons maybe considered to have *three* weights: (1) one which corresponds to the weight of first-order reasons it can suppress; (2) one which corresponds to the weight the suppressory reason will have in the final balance of reasons made necessary because of its inability to suppress other reasons; (3) its weight vis-à-vis other second-order reasons if all first-order reasons have been suppressed (this raises in a different form the part content plays in the determination of law and the problem it creates for positivists). Such suppressory reasons are more difficult to fit into systems than exclusionary reasons. However, they have an important part to play in the nonsystematic theory of law outlined in chapter 7.

This quibble aside, the problem is not with Raz's account of these phenomena, it is with his claims to find system in them and to see them as either systematizable or sufficient for an adequate theory of law.

Relations and Structure

Raz sees the elements of law as a set of norms practised by a distinct set of persons. He acknowledges that this does not entail that these rules are related to each other, and that such relations are necessary for the presence of a legal system (1975, p. 197).

Like Harris, Raz sees these relations linking the parts into two structures. Like Harris, Raz calls them momentary and nonmomentary systems. But there are few other similarities. Raz's nonmomentary system is a system of authorizing relations that link source rules, power-conferring rules and substantive rules into a 'genetic structure' similar to the pyramidal structures of Hart and Harris. Raz's momentary system relates all the substantive norms that are in operation (i.e. used as reasons by the courts) at any one time into what he calls an 'operative structure' (1970, p. 185).

As these structures differ greatly, so do the relations that form them. Genetic relations link elements of the nonmomentary system. These were initially described as relations between one law and another law authorizing its existence. Put into terms of reasons it is the relationship between a reason and a reason for holding it as a reason. This can be illustrated with Hart's Oxfordshire by-law. The judge will regard certain facts about the behaviour of members of the County Council, resolutions voted on in meetings, etc., as a reason for fining parking offenders. This is because he believes that such facts constitute a reason for action, i.e. he adheres to a power-conferring norm. The genetic relation links those two reasons. The same sort of relation links the normative power of the minister to give ministerial orders to the normative power of the council to make by-laws. Hart's chain of valid rules becomes a chain of reasons that ends with a source. The chain of reasons constitutes the answers to the chain of questions 'why?' that might be asked of a judge to justify his official behaviour. As we go further up these chains they begin to converge, forming a pattern that constitutes the genetic structure of the non-momentary legal system.

The relations of the momentary system link norms on the basis of content, thereby recognizing an importance lack in Hart's theory. They relate the potential effects of various rules. Thus a permission for A to ø is related to a mandatory norm prohibiting a class of persons that includes A from øing. These are related in that the reasons contained in the permission exclude the reasons contained in the mandatory norm for A.

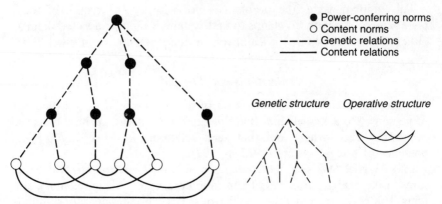

Figure 3.5 Raz's system

Other important content relations can be found: (1) between the mandatory norm prohibiting the behaviour and the (permissory or mandatory) norm imposing a sanction, and (2) where the act involved in the exercise of the power is usually prohibited, between a power-conferring norm and a permissory norm. In all these, the relations are between different reasons that the judge draws from law to decide what action he should himself take. Such relations are extremely numerous and range across the whole of law (e.g. details of property law affect the operation of the laws of theft). They do not fit into a regular pattern, let alone a pyramid. They are part of an 'interconnected web', the operative structure.

Raz's depiction of law in terms of two systems does not split law in the way Harris's theory does. Unlike Harris, Raz includes all the elements in one of the systems. Because all legal reasons must have social sources they will all be linked, by genetic relations, to a power-conferring norm which makes facts about a source reasons for the judge's own action. Thus all legal norms will find a place in the nonmomentary system. The momentary system relates some of the legal norms (the final, 'content' ones) in a quite different way but this cannot detract from any degree of systemness in law established by the nonmomentary system. The legal system would appear like an infinitely complicated version of figure 3.5.

Although the presence of the two systems is not fatal to the overall systematic quality of law, the reason they are needed is. The operative structure is necessary because of the weakness in the genetic structure and Raz's consequent retreat from the pyramidal structures of Hart and Harris. Raz recognizes not only the possibility of several rules of recognition for law in one state, but that this will be usual in complex 'systems'

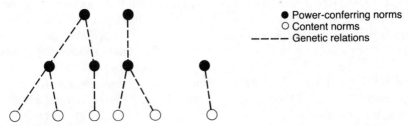

Figure 3.6   The effect of multiple rules of recognition on Raz's genetic 'structure'

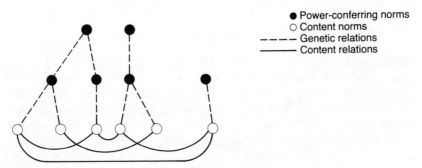

Figure 3.7   Raz's operative 'structure' to the rescue?

like ours. Once there are several 'rules of recognition' the various chains of reasons will not join up, and there will not be one genetic structure but several (see figure 3.6).

The operative structure is necessary to provide extra links between these partial systems. It could not by itself provide an overall structure for law because the operative structure will not include power-conferring norms. No doubt Raz hopes that there would be sufficient operative relations to link the various isolated bits of the genetic structure so that every legal norm will ultimately, if tortuously, be linked to every other in a grand interconnected web of both genetic and operative relations (see figure 3.7).

The key question is whether this interconnected web of relations can usefully be said to amount to a 'structure'. All Raz has given us is a completely unpatterned web of relations. It is a bit like saying that a pile of bricks is structured in that all the bricks are related to others (by being in contact), and that these relationships fall into categories (frictional, gravitational and being stuck together with old mortar). You can even find identity and membership criteria by having a 'primary brick-discerning institution' – the subcontractor who has dumped the bricks in a pile. Perhaps nothing can be ruled out on definitional grounds but this is certainly a very different kind of structure from those of other theorists and from the kinds of structures that spring to mind when the word 'structure' is used. Does such an 'interconnected web' fall within the borderline of what might be considered a structure? If not, then Raz's theory has provided no justification for either legal actors or social observers to find system in law. Even if it does, the question still remains whether, with such a different kind of structure to that of other systems, describing it as a 'system' is helpful or not.

Wholeness

Without a sovereign, ultimate rule of recognition, a basic norm or a legal science *fiat* to place at the apex of his system, Raz has denied himself the traditional positivist's answer to the system's unity and wholeness. Raz offers three other answers. The first is the 'pattern of relations' between the norms (1975, p. 9), but, as seen above, the structure is too weak to bear that burden. The second would seem to be provided by the courts who practise law (1975, p. 124). Yet courts practise much else besides law (including the rules of grammar and occasionally mathematics), but frequently do not practise all of law because they are confined to applying only a part of it (chapter 3.6). The practices of the court may provide an imperfect criterion of *identity* for law by determining which norms are legal ones, but it does not turn them into a whole unless courts *practise* them *as a whole*. In fact, as seen in chapter 3.4, the very opposite is the case. Judges tend to draw on only a part of the law, using only a very few norms at any one time, leaving the rest undisturbed. This allows judges to avoid potential conflicts between various reasons for their decisions, and to pick and choose, from the myriad of legal reasons available, a manageable set that can be applied to the case in front of them.

The third way in which Raz's legal system may be seen as a whole is provided by the position he claims these rules have within the overall social system (1979, p. 99). He describes the legal system as a sub-system of the political system, which is in turn a sub-system of the social system. This view of law will be rejected in chapter 5.

As none of the three dubious wholeness factors can be made out, legal actors and social observers would find even less reason for seeing law as systematic in Raz's terms. Having abandoned the traditional citadel of positivist systems as indefensible, we find that the new lines of defence cannot hold.

The Social Observer's View

Raz has set out a system which has clearly defined elements and relations, yet his retreats from the pyramidal simplicity of earlier theories lead to an indefinite structure with no clear or defensible wholeness factor. Thus it is not a system in the sense used in this book. But can the social observer be persuaded that even this 'system' exists in a society such as ours, and can such an observer be persuaded that it can provide an adequate account of law from his point of view?

The first problem for our social observer is the extremely internal and individual nature of the elements and relations comprising Raz's system and the different ways individual practical reasoners structure them. For the social observer the trite statement that law is a social phenomenon is more than usually true. His problem is to convert such an internal phenomenon into a social one.[4]

The (contestable) answer that these phenomena will be similar merely emphasizes that any system will be the system for the legal actor rather than law the phenomenon of which those actors are a part. There is another problem in converting Raz's model into a social phenomenon. The crucial division of the social decision-making process into deliberative and executive stages is based on an analogy with the way individuals sometimes make decisions (1970, p. 213). At worst, this amounts to an anthropomorphic view of society with hints of a 'group mind'. At best, the analogy is a very strained one, as the quality of a 'decision' taken by society is very different from that of one taken by an individual. This is doubly so when the two stages involve different persons with different views of what the decision was once it was made. It could be answered that although no social observer could see law as this two-stage decision process, the members of the courts see it as such and see themselves as the executors of social decisions already made. But this merely turns the allegedly social phenomenon back into an individual one.

Raz adds to the social observer's problems by providing him with two sets of tests for the existence of legal systems. One set involves two tests to be applied in sequence (1970, p. 205). The first test is the familiar one of efficacy, 'How many of the duty-imposing laws are obeyed?', which he has expanded by also asking, 'How many power-conferring rules are used?' This is used despite all the classic problems he admits it faces. This test determines if any legal system exists in society. If only one system passes the test then that is the legal system (1970, p. 206). The second test comes into operation only if more than one system has passed this test. Although called a 'test of exclusion', it in fact comes in two parts, the first part being a compatibility test and not exclusionary at all. If two legal systems do not contradict each other then both exist; law is split into two different entities and hence is not systematic as a whole. But if the legal systems do contradict each other, the exclusion test proper comes into operation. It examines the attitudes of the population to the legal systems, especially where the norms of the two systems conflict. If the population does not regard law as systematic then this test cannot be met because the population cannot have an attitude to something they do not know exists. But perhaps attitudes to the various institutions might be substituted. Even then the test is difficult to apply (do you look to the so-called 'deliberative' or 'executive' institutions?) and quite possibly unreliable. Considering the contempt so many hold for both legislators and the legal profession from whose ranks judges are drawn, the system whose institutions are held most in contempt might nonetheless be the system most theorists would want to call law.

At first sight both these tests seem to depend only on the behaviour and attitudes of the general population. While making life a little easier for the social observer, this does seem to contradict Raz's emphasis on law-applying institutions and the internal reasoning of its members. But Raz's description of the elements of a legal system mean that legal norms are, by their very nature, reasons for action applied by executive institutions. Thus a judicial-acceptance test is built into the description of the system itself. Raz acknowledges this and presents his second set of existence criteria (1975, p. 131), as a statement of Hart's dual test. Members of the norm-applying institutions must practise, and the population must conform to, the norms of the system.

However, this test by itself is only sufficient to establish the existence of a *set of norms* rather than a *system*. At the very least, the relations and structure would have to exist in some sense or for someone – presumably the members of the 'executive' norm-applying institutions. Not only would judges have to share reasons with the same form and content, but they would have to see them linked by the same relations into the same structure.

The earlier discussion of similar claims about the commonality of judges' practices and perceptions should make us just as wary of these. The content of the reasons may be *similar* but is likely to vary in significant ways, just as did the content of Hart's primary and secondary rules. The structures of judicial reasons are likely to vary enormously, because the chains of reasons justifying an action in Raz will deviate as surely as the chains of rules justifying a decision in Hart.

The nature of the structure of relations between judicial reasons as depicted by Raz is also subject to challenge. Raz pictures them integrated into a complex structure by genetic and operative relations. This suggests something more permanent and all-encompassing than the practical reasoning in which judges are involved. It is not so much that reasons are in existence and interrelated, but rather that judges are skilled in generating reasons and avoiding or resolving any conflicts which appear between them. Rather than holding a power-conferring norm which is genetically related to the reasons which are provided by the institution upon which power is conferred, judges are skilled in drawing reasons for their actions from facts about, and actions of, other social institutions. Rather than judges reasoning that mandatory and permissory norms are operatively related (because the latter reason excludes the reasons for conformity contained in the former), judges possess the skill of removing conflict between rules they have derived by making such interrelations. Rather than delving into a structure of reasons to find a system of reasons appropriate for the case in hand, judges make a partial, temporary structure out of the reasons they bring to bear on the case. In chapter 7 it will be argued that the positivist image of a system of rules, norms or reasons should be replaced by a set of skills that allow judges to create individual and differing internal phenomena to help them decide how to act.

Raz's theory also faces the same two fundamental obstacles that Hart and Harris had in persuading the social observer to see law as systematic. The first is that, even from Raz's point of view, there is much more to law: a theory of adjudication is also required in order to provide even 'a conceptual foundation of an understanding of law as a social institution of great importance to society' (1970, p. 209). No doubt this would include a great deal of material that was not source-based, and would include all Dworkin's principles and Harris's 'congerie' which did not fit into other positivist systems either. The second criticism is Raz's concentration on courts and judges rather than the other institutions of law. Although this criticism applies to the other two theories, it is one to which Raz draws particular attention by referring to the judicial institutions as 'norm-applying' and 'executive' institutions. 'Norm-applying' institution is as appropriate a term for the bureaucracy as it is for courts, because it is on the bureaucracy that the principal task of applying legislation falls. 'Executive' institution is a term used almost exclusively to refer to the ecutive' institution is a term used almost exclusively to refer to the bureaucracy and rarely to courts. Raz also draws attention to other institutions in law by specifically referring to them; he even gives them a special name, 'deliberative' institutions. Why should law be the acts of deliberative institutions as seen through the eyes of members of executive ones, rather than *vice versa*? Raz says that to understand authority it is necessary to look at how it appears to the person who regards himself bound by it. But to prefer the view of law from one institution is to acknowledge that there is a difference, and to raise even more forcefully the question of why we should look from one rather than the other.

Surely the study of social organizations should note the views of both and study the way in which the interaction of the two institutions produces different views, rather than to examine the view of one to the exclusion of the other. The former is certainly the approach adopted in chapters 7 and 8.

3.11   MacCormick and Weinberger

The latest version of positivist theory is to be found in MacCormick's and Weinberger's *An Institutional Theory of Law* (1986). This is a collection of their earlier essays with the addition of a spirited introduction which interprets the collection as outlining a theory of law. Although they are as insistent as any positivist on the systematic nature of law, and still call law a 'system of norms' (1986, p. 18), their concern has shifted away from demonstrating the structure and wholeness of such a system to the epistemological and ontological status of its normative elements (1986, p. 6). As we have seen in discussing Hart and Harris, the existence of individual legal rules was dependent upon the existence or postulation of an ultimate rule of recognition, basic norm or basic legal science *fiat*. Given the problems in constructing such an ultimate rule or norm, this gave the individual legal rules a paradoxically precarious claim to existence. To put these on a firmer footing, MacCormick and Weinberger make the existence of legal norms a matter of 'institutional fact' rather than a consequence of the postulation of the basic norm (p. 20). Like Raz, they concentrate on the elements of law and give an account of them that is much more plausible but less systematizable. At the same time they abandon positivism's key systematizing concept – the basic norm, rule of recognition, etc. It is in effect, if not in intent, a major retreat from the more systematic positivist systems theories in the face of one of their major identified problems. But on account of unremedied problems, it is ineffective to save the theory as a systematic theory of law from the point of view of either the legal scientist or the social observer.

The elements of law include 'norms, goal statements, value standards and criteria of preference', although it is not clear whether the system includes only the norms or all the rest as well (cf. pp. 18 and 19). Certainly they concentrate on explaining norms, and norms are central to their legal theory. Despite being an 'institutional' theory of law, their theory of institutions and 'institutional facts' is in terms of the rules, especially rules which constitute and terminate institutions and determine their consequences (a view criticized in chapter 3.7).

Norms exist only as part of the practical reason or 'action guiding system' of a person or group. They can be understood from the internal point of view, hermeneutically or by the Weberian 'verstehen'. This seems to leave open the possibility that these reasons may be either individual or shared. But it is the latter that MacCormick and Weinberger insist upon for law.

Some norms are norms because of the existence of other norms or norm-constituted institutions (e.g. many statutory norms are norms because of the 'institution' of 'the constitution' or 'enabling legislation', 1986, p. 144). However, some 'key rules' (e.g. constitutions, property, judges, kings, p. 14) must be based on conventions or customs that are rather like Hart's social rules. They are 'thought objects' that are shared standards of conduct and part of the 'custom' of 'shared practical reason'. Like Hart, they presume that when we enter the internal point of view, we find that all members of the relevant group (presumably 'legal scientists' or 'lawyers') share norms as standards of conduct. This glosses over the more interesting phenomenon of behaviour that is convergent despite divergent perceptions of it and the variety of internally held rules.

MacCormick and Weinberger emphasize the variety and range of the normative elements including primary rules, secondary rules and principles. They also indicate the range of relations between such elements including logical entailment, validity and justification (p. 18). This richness, variety and range of normative elements and relations is rightly highlighted. The formation of these into a systematic whole is 'understood as a *rational reconstruction* which states the substantive meaning of the law' (p. 18). The problems facing this understanding are even more extensive than those facing Hart's theory. Is such rational reconstruction of the whole of law possible? Certainly no participant attempts it on so large a scale, whatever they may try to do with smaller areas of law, and, as we have seen, the practices of judges, the key legal players, run counter to such systematization. Even if it were possible, the main problem is the sheer variety of rational reconstructions possible with the same material. These will be multiplied by the variety of internally held rules that are possible. There will be one legal system for every individual who manages rationally to reconstruct the law. From the social observer's point of view this again would make law a paradoxically *a*social phenomenon.

Once again, retreating from Hartian and Kelsenian positions and having more plausible elements makes MacCormick and Weinberger's theory less systematized and even less systematizable from the participant's point of view. At the same time, the individuality of any systematic reconstruction makes law, which includes several such participants, unsystematic from the social observer's point of view.

3.12   Conclusion

This chapter has looked at the most influential post-war positivist and his theory of law as a system of primary and secondary rules. We have seen how it incorporated the major positivist insight into the importance of source-based rules in law and some important insights of his own – the social phenomenon of convergent behaviour and normative orientation, the fruitfulness of comparing our own law to that of hypothetical simpler societies, the variety of rules and the use of meta-rules. However, the attempt to force these insights into a system caused many of the theory's problems. Much of the potential insight into the above-mentioned social phenomena was missed by representing them as shared social rules and the rest was lost by their unheralded exclusion from Hart's system in favour of more systematizable secondary rules internally held by officials and primary rules that are validated by such rules. The secondary rule of recognition is crucial to Hart's system but the necessary official consensus seems lacking. Without such rules of recognition there is either no system or a system for every judge. The limitation of the relations to validity relations between rules makes them potentially more systematizable but at the cost of ignoring the wider variety of relations between persons and the varied structures of legal reasoning and justification including, especially, the importance of the content of rules that are valued by individual reasoners.

Hart's comparison between a hypothetical 'primitive' law and our own is challenging but the real difference must be seen in terms of practices, officials and institutions which cannot be adequately captured by rules and certainly not by the system of rules that Hart proposes. In any case, the system Hart proposes covers so little of the phenomenon of law as to throw in doubt whether it could amount to an adequate theory of law at all.

Later writers have consciously or otherwise retreated from Hart's theory without solving its basic problems. Harris's theory is even more systematic but is only seen from the limited standpoint of the legal scientist. However, Harris actually highlights some of Hart's problems (e.g. by specifying what an apex norm has to do to fulfil its function, the problems of formulating one are emphasized). His limited point of view makes us question what he assumes – that judges, practitioners and academics are legal scientists. Without such assumptions there is little point to his theory. Yet, on his criteria, adherence to the principles of legal science is very rare, especially on the bench; and even from the limited point of view of legal science Harris sees law as at least two separate legal systems, one of which is a 'congeries of rules, principles' etc. Having abandoned a single apex norm and incorporated content-based operative relations, Raz's theory is less systematic and concentrates more on the elements of law than on its systematic structure. In seeing the legal rules as practical reasons derived from sources he has deepened the positivist insight. But in trying to see them as systematically ordered, he overstates the exclusionary character of legal norms and ignores the essential individuality of reasons. MacCormick and Weinberger retreat further into a consideration of the elements rather than the structure and wholeness of law. These elements are seen as 'institutional facts'. However, like Hart, their institutional character is seen entirely in terms of rules and they still see legal scientists rationally reconstructing law in terms of a legal system. The individuality of legal reasons and norms, the great variability of legal systems caused by different choices of apex norm, and the different kinds of rational reconstruction indicate an emerging theme. This kind of systematization makes law a curiously asocial phenomenon.

Overall, the retreats have not saved the positivist theory of legal system. Some have highlighted its problems, others have been seen as positive steps in the right direction, but, as steps towards a nonsystematic theory, they are supportive of this book's contention. Some have acknowledged the insights of others but they are either largely excised (content) or incorporated in a completely different guise (institutions). The next two chapters will examine how others have attempted to develop theories of legal system from these rejected insights and show that the same fate befalls them.

Notes

1 Note that it is not sufficient to say that law is the union of social rules and secondary rules and that such a system exists when Hart's two minimum conditions are met. Meeting the two minimum conditions does not demonstrate the existence of social rules, merely that of hybrid rules. It is not possible to define an object as having two attributes and then to set the minimum conditions for its existence as the presence of only one attribute. If only one of the two is discernible then *something* certainly exists, but it is not the thing with two attributes.

2 Roberts argues that the officials' decisions will not be effective unless they follow rules: otherwise they will not receive public support, parties will not come to them and the losing party will not feel bound by their decisions (1979, p. 179). However, what makes official decisions effective is extremely complex (see chapter 8). The public's and parties' attitudes to the decision are important, but are more likely to reflect its *content* than the way it was reached. Paradoxically, following a rule may undermine the perceived legitimacy of an official if (s)he uses rules to decide against a strong or well-respected party.

3 Weber presented the image of institutions running according to rules as the ideal type of government in the capitalist countries, matching the ideology and business needs of the bourgeoisie. But though the bourgeoisie may wish that the bureaucracy deal with them according to rules, the desideratum is only partly realized. Chambliss and Siedman (1983) offer a partial explanation. The same bourgeoisie do not wish legal institutions to deal with the working class according to rules. What they demand is action to protect threatened interests, whether this action is in conformity to existing rules or not (e.g. the demands that crime *must* be controlled, riots *must* be stopped, strikes *must* be broken). If Chambliss and Siedman were right in seeing the various legal institutions as controlled by the bourgeoisie and like-minded running dogs, then some institutions would operate by rules and others would not. But, despite an undeniable overall bias towards 'bourgeois' interests and values among legal officials, there is considerable variation between individual officials. Some avoid rules in pursuing middle-class offenders and some operate by rules in pursuing working-class ones.

4 This is a traditional problem for positivism. Command theory found it very hard to convert the model of one person willing another to do something into an analogous willing by society or an institution within it. Kelsen, Hart and Harris had difficulty with existence tests for systems based on internally followed 'grundnorms', secondary rules and principled practices.

4

Content Theories of Legal System

4.1 Introduction

In the last chapter we saw that positivist systems encompass rules or norms formed into structures by relations which link a rule authorizing the creation of rules to the rules created under that authority. The *content* of the rules of law has no significant role. Indeed positivist systems cannot stand a more significant role for content in law. Where the content of legal rules may lead judges or other officials to disregard them or interpret them out of existence there is an informal content test which cuts across the validity test laid down by positivists (chapter 3.6). For these officials, rules which form part of the positivist system because of the rules of recognition are nonetheless not part of the law. In their stead are rules which owe their place not to any relationship to a rule of recognition but to the judges' approval of their content. If that approval is based on the holding of some other rule (or principle) there is a relation between the two rules. But the relation is quite different from that found in positivist systems. Rather than a relation in which one rule authorizes the creation of another, it is a relation in which the content of one implies or justifies the content of another.

Several theorists have regarded these relations between the content of legal rules as vitally important in understanding law and reject positivist theories of legal system for missing what is for them the key insight into law. Others go further and attempt to use this insight to build a different type of legal system – a content one. Legal rules are related to general principles and the principles to each other by a network of content relations which are integrated into a coherent whole, or even into a 'closed system of definitions, rules of operation and substantive major premises such that any specific legal problem can be solved by deductive reasoning from the propositional system so established'. (Sawer, 1965, p. 17).

4.2 The Variety of Content Systems

Content systems vary as to both the source of the basic principles and the role the content system plays in the overall theory of law.

Some theories of natural law are strong content systems with God or reason providing a set of perfectly reconcilable principles with which all legal questions can be answered. Such theories tend to be more those of straw men, ritualistically burned for jurisprudential heresy, rather than of those who choose to call themselves natural lawyers (Finnis, 1980, p. 26). But writers do occasionally emerge to provide footnotes to pure and extreme statements of natural law content theory. O'Donoghue (1973, p. 150) says that 'human law must recognize that it is but an approximation to a higher system, at once far more unified and far more complex than man with his generalizing intelligence can elaborate.'

Certainly most modern natural law theories see natural law in less systematic terms. Fuller (1969), for example, sees natural law setting out formal requirements for law rather than providing a systematic content for it. Finnis gives natural law content in the form of seven 'requirements of practical reasonableness', but these do not found a content system. Instead they provide a model for what the rules and institutions that make up legal systems should be like (and allegedly generally are like), and provide reasons for accepting its authority. When Finnis uses the term 'legal system' he is not referring to natural law or any kind of content system but to something far more positivist – a system of rules and institutions in which the institutions create rules and the rules authorize them to do so (1980, p. 268).

Finnis effectively uses practical reason and natural law to provide a 'front-end justification' for a system of law identified and constructed on positivist lines.[1]

Many 'formalists', who extolled the virtues of the common law, saw it as a kind of content system without offering detail or elaboration (e.g. Beale, 1907, p. 558). The character of these systems as content ones is borne out by the frequent insistence of such writers that judges do not make law because the content of their decision is already there in the legal system, deducible from pre-existing substantive rules (Bodenheimer, 1977, p. 1146).

Proponents of legal codes claimed that these could amount to content systems – and better than the common law ones because they were more deliberately man-made (Bentham, 1970). Savigny, in defending existing laws against the imposition of codes, claimed similar systematic unity for the *Volksgeist* or spirit of the law (1975). Pound (1954) and Llewelyn and Hoebel (1941) put the idea in more sociological terms – seeking to find a set of 'jural postulates' beneath the law of contemporary American and Cheyenne societies respectively. Parsons includes a similar system of values in his sociological theory, calling it the 'vertical structure' of the social system (chapter 5.3).

Some very ambitious theorists attempt to translate law into formalized sentences and then diagram them using Boolean Algebra. Marsh (1975) attempted this for *Hedley Byrne and Heller* ([1963] 2 All ER 575). Whatever may be said about this attempt, the tiny fraction of law this covers bodes ill for any such systematization of law. In this respect, it is interesting that despite early hopes, especially in code countries, attempts to use computers to systematize law in this way have been discontinued. Computers are instead used for the retrieval of legal documents by the use of key words (Tapper, 1982) – a process which assumes not that the law has any systematic quality but merely that most judges will at some stage use similar words when talking about similar things!

MacCormick included a comprehensive content system in his legal theory – 'a consistent and coherent body of norms whose observance secures certain valued goals which can intelligibly be pursued together' (1978, p. 106). However its role is limited because it is only to be used to fill in gaps or resolve uncertainties. The bulk of law is covered by an essentially positivist system. MacCormick unambiguously limits the content system to hard cases, which he sees as rare. In clear cases, single relevant valid norms, derived via a source system, determine the outcome.

This chapter will concentrate on Dworkin's theory as it is the only current theory which is essentially a content system (without it this chapter would merely be a brief reminder of follies past). Dworkin's theory also offers significant new insights, especially the importance of *individual* value-inputs into the derivation of legal rules and the interpersonal variations in such inputs.

Like many theories, Dworkin's is susceptible to more and less systematic expositions. In fact he does seem to be drawn both ways. He tends to be more systematic in exposition and generally less so in defence. He began with 'The Model of Rules' (1967), in which he vigorously attacked source-based theories of legal systems. His strong anti-systematic sentiments were, of course, directed to such systems rather than the one he later created. In 'Hard Cases' (1975) he saw law through the eyes of a hypothetical judge called Hercules, for whom law was a very strong content system. In 'No Right Answer' (1978) he echoed the claim of the most systematic formalists that the system could produce a single right answer although, very importantly, the system was that of a Herculean judge rather than a system of law shared by all judges. When re-expressed in *Law's Empire* (1986), his theory was more heavily qualified. This chapter will expound the stronger theory and show how its problems from both the internal standpoint of judicial participants and the external standpoint of the social observer are related to the over-systematization of his basic insight. It will show how the qualifications and retreats in *Law's Empire* constitute improvements and in some cases incorporate new insights. As they make the theory less systematic, they tend to confirm this book's contention about the direction that legal theory should take. However, this chapter will also show that this development is inhibited by the systematization of the content of law that still lies at the heart of the theory and which finally emerges in an attempt to incorporate both the systematic and nonsystematic aspects of law into a wider content system of political principles. This prevents the qualifications from rescuing the theory from the problems caused by over-systematizing its insights.

4.3   Dworkin's System

The systematic theory of law that Dworkin offers is of a set of principles that a hypothetical judge called Hercules would create to provide the 'best justification' of his society's legal institutions and the decisions made within them. It must justify a sufficient number of decisions of the courts, the constitutional arrangements and the legislative output of those institutions (1977, p. 107). It need not cover all of these decisions, merely enough to pass a threshold of 'fit'. If more than one theory passes that threshold, the most attractive must be chosen. The theory can then be used to justify Hercules' future decisions, providing a single right answer in all cases. This system of principles links the content of new decisions to that of the old by justifying both. Dworkin has redescribed the enterprise a number of times in an attempt to convey what he sees as an essentially unchanging message. Since 1977 he has seen Hercules providing an 'interpretation' of those same institutions and decisions analogous to the interpretation that a critic makes of a work of art or literature in order to show it in the best possible light (1977, p. 331). Hercules' interpretation of law shows it as the best system of law it could be.

Because law has many 'authors', Dworkin modified the analogy to the interpretation of a chain novel in which all chapters are written by authors who attempt to make their own chapters follow on from earlier ones by interpreting the pre-existing chapters as a whole (1980).

In *Law's Empire*, he offers his systematic theory as a conception of law that can provide a general justification of official coercion, especially the individual judge's own coercion of others. The best justification is one that assumes, as far as possible, that the law is created by a single author, the community, expressing a coherent concept of justice and fairness (1986, p. 225).

Law as integrity asks judges to assume, so far as this is possible, that law is structured by a coherent set of principles about justice and fairness and due process and asks them to enforce these in the fresh cases that come before them. That style respects the ambition to be a community of principle. (1986, p. 243)

Dworkin's theory claims for law all four characteristics of a system – elements, relations, structure and wholeness.

Elements

'The Model of Rules' emphasized important and allegedly disregarded elements in law – *principles*. Principles are moral judgments about what is right and what is wrong made by a judge to justify elements of his 'best theory' of law. Principles can be sub-divided on the basis of what they must justify.

1 Principles of political morality and political organization justifying the constitutional arrangements (1977, p. 106).
2 Principles that justify judicial methods of statutory interpretation (1977, p. 108) – i.e. the way in which the output of other institutions in those constitutional arrangements is interpreted.
3 Principles about substantive human rights to justify the content of (most of) the decisions of the courts (1977, p. 112).

The place of the actual statutes and decisions of the courts, as opposed to the place of the principles that justify them, is problematical. These might be regarded as elements of the system, linked into it by the principles which justify them. Alternatively, they could be seen as non-legal 'preinterpretive' sub-strata which the legal system of principles justifies, part of the environment of the legal system with which it interacts, but not part of the system itself.

The place of rules is also unclear. Perhaps rules should be seen as similar to principles, as narrower, and more closely defined, justifications of either a few decisions or a part of an institution. But again, they may be seen as the sub-stratum to be interpreted.

Relations

One of Dworkin's most important claims is that these principles are related to each other by 'intense intersections and interdependencies' into a systematic whole (1978, p. 81). The exact nature of these relations, and the structure into which they fit, is not spelled out but it is possible to infer something about them.

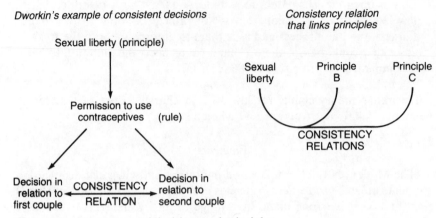

Figure 4.1 Consistency of decisions and principles

Some kind of consistency relation between the principles is indicated by the various claims of consistency and coherence that Dworkin makes for the system as a whole.[2] This systematic consistency is called 'articulate consistency' in 'Hard Cases' (1975), 'normative consistency' in *'No Right Answer'* (1978) and 'integrity' in *Law's Empire* (1986). It is supposed to be a strong requirement which binds the principles tightly together. One example he gives (1977, p. 88), that a judge should not allow one couple to use contraceptives on the basis of sexual liberty then deny their use to the next couple coming before him, merely requires treating identical cases in the same manner. This links a few cases and one rule to a single principle rather than linking principles to each other (see figure 4.1).

'Normative consistency' is likened to 'narrative consistency', in which a proposition about a character in a novel or play that is not stated by the author is inferred because it fits the picture of that character built up from what the author *does* say. Thus the consistency relation is an indirect one (figure 4.2).

The nature of the relationships involved is reasonably simple, involving causal inference, probability theory and psychology. It is only difficult in practice because of the controversial nature of the last. The theoretical problem is to translate the analogy into a model of relations between legal principles. Dworkin tells us little about normative consistency and explicitly acknowledges that normative and narrative consistency differ – but without enlightening us as to how. Nevertheless, he clearly has something like the following in mind: several existing decisions can be justified by a moral principle, and that moral principle will also justify the new decision (figure 4.3).

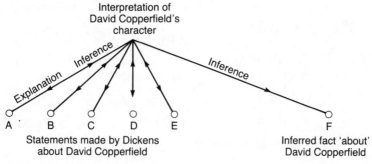

Figure 4.2 Narrative consistency

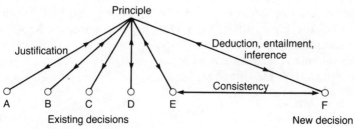

Figure 4.3 Normative consistency

Thus the horizontal relation of consistency is based on a vertical relation of 'justification'. This latter relation is the key one in Dworkin's system. It not only makes the horizontal consistency relation possible, but also links rules to principles, principles to higher principles, and finally provides the single right answer to legal questions that Dworkin so controversially claims for it. The relation of 'justification' may be likened to the 'logical' relations of 'deduction' or entailment which joined the general and specific rules in earlier common law content theories. Where deduction looks down from the general to the specific, justification looks upward from the specific to the general. But Dworkin's relation must look down as well – when the general principles are used by the judge to justify the new decision in the case before him. Furthermore, although the notion of justification might seem to denote a much weaker relationship than 'entailment' or 'deduction', it must be strong if it is to furnish a single right answer for legal questions. Indeed if the principles cannot justify one rule only (Rx) out of the several possible (R1, R2, R3, R4 ...) then they cannot be said to justify following Rx.

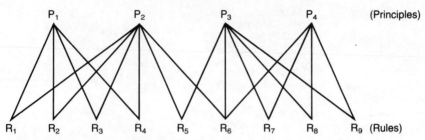

Figure 4.4 A truncated pyramid lattice

That this, or something like it, can play an important part in legal reasoning is one of Dworkin's most important insights. Judges use this technique to fill apparent gaps in the legal rules and to dispose of unattractive existing decisions. If it appears to a judge that the rule he derives from the apparently most similar case is unattractive he will often look to less similar cases, derive a general principle from those cases, say the relevant rule is inconsistent with the principle and either overrule or confine to the facts the offending rule.

Structure

Dworkin frequently emphasizes the structured nature of law as integrity (e.g. 1986, p. 243) and that the principles, and the decisions that are justified, form part of an overall structure. The form it takes appears to be that of a truncated pyramid lattice with a few principles at the top and the many individual rules at the bottom. Although basically pyramidal, it does not have the tree-like simplicity of some positivist systems because many lower principles and rules will be justified by several higher principles (the pyramid will get wider at the bottom because principles will justify more rules than rules need principles to justify them). (See figure 4.4.)

This structure is complicated by the various 'layers of authority' (1977, p. 117) found in the law of modern states. Dworkin refers to four levels in the USA – the constitution, constitutional decisions of the Supreme Court, statutes and common law decisions. Hercules must create a theory to justify the rules to be found at each level. Furthermore, the theories he creates at lower levels must be consistent with the theories he has created at higher ones – for example, a judge finding a privacy principle in the constitution must also find one in torts (1977, p. 117). Thus Hercules must first choose a 'background theory' comprising substantive principles of political philosophy to justify the 'constitutional structure'. He must then choose the best theory he can which incorporates the first theory but

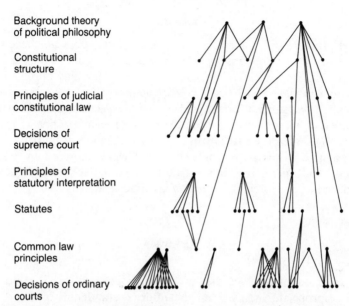

Background theory
of political philosophy

Constitutional
structure

Principles of judicial
constitutional law

Decisions of
supreme court

Principles of
statutory interpretation

Statutes

Common law
principles

Decisions of ordinary
courts

Figure 4.5 Hercules's entire theory of law – his legal system (Only a few symbolic lines have been drawn to represent the many intersecting lines linking levels with each other and with higher ones)

also justifies the decisions of the Supreme Court. The next theory must incorporate the previous ones and justify the various statutes as a means of interpreting them. The final, grandest theory of all is the best theory which incorporates the above three theories but also justifies a certain percentage of decisions the courts have made in the development of the common law. Hercules need not justify all earlier decisions because Dworkin allows him to dismiss some of them as 'mistakes'. (Note that the decisions so dismissed are not part of the legal system because the higher principles do not bind them into its structure.)

This indulgence cannot be extended to Hercules in respect of constitutional arrangements, statutes nor, unless he is judge of the highest court, decisions of that court. That which a judge has no power to overrule, he cannot officially call a mistake, and he must tailor his theory to 'fit' it completely.

Thus there is a series of theories to justify the 'institutional history' of law at progressively lower levels of authority, each incorporating theories used to justify the higher levels. The first of these theories looks like figure 4.4 above but the whole structure of the legal system would resemble figure 4.5.

Wholeness

The fourth feature of a system, a 'wholeness factor', does not have to be inferred from Dworkin's writing – he insists upon it and criticizes other theories for lacking it (1986, pp. 10, 226, 274). Hercules must create a *single* theory of law which as a *whole* justifies *all* of the statutes and non-mistaken decisions of others and all his own actions as well. It must be grounded in his convictions about the point of legal practice as a whole (1986, p. 87). According to Dworkin the justification of judicial action is only possible if law is interpreted as if it were authored by a single individual. And, in a sense, this is true because the system is created by the single mind of Hercules to justify his official actions.

4.4 Criticism

Dworkin's standpoint is not that of a social observer. He is concerned with the appropriate theory from the internal standpoint of a judge or other participant in the practices of arguing about law that constitute Law's Empire. But as such he is not strictly using Hart's internal point of view because he is not much concerned with the actual internal attitudes of participants. He seeks an *interpretation* of such attitudes which both fits and is more attractive than the alternatives. Indeed, ever since 'Hard Cases' (1977) he has made the stronger (and interpretively unnecessary) claim that it fits better than other theories. Participants in judicial activity may be interested in both questions. The social observer is mainly in- terested in the former question, especially in its stronger form, because accepting Dworkin's answer to it would entail the existence of a legal system *within* law, in the practices of judges. Furthermore, if the rest of law can be either incorporated into Dworkin's system or dismissed as peripheral, the social observer will accept that law is best seen as a system of Dworkin's type. Consequently, the criticism will begin in the next section by countering Dworkin's claim that his theory fits judicial practice. Not only is judicial practice far less systematic than Dworkin's theory port- rays it, but much of it is antithetical to an overall systematizing of law's content. However, Dworkin's main argument for his theory will be con- fronted four-square because in chapter 4.6 it will be argued that one of the reasons for this actual divergence is the theory's unsuitability and unattractiveness to judges. As the reasons given apply to the suitability of *any* such interpretation, the attack will apply as much to the kind of interpretation used as to the particular interpretation advocated. Chapter 4.7 will examine some the defences, modifications and retreats that

Dworkin has tried. Finally, in chapter 4.8, it will be argued even if the interpretive description given by Dworkin *were* suited to judges this would not make a good description of law for the social observer.

4.5 Dworkin's System and Judicial Practice

Dworkin claims that his theory fits judicial practice – i.e. that judges attempt to interpret law as if it were such a system. Judges certainly use the elements of Dworkin's system in their reasoning, the problems lie in the way they are related and structured.

Relations

If principles are to be related by horizontal consistency relations, then there must be some meaningful way in which legal rules and principles can be inconsistent and contradict each other. The alternative rules between which judges have to choose are rarely expressible in terms of opposites (the decisions for or against parties may be opposites, but the *rules* on which they are based usually vary little). When it *is* possible to set up principles or rules in terms of opposites, judges frequently avoid doing so (chapter 4.9). Although they sometimes set up a rule to knock it down, they normally attempt minor modifications to avoid the contradiction or merely ignore the contradiction altogether. Instead of relating consistent rules to each other or rejecting one of a pair of rules that contradict each other, judges tend to reformulate the rules to effect a compromise, or just distinguish the facts of the case from which an inconvenient rule comes. This does not so much *relate* the two rules as confine each in such a way that they do not interact at all. The widespread practice of 'distinguishing' completely contradicts any desire to make law as a whole consistent. If law really were interpreted as a consistent and coherent whole then judges would insist that legal rules from widely differing compartments of law be consistent.

The informality of judicial formulation of legal rules also affects the strength of the vertical relations of justification by which lesser rules, and ultimately the 'right answer', are supposedly derived from higher principles (Farago, 1980, p. 409). Although it is certainly true that judges often talk as if one rule followed inexorably from another, they also recognize the variety of answers which could reasonably be expected both explicitly (Harris, 1979, p. 191) and in practice (e.g. by limiting the retroactive effect of their decision: Brilmayer, 1977, p. 1190). There are many legal statements that judges, barristers and solicitors would call 'arguable' or 'unsettled'. If lawyers *did* believe there were a single right answer, and they agreed with Dworkin that such right answers had moral force, would it not be immoral for them to argue against it for money; could they so easily respect, fraternize with and show courtesy to those who accepted the brief from, or decided in favour of, sides that did not 'deserve to win'? It would rather seem that they all see themselves as having the job of arguing for their client, or deciding as best they can. The answer they give is theirs. They stick to it not because it is *the* law or because it is morally right, but because it is their best attempt.

But even if the central principles were more formally stated would it be possible to derive the right answer from them? It is difficult enough to derive a concrete practical conclusion from a technical rule drafted with great care and skill, but to derive such answers from general moral principles seems fanciful. If it were possible to do this, one wonders why parliament and draughtsmen go to so much trouble. Why not merely legislate the central principles and then go home? Of course some have hoped to do this – it is the great dream of the code-maker. But the principles and rules the latter set out were quite insufficient to provide the host of required answers, even with massive additions of commentaries and court rulings. The same fate awaits Hercules' system of principles.

Structure

However judges and other lawyers may regard the relations between rules and principles, they certainly do not treat them as systematically arranged into a content-structured whole. In 'Hard Cases' the judge who creates such a system is a mythical creature and is clearly labelled as such. The best Dworkin claims for mortal judges is that they seek to go as far as they can towards systematizing law. The furthest they could go would be to construct several internally coherent sets of legal principles which do not cohere with each other into a content system because of the judges' unfortunate shortage of super-hero powers. But few judges go anywhere near as far as they could. Most look for a single overriding authority, or for several authorities that appear to say the same thing. They seek a single rule under which a case can unambiguously be stated to fall. It is usually only when the rule based on the most directly relevant and/or authoritative cases does not appeal to the judge that (s)he starts looking more widely – in search of other case(s) which will support a principle that can be used to contradict the offending rule. (S)he will have indulged in a very small exercise in something like Dworkinian system-building, but (s)he will only have gone so far as is necessary to achieve what appears to him or her to be a satisfactory result. The most that is systematized is a tiny part of the law several orders of magnitude less than the Herculean dream, and even such limited efforts are rare. Indeed any attempt to suggest a grand system would be treated as the most eccentric of *obiter dicta*. This may be an unjust reward for one of the labours of Hercules, but any judge with the wisdom of Hercules would undoubtedly realize this and abandon the effort.

As argued in chapter 3, judges do not tend to build systems of any kind. Those in the Anglo-American tradition do not see that as their 'rational strength' (Cotterrell, 1984, pp. 3, 18). Rather they see themselves using (conveniently ill-defined) judicial techniques to deal with the material presented to them during the arguing of cases. Some of these techniques involve authority- and source-based argument. Some involve content- and principle-based argument. Some involve consequentialist and pragmatic argument. Each technique is available, and judicial discretion exists as much in the choice of technique as the different uses to which it is put.

4.6 Hercules as Myth

There are many reasons for this reluctance to systematize. These reasons are offered primarily as part of the explanation of why judges do not practise Dworkinian system-building and hence why his theory does not fit. However, to the extent that these reasons appeal to the reader, they count against Dworkin's central claims that the theory is attractive, that judges *should* practise it, and that such a system would be the best possible interpretation of the law.

Although Dworkin advocates this system-building as a necessary part of adjudication, one of the major reasons for judges to shun it is how far it takes them from the task of adjudication. Judges perceive this task, especially in the face of large case backlogs, as very onerous, leaving little time for chasing even the worthiest of impossible dreams. But it is not just a problem of time. Judges see themselves as primarily adjudicators rather than justifiers and their principal task is to settle the case in hand. The judge is *functus officio* when the order has been made, whether or not any justification has been given. The judge will usually seek to do more, to settle the point of law involved, but (s)he is usually reluctant to state a rule which goes much beyond it. The judge may offer a justification, but it will usually be extremely limited in scope and there is no obligation to 'sell' the decision. Indeed there is a very good reason for avoiding the full-blooded moral justifications of law that Dworkin urges on judges. Like any reasonably successful exercise of power, and like most such exercises, it is a mixture of force, sanctions, manipulation, persuasion, etc., because of the different reasons citizens have for obeying it (chapters 3.5, 8.2). Not all citizens can be persuaded to obey, so an emphasis on justification may lead others to forget the other resources that legal institutions have to compel compliance. Furthermore there are numerous justifications that might be given for obeying laws. Many of them will be incompatible – by tying law to one it loses the support of the others. Thus judges have an interest in laying down rules and leaving it to others to invent reasons for following them.

A second reason for judges to reject Dworkin's system-building is his major claim for it – that it provides a single right answer in hard cases. This would destroy the flexibility that so many judges like to retain and possibly even promote (Munzer, 1977). It would also make legal change extraordinarily difficult because if the whole system produced a single right answer A, to change the law to produce −A would require changing the entire system. This is not the way judges change law and it is completely contrary to common law traditions of change by accretion and piecemeal modification rather than root-and-branch systematic change. Indeed *all* law exhibits this quality – new ideas are not introduced simultaneously throughout the law but percolate gradually.

The main reason against judicial attempts at Dworkinian system-building is that the nature of the material sought to be systematized makes it impossible not only to complete the project but to make any real headway at all. The further one judge goes, the more difficult the task becomes – there are more cases to reconcile, more rules and principles to incorporate. Having organized one compartment of law around a set of principles, the attempt to relate it to another set of principles means further adjustments to each set. Hard cases are hard precisely because they involve integration of differing cases and the rules, principles or ideas behind them. The more integration involved, the harder it becomes. Anything like the integration required by Dworkin is impossible.

The problem is that the material sought to be systematized has been created in attempts to realize a multitude of values. This is because the creators were different people (with consequent variation in personality, point of view, etc.), at different times (with consequent variation in the then current ideas and concerns), in different cases (where the peculiarities of the case or the disputants, or the consequences of alternative decisions sway the judges), relying on different information and with different paradigms in mind (e.g. in commercial law one judge may be thinking in terms of massive conglomerates and poor consumers, and the other of harassed small businessmen with pernickety customers). Many of these values will be contradictory to each other, so many values will be inimical to the values contained in any system of principles a judge might create.

This problem will be aggravated by any attempts at systematization by earlier judges. These will have created blocks of rules, decisions and statutes, representing attempts to institutionalize different values. Thus the more people who embrace Dworkin's theory, the more problems it creates for each of them and the weaker is Dworkin's normative claim. Of course if no one has attempted such systematization this aggravation (though not the problem!) disappears. But in that case his claim that it fits judicial practice would have to be abandoned too.

4.7 Dworkin's Defences

Dworkin offers several defences against the problems caused by the diversity of material created by judges and legislators operating under their different values.

One is to argue that Hercules 'tries to impose order over doctrine, not to discover order in forces that created it' (1986, p. 273). This is true; however, a disordered process is likely to produce a disordered result unless there is some mechanism counteracting this. Dworkin suggests some tendencies to convergence in judicial convictions about the purpose, goal or principle of legal practice as a whole. But he himself warns against exaggerating their effect given the variety of judicial ideologies, concepts of justice and, not least, theories of law which he asserts they hold (1986, p. 88) and even lauds (p. 89).

The second defence is that the judge can characterize a certain proportion of the judicial decisions as 'mistakes'. However, the further the judge goes in attempting to systematize law, the more mistakes (s)he will have to declare, whereas judges are usually at pains to minimize the number of their peers they say are wrong. Furthermore it is a very limited device. A judge cannot exclude statutes, 'embedded' (long-standing) mistakes, mistakes of superior courts or rules within their 'enactment force' from the decisions to be justified. Statutes are particularly troublesome. They are very numerous and their impact is multiplied in the areas of law they affect because judicial decisions in those areas must be tailored to fit in with them. Furthermore they are passed by a succession of governments, often attempting to implement clearly conflicting values. Statutes passed by successive Conservative and Labour governments may be very easily justifiable in terms of principles – but not compatible ones. Where the statutes are *not* passed with clear principles in mind, the contradictions are not so much between the statutes as built into them.

Dworkin's third defence to the problems caused by the variation in the values of those who create legal materials lies in his explanation of how a chain novel might be written and interpreted and the analogy he draws for law. In Dworkin's chain novel, the first chapter is written by one author who sends it on to the next author. The second author writes chapter 2 as if it followed from the first, and so on. Dworkin argues that it is possible at any time to interpret the whole of what has been written so far, and that each successive author must so interpret it in order to relate his own chapter to those which have already been written.

Much depends on the compatibility of the writers. Suppose D.H. Lawrence writes the first chapter and introduces two women who take two men as lovers. Gore Vidal's chapter 2 changes their sexual orientation and Waugh's chapter 3 their religion. In chapter 4 Agatha Christie has one of them murdered but, with all the other three having motives by now, leaves us guessing who did it because in chapter 5 Tolstoy asks what all these shifting relationships in the midst of bloodshed could mean. How can we appreciate or interpret such a work which seems to be a combination of love story, satire, mystery thriller and philosophical musing? Should we attempt to impose some thematic unity on the whole by seeing one genre as dominant or by inventing a new hybrid genre? Or should we appreciate each chapter with its own style, point and purpose? Dworkin ridicules the idea of interpreting a mystery thriller as a philosophical novel, but it would be exactly the same mistake to interpret a mystery thriller *chapter* as either philosophical or hybrid – and for the same reasons. Even if there were some apparent, or even deliberate, philosophical aspects of the chapter resembling novels from the philosophical or hybrid genres, to regard it as part of either kind of novel is to give such an incomplete and unsatisfactory account of the chapter as not to fit the facts. The price of seeking an interpretation that fits the *whole* of the novel is that it does not really fit any *part* of it. Even if some hybrid genre could be concocted which did meet Dworkin's standard of fit (or if Dworkin dropped the standard of fit sufficiently to pass the concoction), the price must still be paid because the interpretation that fits the whole does not fit nearly as well as separate interpretations of the parts. Furthermore, although Dworkin wants to find the interpretation which renders the whole enterprise the 'best and most successful it could be', he rules out the most complimentary thing that could have been said about it. It may be a very bad *novel* but a great series of barely related essays. Even before this point has been reached we may come to see that holistic interpretation will involve a worse fit and, at any level of fit, a less attractive interpretation than interpretation of the separate parts.

At this point, it might be argued that law could still be interpreted as if it were the work of a single author, because there is less variation of purpose among judges than among the different writers in the multi-authored book I describe. However, we have seen Dworkin specifically accept that judges do operate under at least three significantly different theories of judicial role, different theories of justice and, in general, different ideologies. Most importantly from Dworkin's standpoint, judges operate three radically different theories of rights which he calls conventialism, pragmatism, and law as integrity.

In fact the complexity and variation of legal material will be far greater than in my version of Dworkin's multi-author book analogy. Interpreting it as if it were written by a single author will be much more difficult because my variation of Dworkin's analogy still does not take account of five further facts about judicial decisions.

1 The authors read all the previous chapters by other authors whereas judges do not read all the previous judgments by other judges.
2 Judicial decision follows an adversarial argument and in general addresses only the issues and cases raised in that argument. This is like the new chapter in the chain novel being written by an author who had read *not* the previous chapters, but only criticisms of the earlier chapters written by critics with violently opposed prejudices e.g. Levis and Forster (or, to bring the analogy closer to home, it would be like chapter 2 of *Law's Empire* being written by someone who had read only Posner and Hutchinson's criticisms of Dworkin's chapter 1).
3 There is nothing in law comparable to the sequential development of the plot in the chain novel. Questions in law are less analogous to 'what happens next' than to questions about what has already been written in the novel, what has not been written and how these two relate.
4 More than one judge writes about the same part of law. Thus its interpretation is not like the best theory of Hamlet's character but the best theory of Faustus' character taken from the plays of both Marlowe and Goethe. We would need to alter our chain novel analogy by having two chapter 5s – one written by Tolstoy and one by Vidal.
5 The time span for 'writing' the law is so much greater than that for the chain novel.

Perhaps a truer parallel to law would be an attempt to create a theory of 'art', or 'literature', or of all the plays currently showing in London's West End. Such exercises would be considered at best worthless and eccentric, but more often simply misleading. I can find only one example that Dworkin has offered at this level of complexity – that the meaning of modern painting is 'negation' (1981, p. 36). But so much of the meaning of modern paintings would be missed in the attempt to encompass it under that one umbrella that such an interpretation would be a serious encumbrance to its understanding. Even more than in a single chain novel, the incredible variety of artists' approaches and purposes requires separate treatments of their work rather than an attempt to bundle them all into 'modern painting'.

And so, I would argue, it is with law. It may be quite possible to interpret various segments of the law (e.g. legislation on a topic during a party's term of office or a series of decisions on an area of tort law) by providing one or more related principles to justify it. Let us imagine that a judge has picked three areas of law involving some Conservative legislation, some Labour legislation and some House of Lords decisions and has chosen the best principles (according to his or her own values) that fit each. If, as is likely, these principles are not compatible, the Dworkinian judge would have to look for other principles that are. Assuming that (s)he can find these principles, they will inevitably either fit each area less well, or be a less attractive justification of them – possibly both. The judge will have to make the same sacrifice as a chain-novel critic – to give up a *better* interpretation of the *parts* in order to furnish *some* kind of interpretation of the *whole*. Consequently any decision (s)he makes in areas in which (s)he had to choose less attractive or less well-fitting principles will itself be less attractive and more loosely aligned to its neighbours. Furthermore, in adding such a decision to the body of decisions in that area, that decision shifts it slightly in the direction of unacceptability or incoherence.

Some judges may not find this too great a price to pay – they may not be too concerned about fit or they may have fairly catholic tastes in what they consider acceptable. But what about those judges who can find justification for many parts of the law but for whom the best set of principles that fits the whole of law is just not acceptable? Dworkin considers such cases confined to completely intolerable regimes like Nazi Germany (1977, p. 326; 1986, p. 105), but more radical lawyers would see it as true for their own countries. Dworkin offers them little. He suggests they either lie about the principles embedded in the law (i.e. use principles that do not 'fit') or resign in protest. He offers the judge the choice of pretending to judge or not 'judging' according to his theory at all. But Dworkin not only denies *judgeship* to radicals – he even makes it impossible for them to be good *lawyers*. This is because providing the *answer* to a legal question requires the same theory-building as judging does, since the correct answer to a question of law is the one a judge would provide using the 'correct' Dworkinian theory of adjudication.

This reflects a generally conservative bias in the theory. There is very little room for radicals. From the first page of the preface to *Law's Empire*, he assumes or implies more commitment to law than many lawyers are willing to give. 'We are subjects of Law's Empire, liegemen to its methods and ideals, bound in spirit while we debate what we must therefore do' (1986, vii). 'We think the law should be obeyed and enforced ... there would be little point to treating law as an interpretive concept if we did not' (p. 111). 'Good citizens interpret the common scheme of justice to which they are committed just in virtue of citizenship' (p. 190). Those who cannot justify law as a whole or a sufficiently large part of it (he cites Marxists as examples, 1986, p. 408) are defined out of the enterprise. Even Kelsen, who was an implacable opponent of Marxists (1980), acknowledged that they could be very good lawyers (1970, p. 218n.).

While not excluded like radicals, reformers will find Dworkin's theory a poor critical tool. Institutions, rules and practices may have several justifications. Suppose Hercules adopts a minority, or even idiosyncratic, interpretation (indeed, if such an interpretation fits and is preferred by Hercules, he must). A majority of judges may adopt repugnant interpretations to justify repugnant decisions. But Hercules is oblivious to the problem. Dworkin's theory prevents his seeing the need to change the institution, rule or practice to one the repugnant interpretation will not fit. Ironically, once the repugnant decisions have been made, Hercules' interpretation may no longer fit so 'Law as Integrity' will tell him to abandon it. Like most theories of law that consciously mix fact and value, Dworkin's provides a poor basis for criticizing law because the critic's values have already been built into it and hence the law is seen in a better light than it otherwise might be. It also provides a poor basis for understanding the way the law operates, because law operates according to the values of the officials rather than the values of the critic.

In addition to its inbuilt conservative bias, there is a massive and anti-social assumption in Dworkin's view that the best interpretation of his multi-authored book is a 'novel' written by a single author. This is really rather strange. One would hardly expect a single-author interpretation to fit a multi-authored book well. Given the difficulties involved, it will never be able to match the virtues of a single-author novel. However, such a book may have other, possibly greater, virtues – it may provide different angles or points of view on the same events (and do it better than a single author's attempt, e.g. Fowles, 1971), it may provide argument, it may allow the authors to hone and express their own views better by virtue of reading the pieces written by others, it may provide a genuine experience of the pluralism of authors. The most attractive interpretation of a multi-author book may be as a moderately successful single-author work, but one would hope that in some cases a more attractive interpretation would refer to values which *only* a multi-authored book could have – only such an interpretation justifies having multiple authors at all.

Dworkin seems blind to the possibility that social phenomena may have virtues other than those of individuals. When he interprets law and community so as to show them in their best light, he portrays the former as if written by a single author and the latter as the author. The virtues of each are the virtues of highly principled individual moral theorists. However, the virtues of community may well be the vices of individuals and *vice versa*. Pluralism may be a communal virtue but for an individual it equates to schizophrenia. Checks and balances *may* be good for law but they may incapacitate an individual. Self-mastery for an individual may equate to facism for a community, decisiveness to authoritarianism. For an individual, systematizing values and beliefs by making them consistent and coherent is broadly achievable and highly desirable. For a community it is impossible and perhaps highly undesirable because only pluralism of values and value-combinations provide the material from which an individual can choose. If such be the community, a consistent and coherent law may be possible only by the inclusion of only one system of beliefs within it.

There is something descriptively and normatively archaic in Dworkin's interpretation of law as if it came from a single author. It harks back to the long-rejected metaphor of an individual sovereign and the long-rejected preference for potential consistency provided by a single individual for the pluralism of a democracy. Of course Dworkin imagines the single author to be the community rather than an all powerful Leviathan within it, but that again fails to see the community as having virtues different to, and perhaps greater than, those of an individual.

Back to the Checkerboard

The piecemeal treatment of law offers an alternative way out. Law might be seen as part good and part bad, part justifiable and part not. The parts that are considered good can be used by judges and lawyers to justify their continued participation in legal institutions – something that can be achieved through law. The parts that are considered bad can also justify continued activity – there is much work still to be done. Furthermore, such piecemeal treatment becomes a valuable critical tool. The justifications that can be given for one area of law can be compared with the poor justifications that can be given for another. In interpreting law as part good and part bad, and in subjecting the bad to criticism, lawyers will probably abandon not only Dworkin's holism but also his insistence that law be interpreted in the 'best light'. This abandonment allows a judge to interpret decisions (s)he regards as mistakes as well as those (s)he can justify. 'Mistaken' decisions are made by those with different values and interests or influenced by differing groups (as such it is useful to conservative as well as radical judges – they just don't need to use it so much).

Dworkin rejects such checkerboard solutions on the grounds of intuition and principle. I cannot share Dworkin's intuition. I would prefer to make the best decision according to my values rather than suppress those values and choose a decision that will cohere with the bulk of decisions made by those with whom I disagree. The principle he cites is that of 'integrity'. But this depends on treating the state as if it were a single principled individual and treating judges and lawyers as if they had to justify most or all the actions of state officials, rather than the actions that are actually within their power. These propositions were dealt with above.

This piecemeal treatment of law also leads us to a new insight into the way judges respect the institutional history of law. They do this by avoiding wholesale changes and by their already noted reluctance to declare mistakes, rather than by attempting to justify them. Their respect is much more neutral than Dworkin implies. Conservative judges and lawyers would probably approve of most of the decisions already made, though most still like to retain their flexibility and do not want law to have to live up to any extravagant claims about how good an institution it is. Reformist judges and lawyers know that they cannot achieve instantaneous wholesale change. They thus cannot be responsible for the whole and should feel no need to justify it. All they must justify is the individual decision. Consequently, radical and reformist judges are silent about the many decisions of which they disapprove, nibbling away at them case by case. Their 'best theory' of law, if they had one, would be that law is an institution with great potential as a civilized and democratic way for human beings collectively to control their individual behaviour – a potential that is rarely achieved but which is worth striving for, and an ideal to be contrasted with the failures of existing practice.

Confess and Counter-attack

In *Law's Empire*, Dworkin has acknowledged some of the problems his holistic theory has encountered. He recognizes that some 'mistakes' will have to be enforced because they stem from statutes or judicial decisions which the interpreter is powerless to ignore. He also acknowledges that judges are not attached to the idea of interpreting the whole of law – their interpretations 'fan out' from the cases immediately in point, only so far as 'seems promising' (p. 245) and, indeed, only so far as is necessitated by dissatisfaction with the content of the rules, which would otherwise seem to be most in point. This gives decisions in similar cases 'local priority' and tends to compartmentalize law and limit interpretations to those compartments (he does not seem to appreciate that this runs completely counter to the chain-novel analogy). He even admits that law is 'far from perfectly consistent overall' and that there are frequently competing principles. However, despite these admissions, he returns to an insistence on holistic interpretation (p. 255) and is particularly insistent that 'depart-

ments' of law can be interpreted in a systematic way with even contradictory or 'competing' principles being incorporated by the different
priorities or weightings given to each.

And then he counter-attacks. Anyone who does not accept that this
systematic interpretation of law is possible is a 'sceptic' (p. 271), which in
this context seems to mean no more than someone who doubts and
demands reasons for that which Dworkin takes for granted. He acknowledges the reasons that some in the critical legal studies movement (CLS)
might have, says they might be valid but that they are unproven (p. 273).
This is an astonishing argument to use against a 'sceptic' because it is,
itself, a sceptical argument. He insists that the sceptic should show not
merely that an unsystematic interpretation is plausible, but that it is the
only plausible interpretation, by trying to create a systematic interpretation
and find it wanting (pp. 237, 274). This really must be one of the most
unreasonable requirements that Dworkin could make. The 'sceptics' must
have tried to do a Hercules and found it impossible. But then, according
to Dworkin, no one can do a Hercules. Thus no one can have met the
minimum conditions Dworkin sets for the right to challenge Dworkin. It
is a bit like Dworkin saying: if you walk for five thousand years your feet
will turn into wings and you will be an angel. The CLS scholar denies this
and Dworkin says he is therefore a sceptic. The CLS scholar offers
reasons. Dworkin says that those reasons might be valid but then they
might not. Dworkin then says that his explanation must have first been
tried and found wanting. Why? Because his kind of explanation is to be
preferred.

The answer of course is that we do not have time to waste on embark-
ing on the impossible as a prelude to rejecting the unreasonable. Dworkin
needs reasons for his theory, CLS needs reasons for its theories, I need
reasons for mine. We are each entitled to doubt those statements which
do not fit in with our overall views of the world and which we have
reasons to suspect would not fit in. We can evaluate the reasons according
to our own knowledge and view of the world. We may not have enough
information (we couldn't without doing a Hercules) to be certain that
Dworkin's theory is wrong. But we can have good enough reasons to
reject it.

Retreat to a Higher Plain

In his final chapter, Dworkin changes tack, retreats and mounts a final
defence from a hastily prepared position. Dworkin has by then admitted
many of the factors that build inconsistency into law and which prevent
judges finding, or even wanting to find, a content system in law (notably
local priority, legislative supremacy and binding precedent). He accepts

these as part of judicial practice and hence as something to be interpreted. Thus principles must be found which provide the best justification for the inconsistency which deals such a blow to law as integrity. Dworkin suggests that other political ideas may perform that function. A concept of fairness could justify legislative and constitutional supremacy and a conception of due process could justify binding precedent. He suggests that these larger ideals could be incorporated with integrity into a coherent scheme of political principles at a higher plain which he calls 'inclusive integrity'. Thus even as the content system he has expounded for sixteen years falls to pieces and he admits it does not 'fit', he is looking for a higher, more comprehensive content system which will provide an interpretation of everything, including the earlier failures. Such is the faith some theorists put in the necessity of systematic theory and, in particular, their own kind of system! For them there must be a content system out there somewhere. As this larger inclusive integrity is suggested as something of an afterthought and is not expounded, it will not be further discussed – except to make the comment that it is highly unlikely that an overall content system can bring coherence to a set of incoherent sub-sets of rules and principles.

4.8 Dworkin's System and the Social Observer

Even if judges overcame the many difficulties and objections to Dworkin's legal system, thus validating Dworkin's claim that his theory fits judicial practice, the social observer would still not view law as systematic. First, as already argued, law is far more than mere judicial practice, so that any systematization of that alone will systematize only a small part of law. But from the social observer's point of view, even if all the judges fell under Dworkin's sway, the judicial institutions would not be systematic because, *if Dworkin's system exists, it exists only for individual judges.* Dworkin's system must necessarily be individual because its creation requires the injection of an individual's moral values – when the judge chooses, from the several systems that pass the threshold of fit, the one he considers best (1977, p. 117; 1986, p. 255). In fact Dworkin's theory is more subjective still – because the standard of fit a successful theory has to pass will itself be determined by the judge's normative theory (1986, p. 231).

This necessity for individual value choices to be made by the system-creator means that there can be *no* system until those choices have been made. Because Hercules is mythical he cannot have made those value-choices, so it is not possible to assert that Hercules' system exists and that it is only our lack of superhuman powers that prevents us discovering it.

Likewise, we cannot say that any *real* judge's system exists because *s(he)* has not yet made all the necessary value-choices (including the crucial final one of the 'best' theory of law out of those that fit). We cannot even say that *elements* of such a system exist. Even if the judge has chosen the principles (s)he regards as best justifying one or more areas of law, (s)he might later reject them in favour of a justifying principle intrinsically less appealing but which fits in with principles (s)he later uses to justify other areas of law. Finally, the requirement of individual value-choice makes it impossible to cobble together a composite system by linking partial attempts at systematization made by different judges. Partial attempts are based on the value-preferences of their creators among which there is no reason to expect coherence. In any case, the crucial final holistic choice between alternative systems of principles has not been made by anyone.

Nevertheless, let us suppose that several judges overcame or ignored all these problems, reached the stage of finding more than one theory of law that fitted the institutional facts and chose one of these as their best theory. Dworkin accepts that in such a situation different judges would most probably make different choices. Naturally law will appear perfectly systematic to each of them. Our social observer might observe any one of these judges and conclude that there existed a system within the mind of that judge. But for the social observer, law involves more than the contents of a single mind. Law's Empire is broader than that! The social observer will look at other judicial minds. (S)he could not conclude that law as a whole was systematic because (s)he could not but notice that there were different systems, incompatible not only in the observer's eyes but in the eyes of the individual judges who chose one system above the others. Ironically the alleged strength of the system for each individual judge could be the undoing of the system for law as a whole. On the other hand, if the actual weaknesses of the individual judge's systems are acknowledged, this does not make law as a whole any more systematic. It rather acknowledges the failure of this attempt to find system in law at all. When the social observer takes into account the impossibility of actually achieving such systems in *any* minds and the fact that many (reforming) judges could not, and many realist and positivist judges do not, approach law in a Dworkinian manner, Dworkin's system is reduced to an unobtainable and rarely sought goal in the minds of some judges and lawyers, rather than a model for the social observer's systematic description of law.

Much of the problem lies in attempting to turn a theory of adjudication into a theory of law. A theory of adjudication tells an individual how to act rather than describing the institution in which (s)he and others act. Of course Dworkin's theory *refers* to the acts of others, but merely to tell the adjudicator what *obligations* those actions impose on him/her because of his/her duty to respect institutional history. What is included in the system is not so much the acts of others, as the adjudicator's moral reactions to those events. This turns law into a curiously *a*social activity – a moral response in an individual mind, rather than some kind of *social* interaction between the members of a society or officials of an institution.

The social observer will also have problems with the way Dworkin's system ignores the intentions, theories and interpretations of all participants other than the systematizer's. If the social observer accepts the sociological cliché that human action is purposive, (s)he will consider this a major hindrance to understanding those actions. Dworkin defends himself by saying that intention is of no use in deciding the *point* of several decisions *taken as a whole* (1986). However this does not count as an argument against using intention, it merely points to a stark choice. The choice is between treating as purposive *either* the *whole* activity or institution or the *individual acts* that make it up. In order to treat an activity or institution involving several participants as purposive it is necessary to *ignore* the purposes of each individual participant. What actually happens is that the point of the activity or institution is supplied by the observer. This is a mistake that we shall see in the next chapter is repeated by sociological theorists under the guise of ascribing a function to the activity or institution. Surely most social observers, and lawyers too, when faced with this choice between treating individual and institutional action as purposive, would choose the former, and in doing so reject the attempt to analyse law *as a whole* rather than in much smaller pieces. In fact, this is especially true of lawyers. They regard intention and purpose as quintessentially individual, as demonstrated in their approach to guilt in crimes involving several persons.

4.9 Conclusion

Although neither the social observer nor the active participant can accept that law forms a system resembling that outlined by Dworkin, the theory highlights certain very important features of law. First it notes (and in so doing backs up a major argument of the last chapter) the highly individual way in which officials derive reasons for action from the actions of others. Judges do not take the rules from cases and statutes and merely plug them into their practical reasoning; instead they note the actions of others and construct their own reasons for action from them. In doing so they are affected by factors quite external to the statute or decision under consideration – factors which vary from individual to individual and help to explain the individuality of the reaction. Among these factors Dworkin emphasizes the judge's reaction to the *content* of the rule (s)he gleans from the statute or decision, and the part the judge's own *values* play in this.

However, his claim that there is system in the way judges react to statutes and decisions (because they integrate them into a system of principles) cannot be supported. Even if it could, the very individual and varying nature of that reaction would lead us to see the *institutions* of law not as systematic but as the very opposite. Thus Dworkin's system suffers from precisely the same problem as positivist systems, despite the different kinds of elements and relations it contains. Finally, even Dworkin's system includes only some of the external factors affecting the nature of the individual judicial reactions – the others discussed in the previous chapter would certainly not fit into his system.

Dworkin is instrumental in undermining one theory of legal system but fails to establish his alternative. The principles he first introduced in 'Model of Rules' to attack the positivist system did not prove as amenable to systematizing as he later claimed in 'Hard Cases'. Instead they added to the complexity and heterogeneity of what even Dworkin refers to as a 'chaos of legal materials' (1986, p. 91). This is perhaps *the* classic case of a theorist rejecting another theory because its artificial system does not incorporate his insights into law, then failing in his attempts to build those insights into a system. It also provides a classic case of how those insights are so distorted by attempts to force them into a system as all but to lose their original value.

Like source-based reasoning, content-based reasoning is an important part of the activity of lawyers and judges within the institution of law, and Dworkin has provided some major insights into the way this occurs, especially the way some of the content must inevitably incorporate the lawyers' values. But it is only a part of that activity and lawyers have good reason for not aspiring to continue such reasoning until it provides a system covering all, or even the bulk, of law's content. Dworkin's content system takes his insight too far, distorting it, overestimating its importance, then blurring, distorting or ignoring the insights of other theorists.

Notes

1 This is strangely similar to Hobbes's rather limited use of natural law. Hobbes's account of how reason would tell men to seek and submit to an omnipotent sovereign lacks the subtlety of Finnis, and it also lacks the acknowledment that reason might also tell them to disobey at times. But it functions in a similar manner.

2 Dworkin distinguishes between integrity and consistency (1986, p. 225) but the consistency he rejects is consistency over time rather than consistency within a coherent, instantaneous and contemporaneous justification of law (1986, p. 222).

5

Sociological Theories of Legal System

5.1 Introduction

Many legal theorists see law as too intertwined with society to be explicable in any terms other than those they use to describe society and maintain that theories of law must be subsumed within a theory of the society of which it is a part.

This chapter will deal with the possibility of finding system in legal institutions and/or in what they do from the standpoint of the social observer (other standpoints are rarely taken in legal sociology) and will accordingly examine a number of more or less 'sociological' theories of law. None of these contains theories of legal system that are as well developed as the positivist and content theorists discussed (a fact freely admitted by Evan, 1980, p. 31). Some are so undeveloped and undevelopable that their authors' use of the term 'legal system' must be seen as little more than a synonym for law and a vague belief that it is or must be ordered in some way – a matter of verbal habit and/or terminological negligence. Such cases apart, there are two substantial reasons for this relative lack of development. First, sociological theorists are more concerned with elaborating law's external connections to other social phenomena than with its internal characteristics. Secondly, social phenomena can be described at several levels of generality. 'Macrosociology' deals with phenomena of culture, ideology, the economy and law, their interrelationships and the way they mutually influence changes in, or the stability of, each other. 'Microsociology' deals with the constitution and interaction of individuals and examines how citizens, judges and other officials are curbed, circumscribed and influenced. Sometimes an intermediate level that deals with the constitution and interaction of institutions can be distinguished. Most theories tend to concentrate on one of these levels and are usually founded on an apparent insight into that level. The problem is to synthesize a sociological theory of legal system that spans this range of social and legal phenomena. A theorist might build up from the microsociological phenomena to the 'macro' phenomenon of law as a functioning whole – or work down from the postulated social structures, inferring similar lower-level structures in law, until those same individual phenomena can be reached. The problem is that the two theoretical extrapolations may not meet. The construction of a macrosociological theory based on extrapolation of observation of the behaviour and interactions of individuals may reveal not a systematic whole but a disordered mass (as argued in chapter 7); and the lower the macro-theory is taken, the more may its lack of foundations be revealed.

5.2 Sociological Systems

Two kinds of system are found within sociological theories of law – functionalist theories and content theories. Functionalist theories have, as their elements, facts about the actions of individuals and their effects on others. These elements may include values and rules but generally only as facts about the actual values held by social actors and the rules they follow (rather than as posited by legal scientists or interpreted by a Hercules). These facts are related by the mutual effects they have on each other.

These elements and relations are structured into institutions by the way each actor's actions help the institution perform its allotted 'function'. The institutions are similarly structured into sub-systems by the way the institutions' joint performance of their functions allows the sub-system (e.g. law) to perform its function within the overall social system (e.g. reducing conflict, integration or reproducing the relations of production).

Some sociological systems resemble a classic content system whose norms embody and reflect a coherent set of values. Their sociological credentials are based on their claim that there is a link between these values and wider social values or interests or because they claim that this system has certain effects (or 'functions') on law for the rest of society. The Parsonian theory with which we begin this chapter involves both.

Some sociological theorists – including many realists, critical legal scholars, conflict theorists, symbolic interactionists, ethnomethodologists and deconstructionists – do not see law in systematic terms at all and do not address themselves to the task of constructing systems. Increasingly, sociological theorists, especially microsociologists, do not see law in systematic terms and more or less explicitly say so, often for the same reasons as the present writer; because societies are unsystematic and disordered, law, as an integral part of that society, cannot escape being unsystematic and disordered too. But that is the subject of chapter 7. This chapter discusses those sociological theories which do refer to 'legal systems' and do appear to see law as systematic in some way.

This chapter will not discuss all such theories or possible theories. Following the pattern of other chapters it will begin by expounding and, where necessary, elaborating a prominent sociological systems theory. In this chapter the Parsonian structural functionalist theory as developed by Evan and Bredemeier will be chosen as the highpoint of post-war systematic sociological theories of law. I will show that its key insights – the place of law within society and the effect this has on law, the institutional character of law, the importance of the relationships between the actions of officials rather than between the rules – are distorted by the attempt to systematize them and that subsequent sociological theories of law (Marxist, process, pluralists and some CLS) retreat from this highpoint and provide insights that could not be included within its structural functionalism yet still try to create systems of their own. By the time we reach the CLS theories, the systematic character has all but disappeared.

5.3 Parsonian Structural Functionalism

Parsons's structural functionalism is a theory of society and does not include a fully developed theory of law. Bredemeier (1962) and Evan (1962, 1980) went a long way towards producing such a theory, but the latter freely admitted that the task was not complete (1980, p. 31). Accordingly, the synthesis of a functionalist theory of law involves some interpretation and expansion. Nevertheless, the lines are clear and the views of other structural functionalists can be incorporated.

Parsons believed that a Hobbesian state of nature can only be avoided, and society can only continue to exist, if society is structured vertically and horizontally into an internalized hierarchy of consistent *values* (normative beliefs, at a very high level of generality, about what is desirable), *norms* (more specific formulations of what is acceptable behaviour in given circumstances) and *roles* (which specify the duties of individuals in particular positions or circumstances). At the same time it is horizontally structured into several sub-systems – political, economic, legal and educational. Each of these systems is itself vertically structured into values, norms and roles which are incorporated into the larger vertical structure of society by being related to ultimate values and the values of other sub-systems (Evan, 1980, p. 160). But what distinguishes one sub-system from another is the 'function' it performs within society by meeting one of the four (*a priori*) 'needs' society has for survival – 'goal-pursuance', 'adaptation', 'integration' and 'pattern-maintenance' (socialization) respectively. Each sub-system's function both meets a so-

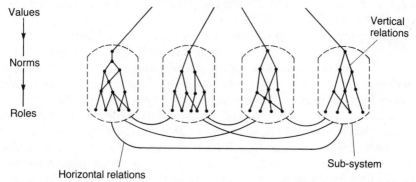

Figure 5.1   Parsons's social structure

cial need and supports the functioning of the other sub-systems, thereby maintaining the system as a whole and helping to preserve and enforce the vertical structure of values, norms and roles.

As these functional needs have been determined (by *a priori* reasoning) and as society has continued to exist, it is assumed that *some* institution must have fulfilled each function and the search for the obliging institution commences. It is precisely and consciously by such means that Bredemeier 'applied' Parsons's theory to law by citing it as the 'integration' sub-system.

Parsons's social system could be represented pictorially as follows. The vertical structure is represented by the pyramid (or more precisely a 'truncated pyramid lattice' – see chapter 4.3) of values, norms and roles. At some level, the bundles of values, norms and roles are seen as sub-systems which are horizontally interrelated by their interdependent functioning. (See figure 5.1.)

The first problem such theories face is to *find* these fundamental values of society and its sub-systems. Evan euphemistically calls it a 'challenge' (1980, p. 141). The problems of knowing the content of other minds, even when they have been verbalized, have already been noted (chapter 3.3). Yet, if there were these consensually held values shaping all our social actions, we should surely be aware of them. We could collect evidence for the consensus by asking those with different backgrounds, jobs and political affiliations if they agreed with us. Unfortunately the evidence points the other way (e.g. Abercrombie and Turner, 1978; Mann, 1970). Indeed, when Evan compiled a book of extracts to *illustrate* the hierarchy of legal values, norms and roles and their linkages with social values, norms and roles, all the articles, revealed a considerable degree of *dissensus*, even among the participants in legal activity (1980, chs 13, 14, 21, 22).

This should not surprise us. We have seen the difficulties another content theorist (Dworkin) had in deriving a uniform and consistent set of principles out of the activity and beliefs of judges. But his problems are multiplied for a sociological content theorist's attempt to derive social values from the activities and beliefs of the population at large (who lack the similarities of background and comparative intimacy of the judiciary). Indeed much of sociology has concentrated on the differences between variously defined groups that lead group members to hold different, 'sub-cultural' values. It may, of course, be possible to formulate propositions with which a sufficient number and variety of people could agree – just as international conferences can produce final resolutions. But just as such resolutions usually had not been internalized before the conference, are given different meanings after the conference, and avoid rather than express the key motivating values of the participants, so such formulations will not express the content of social values. Any formulations of values that could be subject to a consensus are likely to be so vague, or subject to such conflicting interpretations, that they are no guide to action and cannot be usefully related to any specific norms or role-expectations (Prothro and Grigg, 1960). Evan's examples bear this out. 'Justice', 'love and nurturance' and 'the production and distribution of wealth' are the basic values that he claims underlie and structure the social sub-systems of law, family and economy. They are too vague to provide the vertical relations of consistency/justification/derivation needed to create a content system. Any 'social' values or 'postulates' formulated precisely enough to provide those relations would be controversial, selective and hence non-consensual. Sometimes even the vague notions that Evan uses are controversial – Fuller, Unger and Selznick insist on 'legality' rather than Evan's 'justice' as the basic value of law. Consequently, there is no *system* of societal values, norms and roles which law could either mirror (Pound) or of which it could form a part (Parsons).

Even if there were such a system of consensual values, as Cotterrell reminds us, the pressure to create norms occurs where consensus is not attainable and the pressure is applied by individuals and groups who want *their* values reflected in law (1984, p. 106).

The link between the content of values to be found within society and those to be found in legal rules is a common insight on which Parsonians are right to insist. But the attempt to systematize that insight is severely distorting, producing values which are too vague to be of use or which are a partisan selection that ignores many of the values held by others.

Other theories give an inkling of why such systematization would be impossible. 'Microsociological' approaches, like symbolic interactionism,

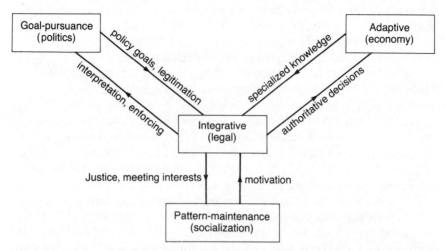

Figure 5.2 Horizontal structure of society showing some of the interaction of its subsystems

exchange and some organization theories, see norms and roles emerging from day-to-day interactions of individuals and responding to their needs, interests and desires. Norms and roles produced by such diffuse and decentralized processes are unlikely to fit well into a society-wide system. Conflict theories emphasize the factors which produce clashes of values, even between those with close contact with each other. Thus values, far from being the great unifiers that turn society into a social system, are its potential destroyers. By insisting on the link between values found in society and those found in legal rules, Parsonian functionalists provide a very good reason why the content of law should not be systematic, and help explain the failure of other theorists to find content systems when they looked at law alone.

Horizontal Structure of Society

Whereas Parsons' vertical structure is widely disparaged for reasons such as those outlined above, similar horizontal structures are much more widely supported. Indeed, Parsons himself shifted his emphasis towards it in his later years (Wilkinson, 1981, p. 78).

There are two aspects to Parsons's horizontal structure: the *joint* achievement of certain functions like system-maintenance, and the effects that the sub-systems have on each other. The latter aspect can be represented diagrammatically using the interactions described by Bredemeier (figure 5.2). Note that he does not include the interrelationship of non-legal systems with each other – e.g. the effect that the institution of socialization has on the economy emphasized by Weber, and the effect the economy has on socialization emphasized by Marx.

The other aspect of horizontal structure could be represented diagrammatically by figure 5.3, indicating how the various functions each sub-system has in relation to the other sub-systems combine to provide the overall function of that sub-system, and these in turn combine to provide the overall effect or function of the system (cf. Roach and Gross, 1972). In particular, law's social function of 'integration' comprises, and is achieved by, the fulfilment of the functions of enforcement, authoritative decision-making, interpretation, and provision of a sense of justice.

The basic structure of complementary and interdependent functioning sub-systems provides the structure of society at the very highest level. It places law as a legal sub-system within the social system. In so doing it also provides the legal system with a *wholeness factor* – the function law has in maintaining the social system. Furthermore, it also provides a model for the internal structure of the legal system at lower levels, a structure that will be elaborated later in this section after more carefully considering the elements and relations from which it is constructed.

The basic *elements* of their systems are termed 'roles'. These are to be found in both the vertical and horizontal structures of society. In the former they constitute the lowest and most specific normative unit. Yet they are also the basic units of the horizontal structure for as we shall see it is only by officials performing their roles that sub-systems are able to perform their functions. In the horizontal structure, roles could be called the '*micro*-functions' of individuals within the functional system of law.

This ability of roles to fit into two different kinds of system alerts us to the different concepts of role used in each case. The elements of the vertical system are more illuminatingly seen as 'role-orientations' (what the role-occupant thinks he should do) or 'role-expectations' (what others think he should do). The elements of the horizontal system are 'role-performances' or 'role-behaviour' (Evan, 1980, p. 242). These three will not necessarily coincide. But it is Parsons's controversial claim that they do. Role-orientation coincides with role-expectation because they are part of a consensually shared vertical structure, the teaching of which is the function of the socialization sub-system and whose protection is the function of other sub-systems. Role-behaviour coincides with role-orientation/expectation, principally because people act on their value beliefs but also because it is the function of certain institutions to ensure compliance with role-expectations.

Relations between roles are established when the performance of a role by A leads to the action of B, and B's role specifies that he act in that way

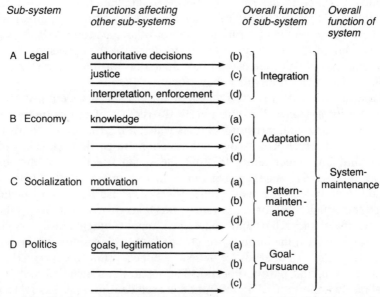

Figure 5.3 Horizontal structure of society showing the joint achievement of social functions

in response to such actions of A's. Two kinds of linkage are common, (1) where B's role is to do A's bidding or follow a rule laid out by A (e.g. the appeal judge's role is to lay down rules and the magistrate's role is to follow them); (2) where B's role is to handle a person or a matter after A has dealt with it (e.g. the arresting officer's role is to take an arrested person to the station where the desk sergeant's role is to charge him). In an ideal Parsonian world this means that the role-expectations are linked in that A is expected to perform the relevant action and B is expected to make the designated response, that the role-orientations are linked because each shares these communal role-expectations and those role-orientations are sufficient to produce role-behaviour in conformity with them. But in the real events from which sociological theorists must construct their systems, what are linked are the role-behaviours of A and B – with the role-performance of B frequently influenced by B's role-orientation, A's and others' role-expectations and usually other pressures as well.

In either case there can be chains of relations, either causal relations or interrelated roles. The form these chains take and the way they converge, split and complement each other is the structure of the legal system.

Many, perhaps most, relations between individual actors are intra-institutional. However, many relations are extra-institutional, either with members of the public or with members of other institutions. The external relations of the institution amount to no more than the sum of such individual extra-institutional relations. It is only through these external relations that institutions fulfil their 'function'.

The legal sub-system is itself a system and the social system provides a model for its *structure*. There is a vertical structure of values, norms and roles and a horizontal structure of roles which are structured into institutions, each of which has its own sub-function which they fulfil in order jointly and interdependently to fulfil the social functions of the legal system as a whole. As Llewelyn put it in one of his proto-functionalist moods, they 'cog together' (1962, p. 234). These institutions include courts and usually one or more out of the following: legislature, police, cabinet, magistracy, bar and some government bureaucracies. Sometimes, several such institutions are grouped into sub-systems of the legal system (e.g. the 'criminal justice system' – police, criminal courts, criminal bar, prisons and parole officers). The institutions included vary, but this is rarely important. If an institution is excluded from law, its relations to legal institutions are merely converted from *internal* relations of the legal sub-system (i.e. part of the structure of the legal sub-system) into *external* relations of the legal sub-system and part of the structure of the larger *social* system. Nevertheless, most functionalists include more institutions in law than the positivists, and emphasize this in their criticism of positivism.

The functions attributed to legal institutions collectively or individually also vary. Bredemeier lists five. However, taking into account other functionalists, the list should probably be nine and each can be attached to one or two legal institutions. For some theorists there is a one-to-one correspondence of institutions and functions (Roberts, 1979, ch. 2) although most would agree there may be variations from one social system to another as to which institution performs which functions.

1 *'Dispute resolution'* – a function of courts and law firms.
2 *'Reinforcement'* or 'reinstitutionalization' (Bohannen, 1968) of existing practices within the community by framing rules that equate to those practices and by providing the means for their 'facilitation' (Summers, 1977, p. 127) – a function of courts and legislatures.
3 *'Change in existing practices'* (Schur, 1968, p. 75) – by legislatures and, sometimes, courts.
4 *'Guidance'* or 'education' (Chambliss and Siedman, 1971, p. 9) – again, by the legislature and courts.

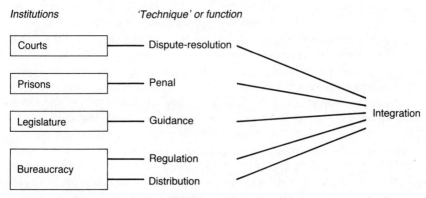

Figure 5.4   Structure of the legal sub-system: version 1

5 '*Regulation*', the administrative control of various private institutions – by the bureaucracy.
6 *Participation by the state in social and economic affairs* by the bureaucracy.
7 *Punishment*, retribution or vengeance against perceived wrong-doers, reinforcement of existing social values – by courts and penal institutions.
8 *Maintaining social peace* (or, more loosely, 'social order' or 'social control') – by police and penal institutions to the extent that they isolate some and deter some other potentially violent individuals.
9 *Legitimation* of existing social institution – supposedly achieved by courts.

Parsonians find two levels of structure in the legal system – the inter-institutional and the intra-institutional. These are intermediate and micro-sociological phenomena respectively.

At the inter-institutional level, the institutions' joint achievement of the social functions of law could by represented as shown in figure 5.4.

The manner in which several institutions can jointly achieve such functions fall into three broad categories: functional chains, functional convergence and functional complementation. In functional *chains* the performance of one institution's function leads to the performance of the second institution's function (e.g. the function of punishment by incarceration is fulfilled when a court functions to convict and sentence and the goal performs its function of isolating the convict). Functional *complementation* (or 'joint causation', Nagel and Neef, 1977, p. 50) occurs when the social function can be fulfiled only by two or more institutions performing their functions (e.g. in bicameral parliaments, legislation is effected only when both houses pass the same Act). Functional *convergence* (or 'cocausation', Nagel and Neef, 1977, p. 50) occurs when several institutions have the same effect on the same subject – each institution would individually have some effect but that effect is reinforced by the effect of other institutions. This is particularly important in the many cases where the effects of the institutions are *individually* less than sufficient to fulfil the requisite function, but *collectively* more than sufficient to do so (e.g. economic stimulation by central bank and treasury).

One feature which crops up in the structure of virtually every systems theory is *feedback*. If one institution acts in performance of its social function it will frequently in turn be affected by its own action, either because it takes notice of its own actions (e.g. the bench remembers how it decided a similar case the week before), or because those affected by the institution's action react to it (e.g. those affected by new legislation put pressure on MPs to have it repealed or modified). Either type of feedback is likely to affect the future performance of that institution.

Most functionalist theories have converging functional structures with elements of complementary functions, functional chains and feedback. Figure 5.5 represents an attempt to incorporate most legal institutions into such a system.

The third and lowest level of social structure is the intra-institutional structure of legal institutions. Functionalist theorists see legal institutions as sub-systems of the legal system, a system of roles which attach to various positions in the institution. As D'Amato puts it: 'the system is so organised that each person working within it – legislators, judges, clerks, lawyers, litigants, policemen, bureaucrats – does of his own accord what is necessary for the success of the system' (1975, p. 202).

These roles are micro-functions for individuals just as legal institutions had sub-functions and the legal system as a whole had macro-level social functions. The structures of these systems of roles are fairly similar to the structure of higher-level systems – the roles are so related that their performance by the role-occupants fulfils the functions of the legal institution within the legal system (as well as the sub-functions of adaptation, integration, etc., that every system, sub-system or, in this case, sub-sub-system 'needs' to fulfil to preserve itself). This is partly achieved by structures of converging and complementary functions – the joint performance of similar roles by those in contact with other institutions or the public (e.g. the resolution of hundreds of individual disputes by individual judges means that the courts perform their function of dispute resolution). But it is also achieved by the arrangement of roles into chains of responsibility so that the role of one official is to respond to the role-

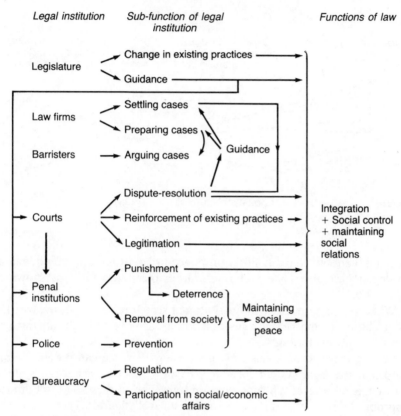

Figure 5.5 Structure of the legal sub-system: version 2

performance of another official. These chains of roles will often be arranged hierarchically into superior roles which involve the issuing of orders or guidelines and inferior roles which require the role occupants to follow them. For instance, it is the role of superior court judges to decide cases before them and it is the role of lower court judges to use such decisions in deciding their own cases. But the chain will not necessarily pass from superior to inferior or *vice versa*. Sometimes it will pass between equals with different functions – as when a detective sergeant hands responsibility for a suspect to the desk sergeant who decides whether and with what to charge him. Similarly the structure will not necessarily be pyramidal in form. The chains of roles may at one point connect one official to many and then from many to one. A prosecutor's role may involve receiving cases from many different policemen and

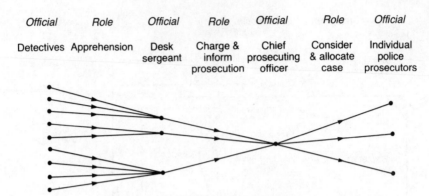

Figure 5.6   An intra-institutional structure of roles (police)

farming them out to many different police prosecutors. This could lead us to depict part of a system of roles within the police force as shown in figure 5.6.

Whatever pattern the intra-institutional structure forms, it involves the interrelation of individual roles that jointly achieve the sub-functions of the relevant institution.

Putting these three levels of structure together, we can see an overall model of the legal system forming part of a functionalist social system. At each level several sub-functions are jointly performed so as to fulfil the appropriate function achieved at the next level (figure 5.7).

5.4 Criticism

The time now comes to pose the same question as was posed for positivist and content theories in the last two chapters: from the social observer's point of view can law usefully be seen as systematically ordered in the way outlined by a functionalist theory of legal system?

This neatest and tidiest of systems incorporates many insights. It appreciates the necessity of understanding law in terms of the part it plays within society and its effects upon other social phenomena (for which purpose laws are created). It appreciates the institutional basis of law and the institutional media and ultimately the human agents through which it must operate.

But it is in forcing these into a system that most of the problems are created. Having a vertical structure of values, norms and roles provides a double systematization of law and helps explain why the horizontal struc-

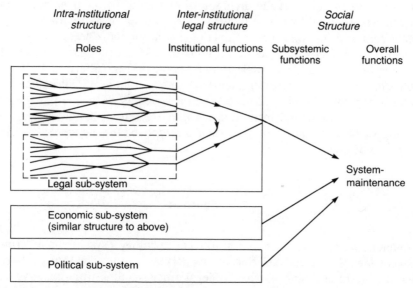

Figure 5.7   Structure of the legal subsystem: version 3

ture exists at all. However, this vertical systematization is untenable. Equating role-orientation, role-expectation and role-behaviour similarly makes system building more feasible but less credible.

Role-orientation will not coincide with role-expectation because, in contrast to Parsons's 'oversocialized' view of them (Wrong, 1961), people frequently resist the imposition of such role-expectations on them (Brittan, 1981, p. 175). They take seriously the differences between persons even if Parsons et al. do not. Role-orientation will not necessarily produce role-behaviour, because there are many other pressures to which the role-occupant is subject (Cotterrell, 1984, p. 98; and Chapter 7 *infra*) and because individuals act and interact as whole persons not merely as the occupants of specific roles (Selznick, 1981, p. 302).

With the rejection of Parsons's vertical structure and its consensus of roles, it becomes doubly important to distinguish expectation, orientation and behaviour. People often differ on the behaviour expected of role-occupants. Thus role-orientation cannot *mirror* communal expectations but must be *chosen from* them. Just as frequently role-expectations are too vague to indicate what behaviour is required, so that if role-orientation is to have any influence on a person's role-behaviour he will have to invent a new one for himself. With conflicting or vague role-expectations we would not expect the pressures placed on the role-occupant to be solely in the direction of one kind of role-behaviour. At the macro-level of social structure, Parsonian enthusiasm for systems leads him and his followers to functionalist accounts of legal and social systems so perfectly designed to preserve themselves that legal and social change is rendered inexplicable (Craib, 1984, p. 50; Cotterrell, 1984, p. 98). However, the greatest problems are to be found at the intermediate, inter-institutional level, and in the central concepts of functionalist legal systems – functions and institutions. These are crucial to the success of their structure and best illustrate their attempts to force system into the disorder of law.

5.5   Function

Function, we have seen, is central to legal sociology's systematic description of law. The social function of law serves to unify law into a whole and the interdependent functions of legal officials and institutions serve to form its structure. At each level of structure the various elements are doubly linked by functions. The functions combine to produce an overall function for the social system, the legal sub-system or the legal institution. These functions are also frequently directed toward other subsystems. From the standpoint of the social observer, the *legal system* exists, as described, if legal institutions singly and collectively really do fulfil their allocated functions, i.e. at each level the institutions, subsystems and individuals really do act as described and have the claimed effects. For *law* to be systematic this system must incorporate most of the phenomena of law.

Our social observer will quickly discover the enormous range of activities performed by those individuals and institutions and the various effects that they have, both singly and in combination. Attention will be drawn to this fact by the variety of functions claimed for legal institutions, the legal system and society as a whole.

Functionalist theories link *some* of the effects into a system, but must be highly selective, including only those which their *a priori* reasoning tells them are necessary for the system's survival.

In so doing they ignore diversity of legal phenomena. Their account is not only impoverished but profoundly misleading as they are forced to ignore the many effects that are partially or wholly contradictory – in the sense that both cannot be fulfiled simultaneously. Of course, some of the theorists postulating contradictory functions may be wrong. But, when roles, institutions and groups of institutions like law are observed, they do appear to achieve opposite effects in many cases. Indeed, for every function listed in chapter 5.3 either that or another legal institution seems to fulfil the opposite. Even where there is agreement by theorists and participants on the function of an institution, it may be the opposite that is *actually* achieved. This is due largely to the nature of legal institutions (*infra*), the variable impact of outside forces on legal officials and institutions and the problem of unintended or unpredictable actions.

At the macrosociological level of social structure, functionalists see the social system's function as the preservation, maintenance or survival of the social system itself. But functionalists see this being achieved (Parsons, 1949) by minimal adaptation, in three radically different ways: by resisting change 'homeostatically' (Laszlo, 1972; Vago, 1981); resisting change where possible but adapting where it is not possible; and by constantly evolving into a more complex and differentiated society (Stone, 1966, Buckley, 1967). These differences fundamentally affect the functions the legal system is expected to fulfil – making it either an instrument (or at least a reflector) of change or an implacable opponent of it. Each suffers plausibility problems. 'Homeostatic' theories find it hard to argue that changes occur only when the system disintegrates in runaway revolutionary positive feedback. But if the legal system's function is to adopt the minimal adaptation necessary to avoid disaster, how *do* the officials know when the eleventh hour comes? Surely some will think that change is necessary and others think not, producing conflicting actions and effects. If the function of law is adaptation to keep pace with social change then how do the officials pick the trends? May not different legislators and judges simultaneously think society is moving in different directions and thereby be making contradictory adjustments? Law and society are characterized by simultaneous moves to initiate and bolster change on the one hand and resist change and reinforce existing practices on the other. This spreads throughout law, producing conflicting effects and partial functioning, even *nonfunctioning*, of legal institutions and officials.

At the inter-institutional level the same theoretical and practical discrepancies in claimed functions are found. Most writers emphasize the function of dispute and conflict resolution for courts. Yet there is tension between this and the function of 'rule creation'. Out-of-court settlement of disputes is encouraged: yet this makes guidance by definitive legal pronouncements rarer. Furthermore, far from reducing conflict, some laws express and exacerbate the conflict in the community. Conflicting parties come to law not to resolve their disputes but to win them. If the losing party feels unfairly dealt with by the legislative or judicial determination, its resentment may lead to other, possibly more severe, conflicts. This danger is exacerbated by adversarial litigation which makes complete victory possible for one party, discouraging the compromises that might otherwise be made. Where the losing side does *not* accept the legislation or judicial decision, then the original conflict continues with the stakes raised significantly by the potential use of legal sanctions – and another of law's functions, legitimation, is compromised. Where an attempt is made to fulfil law's 'rechannelling of conduct' function by *changing* the law, or where no clear solution is provided by law, newer more serious disputes may be created from the indignation of the interests prejudiced by the decision and a flurry of litigation to sort out the details.

The police are generally ascribed the functions of catching lawbreakers and maintaining social peace (i.e. preventing outbreaks of violence). Yet at times these two functions may conflict, as in the 1981 Bristol riots. At other times police may frustrate rather than aid the fulfilment of each function. Sometimes the violence is initiated and performed by the police and peace only returns when the police stop using their truncheons. Sometimes this prevents greater violence, so that they partially fulfil their function. Often the violence used is greater than that averted. This could be due to miscalculation or to a conflicting function, of intimidating oppressed classes, which is pursued even at the cost of increasing the level of violence in the community (Turk, 1980, p. 113). Whatever the explanation, the function of maintaining social peace is prejudiced rather than fulfilled. Similarly, in attempting to catch lawbreakers police frequently become lawbreakers themselves; and because they do not 'catch' themselves, they fail to pursue that social function.

One defence for those who point out that the actual effects of law contradict its claimed functions is to say that ascribing a function to law implies that it has more effects in that direction than in the opposite one, e.g. that courts resolve more disputes than they create, or that policemen reduce the levels of violence and lawbreaking more than they add to them. However, the positive effects do not cancel out the negative effects; it cannot be ignored that law is producing *both* positive and negative effects, especially as these effects fall on different people. Legal institutions resolve disputes between some and aggravate conflict between others, reduce the amount of violence suffered by some and increase that suffered by others, reinforce and facilitate the practices of some while attempting to change the practices of others, and regulate the disapproved practices of some while punishing the disapproved practices of others.

If law as a whole, or a legal institution in particular, achieves both a set of effects and a contrary set of effects, it is very hard to describe the production of *either* as its function. In such circumstances the ascription of a function implies a choice in which some of the actions and effects of law are singled out and others are ignored.

This puts at risk the *wholeness* factor that sociological systems theory

gives to the legal system (and to legal institutions). That which supposedly gives it its unity is the fact that it performs a certain function. Yet it
also does the opposite. This is aggravated by the fact that most of the
actions and effects that are ascribed to law and legal institutions as
functions are also performed and produced by other social institutions.
Not only do the institutions and 'sub-systems' have effects other than
those assigned, but other institutions and sub-systems have those same
effects. The value of seeing institutions and sub-systems as wholes on the
basis of what they are supposed to achieve is rendered highly dubious
because of the poor fit between institution and effect found in practice.

The choice of effects necessary to see legal institutions in terms of
functions is even more disastrous for the *structure* of legal systems. The
structure relates only some of the effects of those institutions into a
system. Other theorists can single out other effects of those institutions
and form them into a system. Thus Parsons builds a system from legitimate authority relations and Quinney (1973) builds a system from the
coercive ones. Parsons makes the function of law the integration of
currently held common values, thus ignoring the new values that law
promotes and conflict over those values. Quinney makes the function of
law the securing of ruling-class interests by the forceful control of the
working class, so he highlights discriminatory and coercive parts of the
law. To do so he must ignore crimes against the person, which seem to
have no class basis, and which are as strictly enforced in all countries.

Dahrendorf noted how such selectivity allowed consensus theorists and
conflict theorists to paint quite different pictures of society. Each of them
drew on observed social facts about the society. He concluded that society
was 'Janus-faced' (1958), presenting different faces to different theorists.
But rather than concluding that both images are true, surely the social
observer will conclude that both are inadequate, observing that institutions
achieve both the effects listed and their opposite, as well as others beside.

Even if there were to be a choice between conflicting images of social
system, on what basis would it be made? The traditional functionalist
answer is that the functions listed are the institution's contribution to the
success, maintenance, preservation or survival of the system. This reply is
often criticized for the overly organic analogy and terminology such as
'needs', 'survival', 'homeostasis' (Buckley, 1967), and for the real uncertainties over what 'survival', etc., entail (Craib, 1984, p. 52), especially
when society can never remain exactly the same, and the *a priori* basis on
which the needs are established. To avoid these problems Cotterrell
rephrases the reply: 'an institution's function is its contribution to the
maintenance of existing social and economic institutions' (1984, p. 74).
But why choose as 'functions' merely these effects? What about the
effects law fulfils in disrupting existing institutions? It is the explicit

purpose of some laws and legal institutions to disrupt the existing social and economic institutions of organized crime and few structural functionalists would not characterize this as one of law's functions (although some would say that the police and political parties in some Australian states *do* contribute to the maintenance of organized crime and *vice versa*). Deliberate attempts to destroy institutions are not confined to illegal institutions, as much anti-union legislation testifies. It is similarly seen as a function of law to change many existing organizations in refashioning society and an accepted side-effect is that those organizations may be irreparably damaged (e.g. in economic structural change).

In the end, the selection of a function from among the many actual effects can only be a value one. The function of society, or law, or a legal institution, becomes not a description of what it *does* and the effects it *has*, but what the functionalist wants it to do and achieve. Desired effects become functions, undesired effects become malfunctions. But the social observer must note that the so-called system is producing *both* the effects labelled 'functions' and the other effects labelled 'malfunctions', and that this tendency lies in the very 'structural' interrelationships which are claimed by sociological systems theory to be producing the functions.

A system built up of the interlocking of such ideal or desired functions is not a system in existence in the real world, but an ideal or desired system. It is a blueprint for society rather than a drawing of it. As such it is much simpler and more systematic. No doubt if Parsons or Bredemeier had the job of designing a society, if one of them could sweep away the products of two thousand generations of communal living, this is just the sort of society he would create, with everyone having a designated place, performing a designated role with sub-systems performing their designated functions. It would be the product of *one* person, just as a computer system may be to the design of *one* person and, as such, the parts can all be made to work towards his or her ends. But societies and legal systems are not the product of *one* person at one time. They are the products of many at different times with conflicting values and ends. Social and legal systems such as Parsons's and Bredemeier's must ignore what does not fit into their preferred system. Such systems may look good on paper, but it is only on paper, and not among the tumult of social life, that they may be found.

5.6 Institutions

Legal institutions are central to the structure of sociological legal systems. By simultaneously performing their allotted functions legal institutions enable law to fulfil its functions within the social system. Images and theories of institutions are adopted which explain how this is possible, involving intra-institutional structures of roles by which the actions of members are co-ordinated and directed towards the achievement of institutional goals or functions. Two mechanisms are suggested for this, based on shared values of institutional members or monitoring and control of subordinate members by superiors. The first mechanism postulates either a consensus over the values to be achieved by that institution or at least a strong tendency to greater convergence of values among members of institutions because of the constant and intensive contact they have with each other (Parsons and Schils, 1982, p. 71) and because they can choose which institutions to join (unlike the choice of society into which they are born and live). Where the convergence of values is insufficient the second mechanism invoking the power of senior officials to control and coordinate the actions of subordinates supposedly is sufficient.

However, just as the last section argued that the functions allotted to institutions involved a partisan selection of their actual effects, including those that can fit into the theorist's pet system, this section argues that institutions are very different from the distorted models that are necessary for the institutions to perform those allotted functions. Indeed, far from explaining how legal institutions perform their functions, an understanding of them will explain why they do not.

Shared Values

There is certainly a tendency for values to converge within institutions (as well as several contrary tendencies). However, one of the factors tending towards such convergence, 'institutional interests', makes the institution less likely to achieve *any* allotted social function. These interests are formed as soon as the institution comes into existence, whether it is deliberately created or merely emerges.

Where institutions are deliberately created they may be planned and given specific functions. But, once the institutions are created and the positions are filled, the individuals who fill them perceive their own interests in the strength of the institution and their positions within it. They then act, at least in part, to enhance them. This is not to say that an institution set up for a particular purpose immediately goes off on its own self-seeking tangent. But institutional interests are a factor in decisions of the institution's officials, so that many actions may primarily further institutional interests while doing little to fulfil the institutional function, and may indeed contradict it. For example, Chambliss and Siedman suggest that, when legal institutions fulfil 'functions' such as dispute resolution, they do so in as complicated a manner as possible, in a language so far removed from ordinary discourse that lawyers' work is increased

(1983, p. 9). Some of the actions which create work for lawyers are either irrelevant to, or derogate from, the functions of legal institutions. The complexities of legal language serve to weaken the effect law can have in guiding the public; the expense of engaging lawyers in all this work minimizes the use of legal solutions in dispute resolution and breeds a sense of grievance which offends the sense of justice and legitimacy which it is law's supposed function to foster.

Many institutions are not deliberately created with a specific or uncontested purpose in mind. Many are not *created* at all. They just grow up from practices that become entrenched, expanded and then institutionalized. As we saw in chapter 3.7, law in less complex societies may involve nothing more than the practice of taking disputes to the rest of the tribe at a particular time. But even then embryonic institutional interests are emerging. Those most influential in the campfire discussions enjoy having their opinion so highly regarded and wish to have disputes settled in this way on a continuing basis. As specialization and formalization take place, these individuals and their successors spend more of their time and effort in these embryonic legal activities, and their interest in the respect and rewards conceded to them because of their involvement grows accordingly.

Such observations are not limited to critics. They are implicit in the theory of functionalism itself. Parsons sees every system as having four 'needs' that must be fulfilled in order for it to preserve itself – pattern maintenance, integration, goal-pursuance and adaptation. It is the function of various sub-systems to meet these needs. Yet these sub-systems and the institutions within them are themselves systems with the same 'needs' for preservation. It is not difficult to imagine conflicts between the function of institutional self-preservation and performance of the institution's social function in the sense that pursuing the latter would – because of resultant controversy, vested interests or a clash with other social institutions – endanger the former. It is hardly a startling suggestion that the social function might take second place! Indeed, the fortunes of many institutions may be enhanced if they do very little because the less that is done the fewer outside interests that are threatened. This challenges the claim by many organizational theorists that institutions are inherently goal-directed (Gouldner and Gouldner, 1963, p. 484; Crozier, 1964, p. 6; Blau, 1976, p. 240). As Crozier has acknowledged, institutions need not fulfil their goals in order to remain in existence (Crozier, 1964, p. 187). It might be added that they might not remain in existence if they tried too hard to fulfil their social function.

Institutions generate more than institutional interests. The prime interest of their members is in enhancing the prestige and rewards that go with their current or hoped-for position. This is generally served if the institution is strong, but it is also served by the enhancement of their position vis-à-vis other positions within the institution. For some this will be achieved if the institution is actually weakened, leading to a loss of confidence in (and by) the institution's 'senior officials', giving more scope for subordinates. In general, the interests of 'senior' personnel lie in being able to direct the institution's personnel and resources to the achievement of their own goals; and the interests of lower officials lie in maintaining their autonomy from central control and in 'empire-building' – expanding the area in which they have control or, at least, discretion (Crozier, 1964, p. 156). Thus the institution will generate conflicting interests which make the smooth interdependent functioning of complementary roles highly problematic.

Once an institution is founded, successors to the initial oocupants must be 'recruited'. Newcomers will not necessarily share the founder's goals or a desire to use their positions to fulfil the socio-legal function of the law, or even to further the institutional and role-interests pursued by their predecessors. Recruiting officers may seek to ensure that they do, but recruiting practices often become comparatively formalized and seek to find those with qualities that are not specific to those with appropriate value commitments (such as formal qualifications or perceived success at a previous job). Choosing someone who seeks to pursue the socio-legal functions of the institution may be put in the 'too hard' basket – too hard to determine what the person's goals are, too hard to guess whether they will remain constant, too hard to determine what the functions of the institutions really are and too hard to determine what the occupant of the vacant position should strive for in order to further that function. Newcomers will join because joining fits their *own* purposes, selfish or otherwise. Those purposes will vary but most will join for a mixture of self-advancement and a vague desire to help fulfil even vaguer personal notions of the institution's functions. These functions may be those assigned to the institution by a different theoretical legal system or they may be those that are set in isolation from any such theory. In fact the nonselfish goals that members pursue will reflect the ebb and flow of ideas both inside and outside the institution about what that institution's functions are. Just as there is debate in the community about those functions so there will be contradictory goals pursued, and some or all of these will contradict the socio-legal function set by the theorists. On joining, the individual's ideas may be modified by contact with other members. But to the extent that the views of existing members vary from one sub-group to another (Roy, 1973, p. 205), the conflicting views of those who see law as a legal system leads to law being nonsystematic (this parallels the problems caused to positivist and content systems by the different systems of rules and principles which different judges would create if they tried). At best, the differences will muffle and dilute the fulfilment of that function but more often they render the institution incapable of achieving it.

Monitoring and Control

Thus it is not in the nature of institutions, legal or otherwise, to produce a convergence of values or interests among its members that will promote the performance of the institution's allotted function. What then of the other hope of the functionalists – the ability of senior officials to control the role-behaviour of subordinates? 'Compliance' and 'organization' theory have devoted considerable speculation and research to this question. Baum (1980, p. 302) summarizes the conditions under which the activities of lower officials will further the goals set by their superiors. The goals need to be *clearly stated* and *communicated*, and either the *subordinates must want to comply* (because it accords with their interests, values or beliefs – including beliefs in the authority of the person setting the goals), or *superior officials must* be able to *monitor deviations* and either *coerce or persuade the subordinates to comply*. On most of these counts legal institutions are weak. The functions of law are highly controversial (*supra*) and the goals to be achieved by individual laws are frequently (though not always) obscure – legislation is frequently the result of compromise and judicial decision-making tends to eschew the setting and pursuit of goals. The language in which they are communicated is, though usually intelligible to lawyers, impenetrable for the many legally untrained officials through whom many of the effects law has on citizens must be achieved. These officials do not read Acts and judgments. If they hear of them at all, they must rely on the often distorted interpretations provided by others. The values of subordinates frequently differ from those of their superiors, and from those of each other. The interests of subordinate officials lie in maximizing their autonomy and resisting control by their superiors. Monitoring of subordinates' actions is a form of feedback that is notoriously weak. Where deviations *can* be monitored, superior officials in legal institutions do have several persuasive and even coercive resources with which to encourage compliance (chapter 8.2). Nevertheless, in such conflicts not all the resources are held by superior officials. Indeed, one of the characteristics of all institutions is that resources have to be placed in the hands of subordinates so that they may achieve their allotted goals, but that those resources will often be just as useful in conflict with superior officials who set these goals. These resources (and others that the subordinate officials bring to the job) are used in an effort to acquire other resources and further to strengthen positions against superiors, subordinates and equals. The strength of subordinate officials vis-à-vis their superiors is considerable in law. Many minor officials, like police, magistrates and prison officials, through whom the ultimate functions of legal institutions must be fulfilled, are given a large area of autonomy and real discretion and seek to carve out more. Where subordinates have this kind of independence and power, many argue that the role they play is the result of 'negotiation' (Brittan, 1981, p. 170) or 'bargaining' (Crozier, 1964, p. 163). Where this is the case, the roles played are those that reflect the interests, values and resources of the bargainers rather than the 'functions' of the institution which can so easily be the first to be ditched in the compromises that result.

Some acknowledge these sorts of factors but try either to play down their importance (Crozier, 1964, p. 167) or to incorporate them within their organizational theory as an 'informal' rather than a 'formal' structure (Selznick, 1981). But the institution is not made of two separate structures; it is an amalgam of both in which the informal element may well compromise the achievement of institutional functions by the formal structure.

Even where members of institutions do attempt faithfully to perform their role within it, institutional functions may still not be fulfilled. Where institutions set both goals for subordinate officials and means by which they are supposed to achieve them then, unless the institution is well designed, it is quite possible that the set means are inadequate for achieving the goal. In such cases an official dedicated to fulfilling his role has to choose between rejecting the goals, the means, or both – between ritualism, innovation and withdrawal (Merton, 1938). Ritualism (not unknown in legal institutions) and withdrawal deny the contribution to the institution's function which role performance would bring. Innovation may restore it but only if the official understands the goals and can innovate successful means without upsetting the role-performance of others.

Even in well-designed systems, in which goals are faithfully followed and limits on means are either conveniently absent or congruent with the goals set for subordinates, the system's ultimate goal may not be achieved. Elliott (1980) considers the example of a corporation whose overall 'function' is to make profits, to which end interlocking subfunctions are delegated to personnel, production and marketing managers. Each zealously pursues his sub-function so that industrial harmony is achieved although the cost in wages and conditions is high, production is maximized (not least because of the former achievement) even though costs are high, and sales are maximized even though margins are low. Despite the successful achievement of all the sub-functions, the overall function may not be fulfilled at all.

Given the nature of their origins and growth, it is doubtful that legal institutions are sufficiently well designed even to suffer this problem. The ultimate goals are too vague and controversial, and roles are set by processes other than the furtherance of goals. But it is a salutary lesson that even the most vigorous and conscientious performance of institutional roles will not necessarily help the fulfilment of an institution's function.

The strength of an institution is also the source of its weakness as a medium for the fulfilment of functions. The action of one person can, through chains of intra-institutional relations, affect the actions of many other members (the basis of the functionalist's claimed hierarchical structure of roles). This means that the institution can have effects far beyond those that any individual could achieve – that is its strength. But these chains of relations must go through several people whose interests, perceptions and values vary and conflict. Institutions must act through the human material of which they are made, rather than through any abstract set of goals or functions which may not be agreed, and roles that may be actively resisted. Furthermore, each actor along the chain is subject to other forces affecting his own action, leading to action that is different from that expected by the initiator of the chain of effects. (This helps explain the discrepancy between 'law in the books' and 'law in action'.)

We can now summarize the reasons why the intra-institutional structure of roles should be rejected and why legal institutions do not appear to perform the functions allotted to them:

1 differences over the functions to be allotted to institutions and difficulties in recruiting only those who agree;
2 unintended consequences that frustrate intentional action in pursuit of functions;
3 institutional interests common to all members;
4 role-interests of individual members;
5 sub-groups within institutions;
6 the effect of outside forces on members' individual actions; and
7 difficulties for superiors setting, monitoring and controlling the role-behaviour of subordinates.

When we consider the nature of institutions and the nature of their interrelationship with other institutions we see that even if institutions did perform a single function they would be unlikely to 'cog together' (Llewelyn, 1962, p. 234) with other institutions to fulfil the social functions of law – i.e. their interrelations would be unlikely to conform to the interinstitutional structure.

The interaction of institutions with which we are most familiar is of institutions in conflict. Yet the various theoretical inter-institutional structures all require institutions to follow the lead of others, respond in certain ways to the actions of other institutions, co-operate in the achievement of a joint effect, or reinforce the activity of other institutions. All of these require a limitation of institutional autonomy and a restriction of their field of operation. Yet institutional interests require the very opposite. The maximization of autonomy and an extension of the area in which the institution may autonomously operate lead institutions to, at best, avoid contact and, at worst, conflict (e.g. especially where institutions complete to cover the same area of social life: Gouldner and Gouldner, 1963, p. 497). In some societies this is not merely a fact of institutional life but actively encouraged by the constitution drafters and interpreters. In proposing the separation of powers between the institutions which later functionalists would attempt to systematize, Montesquieu and the American drafters he influenced relied on conflict and lack of co-operation between institutions whose institutional interest and goals (if any) conflict rather than cog together. It is ironic that Parsons should propose his system in, and applying to, the United States. That country was most influenced by Montesquieu in its constitutional formation, and is the most perfect realization of his ideals with each institution so perfectly and complementarily frustrating the others.

The examples of such conflict are legion: courts and prosecutors over plea bargaining, courts and the executive over judicial control of ministerial discretion, courts and police over interviewing practices, treasury and other departments over anything to do with money, and local and central government over everything the former tries to do.

Llewelyn imagined legal institutions 'cogging together'. A more apt metaphor would be the grating of gears. The appearance of co-operation and interdependent functioning arises only when most of the teeth have been stripped from the gears. At this point the wheels of the various institutions can whir happily, and without friction, because they do not touch. They are either totally ineffective or achieve their effects on society independent of the rest. Only when some of the remaining teeth touch, providing momentary, partial and largely ineffective contact between institutions, does the automobile of law (preferred to 'ship of state') as a whole lurch unpredictably in one direction or another. But this is never for long enough to gain any social momentum.

The various ways legal institutions are supposed to cog together are all seriously damaged by the tendencies of institutions to go their own way so that they either provide no mutual support in achieving their functions or openly conflict.

These tendencies damage 'convergent structures' (*supra*) because institutions will not all play their part in producing similar reinforcing effects on the same person or institution. Different institutions will frequently influence the same citizen in different directions. The legislature may guide him into an activity that the police do not tolerate; punishment may not accord closely with the behaviour the legislature was trying to discourage; and the courts' dispute-resolution procedure may indicate opportunities to the citizen for acting contrary to the guidance of the legislature. Sometimes the relevant institution may affect different people or influence none at all.

Where the structure lies in the chains of functions involving a sequence of institutions, it suffers the same problems as intra-institutional chains aggravated by the greater strength of institutional interests and extent of institutional autonomy. Finally, the conflicting and non-cooperative nature of institutional interaction will be completely fatal to 'complementary' structures which require the performance of both functions before any effect can be achieved.

Consequently the social observer would have to reject the functionalist image of law as a structure of interdependently functioning legal institutions. That rejection joins the rejection of the other parts of the Parsonian structural functionalism – the organic analogy of social needs and 'survival', the vertical structure of shared values, the equating of role-orientation expectation and behaviour, the partisan selection of effects as 'functions' and the view of institutions as structured to perform them. All these were built on insights into the importance of values, institutions and their effects. But those insights were distorted to fit into a system, leading to the rejection of both them and the system.

5.7 Luhmann's Functionalist System

Like Evan and Bredemeier, Niklas Luhmann is much influenced by Parsons and envisages society as a system of 'relatively autonomous sub-systems which mutually interact and furnish the environment for each other'. Such a system is essential to a society's continued existence and in such a system each sub-system fulfils a function that is essential to that survival. For Luhmann, law's function is managing the problem of the complexity and contingency of experience (1985, p. 25). It does this via the stabilization and congruence of expectations of its members and the consequent reduction of disappointed expectations about the behaviour of others (cf. Giddens's function of maintaining 'ontological security', 1984, p. 23). The more complex a society is, the greater is this functional need and hence the greater part law has to play. The more rapidly society changes, the more rapid the changes in law must be, and the more conscious of the alternatives we become, thus leading to increasing 'positivization' of law.

Luhmann claims that social life and participation in group activity are possible only if we can 'expect the expectations' of others about our behaviour. Without this there would be 'disappointment', failed interaction, waste of time in communication of our expectations and too much conflict. To be manageable, expectations need to be relatively simple and general. To be stable they must be normative rather than cognitive expectations because the latter are generally revised if disappointed. Given the potential variety in expectations, every society needs to institutionalize normative expectations by providing third parties who are 'allocated' leadership and whose expectations of behaviour are adopted by members of the group.

Luhmann describes the legal system as a 'structured complexity'. Its elements may be seen as the expectations of an authorized third party about the actions of individuals. Luhmann insists that law is 'structured', although his meaning is not always clear. At one point he seems to define structure merely as 'relative constancy' (1985, p. 31) and at another as a four-level vertical structure of values, programmes, roles and personal expectations (p. 66). But elsewhere Luhmann rejects 'value systems' or 'hierarchies of values' (p. 68), asserting that 'basic principles do not contain sufficient guarantees of order' any more (p. 166) and finally concluding that 'despite all the internal doctrinal "attempts at systemization" only relatively few decisions depend on one another to such an extent that one of them has to be changed if the others do' (p. 255). It is here that he has a particularly important insight in that the positivization of law makes such a system and the consciousness it brings less rather than more likely. He also rejects consensus as a normal phenomenon. Instead he says that legal institutions have to anticipate and *presume* consensus and will last as long as dissenters presume everyone else accepts that which law pretends to be consensus.

Although retreating from a vertical structure, Luhmann retains a Parsonian horizontal structure. Normative expectations are related not so much by 'consistency' as by 'congruence' (p. 73) or 'conditional programming' (p. 174). The normative expectations selected by law from among the possible alternatives are compatible in that A and B expect A's action, and A's expected action fits in with B's. Law increasingly takes the form: 'if A acts in a particular way, then B must make a certain claim' (p. 174). The sequences of congruent expectations are built into structures of 'decision sets' and procedures. Within law, the principle decision sets are the legislative and judicial, of which the legislative becomes increasingly dominant with the positivization of law. These legal structures are possible only with the support of other sub-systems within society (pp. 166, 187).

The wholeness factor is partly provided by the function that is performed by law as a whole. But it is also provided by the legal system itself which, as an 'autopoietic' system, 'constitutes its own unity' (p. 287). It does this by defining its own elements, mapping its own boundaries and regulating changes in itself.

Insights and Retreats

In his system and in his many interesting asides, Luhmann has incorporated many insights. Like all theorists considered in this chapter he centres the understanding of law on the interactions it has with the rest of society (in the functions it fulfils as part of a social system) but he emphasizes that the interactions have effects on law only as those interactions are interpreted by the law. This is, for Luhmann, a part of its autopoietic nature. But it also provides a general insight into the way institutions react with each other. Some of his insights into the nature of the positivization of law are timely, including his insistence that (1) positivization makes consistency less likely and less necessary (pp. 69, 255) because the complexity possible with positive law requires a greater 'indifference to inconsistency' (p. 163), and that (2) positivization of law should make us aware of the alternatives available (p. 161) and that decision-makers have total responsibility for the laws they choose (p. 269). His recognition that social 'evolution' (as he still calls it) is not unilinear and does not necessarily constitute progress, the use he makes of distinctions between cognitive and normative expectations, and his suggested mechanism for the development of practices from cognitive expectations are of great interest.

Many of his best insights are to be found in his retreats from the more extreme structural functionalist positions taken by Parsons. First and foremost is his rejection of the vertical structure and the consistency of legal norms, the existence of consensus (pp. 51, 55, 70), the system of social values, the vertical integration between values, norms and roles, and the determinacy of values (p. 70) which goes with it. Secondly, although a functionalist, he does acknowledge the multi-functionality of law (p. 238) and he does envisage situations in which politics and law do not fulfil their functions and at times implies that they may not do so now (pp. 259, 260).

His problems are found in the parts of functionalist theory which he retains – especially its horizontal structure. Like other functionalists, Luhmann postulates a need that all societies have, presumes that it has been met because society demonstrably continues, and proposes a model of law as the institution that can fulfil it. Yet Luhmann himself weakens any such argument. The claimed need is slightly different to Parsons's and Luhmann has described one Parsonian need as unfulfilled, unfulfillable and, in fact, unnecessary. This raises the question of whether *Luhmann's* claimed need is quite as essential as he claims. Further doubt is raised by his claim that the functions of law are increasingly internal functions performed on and for the institution itself rather than external functions performed on and for the rest of the social system.

The issue, as for Parsons, is whether the relevant institutions really do perform their functions and whether they really do have to be performed by any institution at all. Is the existence of shared beliefs, interpretations, expectations and meanings really so necessary for sustained social life? Given the difficulties which Luhmann acknowledges in establishing consensus, perhaps we can get by without it. Is the reduction of disappointments so crucial to the maintenance of social life? Luhmann himself undermines such a suggestion by pointing to the importance of cognitive expectations. As he points out, we react to disappointments of cognitive expectations by changing the expectation rather than engaging in conflict. Even where normative expectations are disappointed this often means that a period of anger and frustration precedes the alteration of our expectations. Disappointments are part of our life and we get by despite them. We may partially plan our lives and follow role-models as examples of how certain values can be achieved. If we do not achieve those values we learn to live with our disappointments, often internalizing failure and blaming ourselves rather than putting that failure down to the fact that there is no system to ensure that if the same actions are performed by individuals in similar positions the same outcomes will be attained. And even if we do fulfil our expectations it may not be because the system is so well ordered but merely because, when we perform the same actions as the role-model, the outside influences on the outcome were fairly similar in both the role-model's success and ours.

Like some functionalists with their organic analogies, the social and legal systems are seen in very homomorphic terms – as if they were individual human beings – with their human qualities. Law is 'self-referential' (p. 281) and 'reflexive' (p. 167). He tells us what it can do by its own 'action' (p. 283). The existence of conflicting norms 'does not absolve society from the task' of looking for solutions (p. 49). By the time he writes the following passage he seems to have forgotten where the subjectivity lies: 'Each theory, legal dogma and all types of scientific treatment of law can be sociologically understood as forms of self-description of the legal system' (p. 286). In fact it is Luhmann who is 'describing' the law, not law itself. Like other functionalists, Luhmann not only treats society as if it were a single subject, but ignores the real individual subjects without which the claim and system cannot function.

As with any other function law supposedly plays, we see that the effects of law include both the function, its opposite and much else besides. Law for the most part does not structure the cognitive and normative expectations of citizens. This is because of laymen's ignorance of the relevant law and their well-documented tendency to use alternative bases for forming their expectations and for governing their daily interactions (see discussion of 'pluralism' below). For this reason the law when not applied is irrelevant, and when applied is as likely to disappoint both cognitive and normative expectations as to fulfil them.

Luhmann has abandoned many of the more systematic aspects of Parsonian structural functionalism but his retention of function as the key relation between the elements and the use of institutions (or 'decision sets') as the supposed fulfillers of these functions is fatal to the acceptability of his system.

5.8 Law as Process

Several theorists proffer what they call 'process models' of social and legal systems. Among them are Lasswell and McDougal (1970, 1975), J.N. Moore (1968), S.F. Moore (1978), Buckley (1967), Nagel and Neef (1977) and Twining (1973). Law, which they still refer to as 'the legal system' (e.g. S.F. Moore, 1978, p. 3; Lasswell and MacDougal, 1975, p. 465), is seen to comprise 'processes' – regular interactions in which the action of one person or group regularly follows the action of others.

When process theorists attempt to construct legal systems they build them on their insights into the interactions between decisions and processes and how the making of a decision, or the completion of a process, follows on from another. Twining argued that theoretically this is relatively simple and offered a start by providing a flow-chart linking the decision of an offender to offend and decisions by police, barristers, judges, jurors, appeal courts and prison officials. He quipped that this was a 'system of roles' rather than a 'system of rules' (1973). (See figure 5.8.)

Other process theorists like Nagel are concerned with the many influences that actually affect which way each decision goes and hence along which pathways the offender will move. But they are clearly moving towards a similar picture (1977). Process models of the legal system are thus very similar to the intra-institutional structure of law discussed in chapter 5.6. The difference is that process theorists reject views of law in terms of co-ordinated action achieving social functions: they see it in terms of processes by which individuals and groups pursue different, and often conflicting, ends. But in doing so they remove its claim to being a structure, for the mass of actions is only a structure for functionalists because of its combined effect, which could be dubbed its function. This might not appear a problem, as Twining's flow-chart seems to provide a perfectly adequate structure of law by itself. But law involves more than the chains of processes and decisions by which offenders are caught,

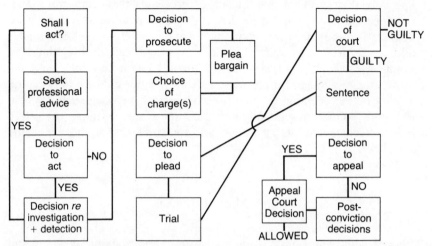

Figure 5.8 Twining's system of decisions, tasks and roles (From Twining, 1973, p. 290; © 1973 by Cornell University. All rights reserved)

convicted and punished. It involves many other chains by which laws are made and changed, contracts are enforced and state corporations are formed. Many of these will not touch or affect the individuals and interactions charted by Twining, but eventually every decision and process will be linked into what will by then have become a tortuously tangled web of processes – 'a complex multifaceted fluid interplay of widely varying degrees of association and dissociation' (Buckley, 1967).

Long before this stage had been reached, many would have failed to discern a structure. Indeed some process theorists criticize the idea of finding *any* structure in legal processes because they are subject to incessant change (S.F. Moore, 1978, p. 47). Lasswell, McDougal and Reisman say law is structured because they see the processes as relatively stable (1967, p. 258). But this does not amount to structure. A crazy collection of lines on a page is stable, but unstructured. Relative stability is important, it means that the sequence of interactions are relatively predictable, but this does not of itself make them structured. Nor is a structure a necessary condition for it – we shall see in the next chapter how such predictability can arise in nonstructured and nonsystematic social phenomena.

The principle objection to process theorists is not what they actually say about law – their descriptions of interactions, processes and pressures. Indeed their insights have been used to criticize content systems and in the next chapter will be used to help build a nonsystematic picture of law (especially their insights into the many processes that *create* disorder). The objection is to calling their description a 'system' at all. There is no recognizable wholeness factor and no structure. Of course, the reader could agree with Lasswell and McDougal and call a 'big blooming ongoing confusion' (1975, p. 465) a 'system', but it certainly lacks the constituents of a system in the sense used in this book. More importantly it cannot be enlightening to attempt to distinguish between such a system and a nonsystem. Consequently such statements merely imply the use of the term 'legal system' as a synonym for, and conveying no more meaning than, 'law'.

5.9 Marxist Systems

Although Marx and Engels made many observations about law (Cain and Hunt, 1979) they propounded no theory of law or legal system. Marx*ist* theories of law either build on those observations or apply to law Marx's insights about society, especially the division of society into base and superstructure and the identification of the dynamics of change in the base. Not all Marxist theories of law are theories of legal system. Many of Marx's insights are used by other Marxists to criticize systems theories and to support nonsystematic theories of law and society (Tigar and Levy, 1977). They emphasize the 'contradictions' of society that lead to endemic conflict, crisis and change. They highlight his insistence that new societies spring from the womb of the old so that, at least during the relatively long transition periods, society is a complex mixture of two or more incongruous elements. Several such insights will be incorporated in the author's theory in chapters 7 and 8. This section will consider those 'Marxist' theorists who do create legal system theories to replace the systems they criticize.

Marxist theories of legal system have fallen into three broad types:

1   those which see law as a superstructural phenomenon that merely reflects the base, an 'ideal expression of the dominant material relations' (Marx and Engels, 1975, vol. 5, p. 82);
2   class instrumentalist theories which see law as a class weapon and part of the repressive bourgeois state; and
3   those which see law as an ideological phenomenon that functions to reproduce the base.

This section will deal briefly with the first two but will dwell on the more systematic ideological theories based on Althusser's structuralism and on the recent retreat from such a theory by most Marxists.

Legal System as a Reflection of the Economic Base

This theory sees the superstructure, including law, as a reflection of the economic base. This suggests a content system of law reflecting the relations of production. Engels seemed to approach this theory later in life: 'law must not only correspond to the general economic condition and be its expression, but must also be an internally coherent expression which does not, owing to internal conflicts, contradict itself' (1975, p. 400).

Such a theory has one clear advantage vis-à-vis other content theories of legal system. Having to reflect neither the values, nor the 'jural post-ulates', but a relatively limited part of society, there is more hope that it is reflecting a system of values and hence can itself be a system. However, this advantage gives rise to a problem. Law covers so many aspects of human activity that it is hard to see the whole of its content reflecting the base. Furthermore, much of law appears relatively unchanging in both content and effect, especially criminal law. This could hardly be the reflection of a changing base. This is doubly problematic because the theory would predict that any such problems of incomplete mapping of economic base and law would be in the opposite direction. Law, being only a part of the superstructure, might reflect only a part of the base. But it could not encompass more than the base's reflection.

This theory builds on Marx's lasting insight into the pervasive influence of economic factors on law. But, like so many other systems theories, the attempt to build a system out of it takes this insight too far and ignores so much else in society and law. As Craib pleads, 'there is a lot more going on out there' (1984, p. 148).

Some theorists are not so concerned to show that the content of law reflects the economic base as that the *form* does. Pashukanis (1978) and some who followed him (e.g. Kinsey, 1978; Edelman, 1979) see the legal form reflecting the 'commodity form' and believe that both are verbalized in the same way (the subject of the legal relation is the individualistic asocial bearer of a right in the same way that the market treats economic individuals as the possessors of rights in the products of labour).

However, this tells us only about the nature of the elements of law rather than the structure of relations into which they must fit if they are to form a system. Once again the essentially outward-looking character of sociological jurisprudence has meant that the external relations are ex-amined and emphasized at the expense of the internal structure that is necessary for a system.

Law as Part of the Repressive Bourgeois State

A second, 'class instrumentalist' (Collins, 1982) theory sees law as an instrument by which the capitalist class maintains its privileged position by force (see Lenin, 1976; Pashukanis, 1978 in his comments about public law; Quinney, 1973). The base provides the resources and the inclination for one group to dominate the other. The relations of production are in turn preserved by the exercise of that domination. This theory sees law as a part of the state, which is inevitably an instrument of repression of one class by another and will wither away when there is only one class.

Society is seen not as systematic but as rent by fundamental conflict that is real and largely conscious. Law, however, is systematic. It is a system of institutions each fulfilling necessary sub-functions so that the legal system and the state of which it is a part fulfil their function of keeping the working classes in their place. Force is central. Legal ideology is, at most, merely a cloak for it.

This theory of law is so widely disparaged, not least by other Marxists (e.g. Sumner, 1979), that little space needs to be devoted to its rebuttal. Problems include the identification of the class which controls law and a mechanism by which the power of that class could be directed to such control (Cotterrell, 1984, p. 116). Perhaps its greatest failing is the extremely limited range of phenomena included within law – the institutions of criminal law and the effects which they have on a few members of the working class and which they threaten for the rest. It even ignores parts of private law that other Marxists like Pashukanis emphasize. Much of the law is neither directed to the working class nor has repressive affects on them, at least partly because of previous efforts to change it, efforts which Marx praised and in which he even played a tiny part. Thus, like most of the functionalist systems discussed in the bulk of this chapter, it cannot amount to an adequate description of law.

This theory is, in a sense, a very old-fashioned view of law in terms of will (of the ruling class or its representatives) and sanction. This might have been excused of nineteenth-century sociologists, but not of their twentieth-century followers. The theory is not convincing because it is patently obvious that force is not the sole or even primary reason for the persistence of capitalism and that the effects of law are not confined to benefiting the bourgeoisie (just as they cannot be confined to the preservation of society and the maintenance of institutions). However, it is important to appreciate that the former popularity of this theory was built on the insight that the interests of powerful elements *are* represented in law and often quite consciously. Even though law may generally be more effective if both powerful and powerless believe in its impartiality and fairness, the direct application of state power is sometimes more certain and those with economic power demand its use to protect their subjective interests. The mistake in the theories discussed above was to attempt to systematize this partial insight about law into a systematic theory. Not only is this impossible but it has tended to discredit the original insight.

Law as Ideology

Many Marxists became aware of the deficiencies of theories which post-ulated a purely reflective superstructure and/or repressive law. In so doing they provided important insights into neglected aspects of law. Gramsci (1971) explained the role of genuine popular support ('consent') for the law and state in maintaining the 'hegemony of the capitalist classes'. Poulantzas emphasized the relative autonomy of the 'juridico-political instance' from the dominant class, and the way it gains legitimacy by according real rights and giving real concessions to the majority (1982, p. 190) – but in treating citizens as individuals it ideologically isolates them from their class and turns social conflict into interpersonal conflict. Hay (1975) saw the operation of law breeding values which support both the law and the social system of which that law is a part. In eighteenth-century England, the pomp and terror of the law produced respect and the frequent pardons and technical acquittals produced a 'sense of justice'. Althusser (1971) saw ideology and practice as inseparable. He emphasized the role of daily practice in the formation and sustenance of the 'knowing subject', the ideas and categories through which it experiences the world and even its subjective conception of itself. Sumner (1979) further emphasized the importance of practice (while seeking to distance himself from Althusser by accusing him of being a recidivist class instrumentalist).

These writers saw the relationship between superstructure and base, and the place of law within them, in a different way. This led to a reversal in the relative importance they gave to ideology and the state within the superstructure. Rather than masking the 'real' repressive manner in which the capitalist mode of production is preserved, ideology is seen as the key to that preservation (at least during the current stage of capitalism). Althusser (1971) saw ideology not as disembodied ideas, but as sets of *practices* which are grouped into structures called 'ideological state apparatuses' (ISAs). The actual ISAs will vary from state to state but for France he lists, nonexhaustively, religious, educational, family, legal, political, union, communicative and cultural ISAs (p. 143). These ISAs preserve, or as he puts it 'reproduce', the capitalist base. They do this by breeding and sustaining men, giving them skills and attitudes appropriate to manual workers, technicians, managers and bourgeoisie, and placing them in approximately the right numbers in the right places so that they can form relations of production of the same capitalist type as those in the rest of the base. Each and every ISA contributes to this process 'in the way proper to it' (1971, p. 154) – it performs its 'function' (a word he uses frequently). What distinguishes ISAs from the rest of society is the predominant *way* in which they function – 'ideologically'. The ISAs involve 'imagined relations' between 'God and His creation', teachers and students, husbands and wives. ISAs 'address' individuals as 'God's creation' (religious ISA), 'students' (educational ISA), 'husbands' (family ISA), etc. Individuals recognize themselves in these roles in a way that seems so obvious that the individuals cannot imagine themselves being other than the subject addressed, or behaving in any other fashion than that laid down by the imaginary relation. Hence they conform to the practices those ISAs lay down for those roles, and the relations are reproduced.

In addition to the ISAs (which he calls collectively the 'ideological instance') and the base (the 'economic instance'), Althusser includes the state (the 'political instance') in his theory of society. Althusser's state is still a repressive one, comprising several institutions called 'repressive state apparatuses' (RSAs). These include the police, prisons, government, administration, head of state, and law. RSAs are unified by the centralized control exercised over them by the 'political representatives of the ruling class' (1971, p. 149). Their 'basic function' is the repression of the working class (p. 137) in order to achieve the political conditions for the ISAs to operate (p. 150)

Thus the reproduction of the economic instance (base) requires the joint function of the state and ideological instance. In its turn the ruling class creates repressive and ideological state apparatuses to preserve the base. Society is seen as a totality, a monolith in which all its 'instances' support each other and preserve the whole. 'They play more or less the same tune' (Law, 1986, p. 2). Although one class is exploited by another and has very different interests, conflict is not a prominent feature of such a society because all its members are enmeshed in the ISAs. Althusser's social system could be represented as shown in figure 5.9.

Law is thus both an ISA and an RSA. As an RSA it has the function of repression, but Althusser does not spell out the sub-function of law as an ISA. Others have purported to fill in the blank. Most merely restate a function of the ideological instance as a whole – reproducing the relations of production (Hunt, 1985), maintaining hegemony, producing cohesion (Gramsci, 1971), or reproducing class power (Sumner, 1979). Edelman (1979) is more helpful. He sees law acting as an ISA *par excellence*, addressing individuals as purchasers, vendors, employers, etc., and spelling out the practices they should pursue so that individuals recognize themselves as purchasers, vendors, employers, etc., and by and large conform to the practices that law lays down for such subjects.

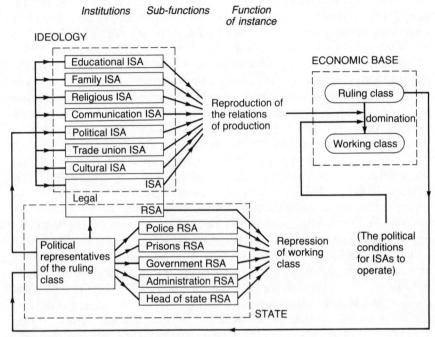

Figure 5.9 Althusser's social system

This dual character provides the first problem for a systematic view of law within Althusser's social system. Either some institutions within law function ideologically and others repressively, or the same institutions within law act both ideologically and repressively. In the former case it will be difficult to relate the two into a single functionalist system. In the latter case the ideological and repressive functions will be difficult to perform concurrently and will lead to tensions between those legal officials who favour alternative approaches, further diminishing the capacity of their institutions to fulfil either function.

Attempts to resolve such problems suffer because Althusser provides no internal structure for ISAs, legal or otherwise. The only structure he refers to is that of the relationship between an ideological practice and an individual (the addressing of the individual as, for example, a creation of God with a set of obligations, the individual's recognition of himself as such, and the performance of those obligations). We thus have elements and relations, but no structure in the sense used in this book.

However, Althusser's main problems are those of any classic functionalist theory. ISAs and RSAs (institutions) have sub-functions which they fulfil in order jointly to fulfil the social function of the 'instances' (social sub-systems). The ideology sub-system has the social function of socializing individuals into the roles it allocates – for Althusser this is the key social function because in doing this it places people into the relations of production and thus reproduces the economic base. He has not claimed that these institutions produce a society-wide consensus. But the claim he makes is, in some ways, far more difficult to sustain. The socialization sub-system is apparently capable of selectively socializing different people (and the right ones at that!) into different ideas. This is a difficult function for any sub-system to fulfil yet the postulated mechanism is highly suspect. The addressing of various individuals as students, husbands, consumers, etc., seems little more than a 'labelling theory' (Sutherland and Cressy, 1974, p. 194). As a part of functionalist criminology it was severely criticized. Individuals *resist* the labels that others attempt to impose on them, and even if the role-occupant accepts the label he negotiates the meaning with those who impose it. Althusser has 'over-socialized man' all over again. As part of a Marxist theory it has been attacked for the pure idealism of its conception of social relations (Sumner, 1979), its dehumanizing of human beings and its removal of class conflict, the Marxist mechanism of historical change. It seems to give law a greater effectivity than would be expected in a Marxist theory (Hunt, 1985, p. 19). Human beings cannot be drawn into such 'flawless subjugation' (Cousins and Houssein, 1986, p. 164). Indeed, not even the greatest apologists for capitalism would claim this ability of the market economy to match jobs and applicants so successfully.

In fact, there will be multiple ideologies available, multiple interpretations of the same practice. There will be oppositional ideologies, there will even be conflicting interpretations from within law (Sumner, 1979, p. 171) – law is not sufficiently unified and coherent to address the subject with one voice. The individual may not have a 'free' or infinite choice of interpretations, but the selection and perhaps modification of interpretations is affected by the self-images generated in previous and concurrent exposures to other practices and the ideologies to which they were thereby exposed. The problems that Althusser has in this area result from his mistaking the insight he has achieved into the nature of law. He has seen how individuals need some imagined conception of themselves and their relationship with the world and how such conceptions can be formed only from interactions with others and are inevitably influenced by their conceptions of those relations. But this is distorted into a view of society and law by which a single conception of the subject and its relations is presented to each individual by a systematic ideological totality.

Other problems of structural functionalist theory are, perhaps unsurprisingly, repeated. For example, how is it that the ISAs all 'play the same tune'? There is no conductor (unless there is some Marxist 'unseen hand' to hold a baton). The variety of ideas which made nonsense of Parsonian consensus theories throws up a multitude of different conductors which bring many an ideological discord. Rather than 'playing a tune', ISAs in modern western societies produce a cacophony, providing snatches of a thousand tunes that are music only to the ears of a pluralist.

Of course, there are significant differences between Parsons and Althusser. In particular, the latter identifies the mode of production rather than the core of values as the key to the nature of society and its continuity, and sees the mode of production as an exploititave one that benefits a dominant class. But these differences highlight the problems of placing such functionalism within a Marxist theory. Having pointed out the role of *one* class in controlling the state and setting up the ISAs, attention is immediately drawn to the *other* class or classes. Their different objective interests are always liable to break out into subjective ones, leading to 'class struggle', some of which will be directed at law. To the extent that such struggle is even partially successful (and even by the mid-nineteenth century Marx himself thought it had been and could be more so) law will be functioning either to *change* rather than merely reproduce the relations of production, and/or to perform other unrelated functions. The conflict between these new functions and those listed by Althusser will be another potent source of internal tension and disorder within the ISAs and RSAs of law. Other Marxists see the same problem for Althusser and ask where is the room for class struggle in his theory (Larrain, 1979, p. 162; Hirst, 1979, p. 52; Sumner, 1979, p. 260)? In fact, Althusser does include the notion, saying that ISAs are the result of the class struggle. But unless the dominant classes are completely successful in those struggles, this will imply a role for other classes in the construction of the ISAs. Thus in referring to class struggles he has made an admission fatal to his functionalist system.

Later ideology theorists have come to appreciate the nonsystematic nature of ideology. Sumner (1979, p. 5) accepts that ideology is not *necessarily* systematic. Hunt goes further. Far from being a unity, ideology operates in a state of disorder. Ideologies are 'constantly communicated, competing, clashing, affecting, drowning and silencing one another in the social processes of communication' (Hunt, 1985, p. 6). He stresses the ideological processes by which ideas and institutional practice affect each other, how the ideas so generated are related, and how they have the power to reorder pre-existing ideas. Further, aware that both the generation of ideological interpretations of particular practices and their reception by the individual participants is problematical, he urges a closer examination of the *sites* of production and transmission of ideology.

But even these theorists stop their retreat and start talking again of legal systems. Sumner still sees law as a 'systematized and complex ideological formation' and a 'technical unity' (pp. 20, 293). Poulantzas returns to an extreme content system describing law as 'an axiomatic system comprising a set of abstract, general, formal and strictly regulated norms' (1982, p. 191).

5.10 Pluralism and Many Systems

Some of the earliest and most persistent attacks on the various theories of legal system came from those who saw a kind of law arising from and operating through social groups from which people come, the associations they form, or the regular interactions they enter. Savigny (1975) pointed to the role of custom in law and its incompatibility with the formal codes whose introduction he opposed. Ehrlich (1936) distinguished the 'living law' (the rules used in ongoing living relationships) from formal legal rules (the rules for decisions, used in official post-mortems of dead relationships). More recently, Macauley (1963) saw the way business avoided law in ongoing business relationships, frequently not enforcing legal rights because the preservation of the relationship was more important to both parties. Law was used in one-off relations (e.g. consumers making major irregular purchases) or when a relationship had been terminated. A recent theme in legal history has been the way significant areas of business activity developed without any formal sanction or support of law and frequently contrary to it (e.g. the nineteenth-century London Stock Exchange where futures and options were freely traded despite the unenforceability of such trades, Ferguson, 1984). Anthropologists studied the law of social groupings without formal legal institutions and observed the persistence of such law despite the introduction of formal rules. The interaction of the two kinds of law proved a fascinating and fruitful study, showing how each deflected the operation of the other and how disputants tended to use each kind of law as it suited their interests and the conduct of their disputes. Some of those anthropologists, such as Sally Moore, Marc Galanter and Peter Fitzpatrick, turned to western societies and saw similar phenomena at work. Like Hart, they found a comparison with law in less economically differentiated societies fruitful, but rejected his central claim that 'primitive law' had been supplanted, rather than supplemented, by formal rules.

The study of these phenomena revealed many insights into law and posed acute problems for legal systems theorists. The law of those groups performed many of the functions attributed to law, so that any functionalist theory would have to take them into account. However the different groups and their laws were likely to interfere in the 'functions' of the laws of other groups. The ability of any social system to socialize citizens into their roles is frustrated by the overlapping membership of groups and the different kinds of rules group members derive from their membership and participation in the 'law' of those groups. Awareness of the different rules would make individuals more sceptical of claims about the naturalness or obviousness of law, and make them more likely to *use* the rules of each kind of law as it suited them in the conduct of their disputes (Galanter, 1981). Content theories of law suffered from the difficulty of finding coherence in rules with such different social bases. Positivist authority systems of law have real problems because these phenomena do not derive their authority from any grundnorm.

However, as always, the tendency to seek system in the very phenomena which made pre-existing systems untenable remains strong. The conclusion drawn by many pluralist theories is not that we have no system but that we have many. For many theorists, law is a 'plurality of interlocking legal orders' (Cotterrell 1984, p. 30; Snyder, 1981, p. 155). Savigny's custom was ordered by the *Volksgeist* or spirit of the people and was praised for its greater capacity systematically to represent it. For Ehrlich (1936), the living law was 'an inner order of associations' and it was that which structured society rather than formal legal rules (which were merely the official interpretation of the rules of living law).

Given the nature of the phenomena uncovered by these pluralists, systematizing is impossible and is rarely attempted (Cotterrell, 1984, p. 33). Even if the phenomena were capable of systematization in isolation, their interaction would destroy it. For example, any systematization of formal law would fail as the values of plural groups and interests of plural groups were incorporated and reflected in the formation of legislation and in the operation of legal institutions. For these reasons some pluralists now talk of 'action areas' or 'semi-autonomous social fields' rather than 'systems' (e.g. S.F. Moore, 1978; Fitzpatrick, 1983). Finally, even if these fields could be seen as structured into separate systems, their incorporation into an overall system for law is hardly plausible. However, freed from the attempt to systematize pluralist insights, those insights can play an important part in the nonsystematic theory of society and law expounded in chapters 7 and 8.

5.11 Unger and Critical Legal Studies

The critical legal studies movement (CLS) has quickly emerged as one of the most dynamic forces in current jurisprudence. Formed by a group of American legal academics who shared a dissatisfaction with what they saw as the current state of legal institutions, legal theory, legal methodology and academic political conservatism, CLS has struck a chord with many other academics and students. They have provided or reinforced many insights into law: the indeterminacy of legal argument; the political nature of much legal decision-making (and the suggestion that the latter may be how judges and lawyers cope with the former); the possibility that the conflicting content of legal doctrine may allow the use of law for leftist ends; the capacity of the mind to imagine alternatives to current social arrangements (a capacity in constant tension with our more limited capacity to alter them); and the placement of social relations between individuals at the core of social description and their elevation to 'the ultimate stakes' in politics (Unger, 1982, p. 587).

CLS is very much a movement with a strong sense of identity. This is in spite of the wide range of frequently incompatible strains of twentieth-century thought on which they have drawn – American realism, structuralism, post-structuralism, post-modernism, deconstruction, linguistic philosophy in general, Frankfurt critical theory and, sometimes, Marxism. What they share is a willingness to search tirelessly for ways of criticizing orthodoxy. They also share, of course, the perception that there *is* a shared orthodoxy among their more conservative colleagues – liberal, formalist and objectivist. This alleged orthodoxy is basically an extreme content systems theory. As such, CLS criticisms are useful to the critical part of this book and some of their criticisms have already been deplored. However, because they consider that orthodoxy takes this single form they have done little to criticize the other systems theories outlined above. Indeed the variety of systems theories belies their perception of orthodoxy. The orthodoxy that most CLSers describe was attacked by the realists sixty years ago. The response to realism produced a range of (largely systematic) theories which differ from each other and the orthodoxy described by CLS. Those who adhere to one of these 'newer' theories (like Hartian positivism!) do not feel compelled either to join or to defend – something that has limited CLS's appeal in England and Australia.

Nevertheless, those who are targeted by CLS have fought back in the United States, both in print and, more effectively, on tenure and promotions committees. This has further served to unify the American movement, though not the less embattled English and Australian ones. But that unity is more political than theoretical. As a movement whose organizing principle is criticism rather than critique, CLS does not possess a shared new theory. For such theories one must look *within* CLS rather than *to* CLS and emphasize the plural of the word 'studies'. However, the emergence of such theories is inhibited by the cohesion of the movement, which tends to discourage the emphasis of internal differences that would result from this development of positive theories, and because many CLS scholars deny the need for theory (Kennedy and Gabel, 1984; Tushnet, 1984, p. 241). Of those who see the need, some offer a theory or are working towards one. Some of these theories seem to depict law as disordered, but others still speak of legal systems and seem to follow the tradition of building new theories of system on the ruins of the old. The former will be used in the author's own theory (chapter 7), which could itself be congenial to many CLS scholars. We are here concerned with the latter as further examples of how insights into the disorder of law can be turned or deflected into theories of legal systems – though in CLS examples the degree of order and system is so limited that the trend towards a theory of legal disorder is very clear.

CLS has so far generated one well-developed theory (Unger's, 1976 and 1982) and two theoretical directions that have not yet been built into full theories – law as 'just politics' (Kairys, 1984) and legal institutions as a self-reproducing hierarchy (Kennedy, 1982). Only the first will be discussed here.

Unger's social, historical and legal theories were first combined in *Law in Modern Society* (1976). In that book, he attempted to provide the kernel of a fresh and unified solution to a number of problems in social theory – the problem of social scientific method, the problem of social order and the problem of modernity. He believed that the solution to these problems required an understanding of the relation between law and society. In attempting to understand society through its relations with law, he differs from the majority of theorists discussed in this chapter, who try to understand law through its relations with society. Unger offers a typology of three forms of society (tribal, feudal and liberal) matched to three types of law (customary or interactional, bureaucratic or regulatory, and legal system or legal order). The links between the forms of society and the forms of law are described in the very strongest terms: 'each society reveals through its law the inner-most secrets of the manner in which it holds its men together' (p. 47); law is 'the bond between a society and its organization' (p. 250); and the 'rule of law' (the centre-piece of the legal system's ideology) is the 'soul of the liberal state'. Law provides what he later called the society's 'formative, institutional and imaginative order' (1982, p. 649). This order arises by the containment of conflict over the basic terms of social life and the specification of a limited number of alternatives. These, in turn, restrict our ability to conceive of new forms of social life. But the restriction is not as complete as in structuralism because, in containing conflict, law incorporates conflict. In fact, he describes each kind of law, and especially law in liberal society, in terms of the type of tensions it generates rather than in terms of the logical coherence of its ideal type. As such he offers a looser form of 'ideal type' that explains the wide variety of legal institutions in capitalist societies by seeing them as the different institutional results of the tensions and conflicts of liberalism.

Law is also central because it provides a justification of the forms of social organization in any society, something which he claimed (1982, p. 582) is a functional need of every society. However, in all societies to date, law has failed to fulfil this function because they have failed to live up to the ideals contained within law (ideals which, because of their inherent conflicts, are not fully realizable). For example, liberal capitalist society has a hierarchy of positions which not only has no justification in the ideology of a society of free and equal beings, but constantly interferes with the actual operation of the law to undermine liberal legalism's proudest claims about the autonomy of law and the equality of citizens before it. In all previous societies, the failure of society to live up to the justification contained within its law has brought down both. Like Marx, Unger claims to have found the key parts of society in tension and, like Marx, he claims that this tension is the prime motive force in history.

'Legal systems' figure in his theory – they are the form of law associated with liberal society. However, that does not mean he sees law in modern western societies as systematic. First, the law in every society and especially in liberal society and our own post-liberal society is a mixture of forms. Ours has a generous sprinkling of bureaucratic law, because of the development of the welfare state, and the customary law of increasingly significant social groups. Secondly, the failure of law to live up to its claims make it less systematic than it claims to be. Thirdly, the content of law (legal doctrine) represents the results of conflicts in which no group has the strength to win all. In containing the conflict and absorbing the tension between a society and its justification it incorporates incompatible strands. As such it is incoherent, inconsistent and unsystematic. This conclusion opens up great opportunities for radical lawyers, who can find support for their ideals within the conflicting content of law.

This raises the possibility of another kind of system – in the arguments radicals can make for their conclusions in law – what he calls 'expanded doctrine'. This seeks to integrate doctrinal argument with the 'explicit controversy' over the right and feasible structure of society. This makes it possible to justify law, to select what parts of legal doctrine are to be extended and what to be abandoned, and removes the indeterminacy of legal argument – all by putting it within a systematic political context (1982, p. 579). Expanded doctrine has three 'levels of analysis' (rules and precedent; principle, purpose and policies; and an ideal scheme of association), with higher levels being used to resolve conflicts at lower levels. However valuable this may be for providing determinacy for legal argument and integrating it with committed political action, this would be a 'system' not for law but for an individual legal actor or perhaps a group of such actors. If more legal actors adopted this kind of reasoning they would produce a range of doctrinal systems expanded in the many directions the currently incoherent law makes possible. The law that resulted from such conflict would become even more disordered for the same reasons as if it suffered a plague of Hercules (chapter 4).

However, even as an ideal for legal argument, the systematizing influence of expanded doctrine is limited because Unger insists that it be developed from the bottom up rather than from the top down. He dislikes what he calls 'Aristotelian' models of society that conceive of ideal forms of society in isolation from the current one. He prefers to develop the positive aspects of existing law and social relations while loosening the grip of the 'formative institutional and imaginative order' on the range of conceived schemes of association, thereby removing constraints on how far the development of expanded doctrine can go.

In 1976 Unger saw an end to the tension between the forms of law and the forms of social association (although, unlike Marx, he did not think it inevitable). In this society, the emergence of just social arrangements would mean that their justification matched their reality. Furthermore, because society served all citizens' interests, there could be both a true consensus and an end to the conflicting pulls individuals feel towards individual interest and social obligation. In such a society, subjective and objective meaning would collapse into one and a new kind of social method would be possible. This is a method of 'common meaning'. In this, the smallest unit of social study would be a 'meaning' – a correspondence between action and belief (1976, p. 246). These would cluster into social wholes where they are capable of being interpreted within the same code of meaning. These common meanings require that the 'universal community of experience, understanding and value comes into existence' (1976, p. 258), which he sees as a political possibility, unrealizable in post-liberal society split by conscious conflict, but realizable in the ideal society he envisages. Thus society and law might be systematic some time in the future.

More recently, however, he has formulated a different, less ordered ideal, 'superliberalism', in which one of the fundamental and frequently exercised rights would be 'destabilization rights' continually to unmake and remake social arrangements so that even the future and the ideal join the present in being unsystematic. However, even here, the lure of system remains. He rather strangely refers to the collection of rights which include destabilization rights as a 'system' of rights. This indicates once again that the word 'system' can be used synonymously with law and add nothing, except a hint or, in Unger's case, a former hope that there might be some order in it. CLS reminds us simultaneously of the criticisms of systematic theories, the trend away from system in legal theory, and the remarkable tenacity of the belief that law is a system. The next chapter will consider some of the reasons for the tenacity of that belief before the last three chapters act on the conclusion to which the first three chapters have been inexorably moving: that law and society are essentially disordered, and that it is this disorder which needs to be theorized.

6

The Quest for Order

6.1 A Different Start

In the preceding three chapters, three kinds of legal system found in contemporary jurisprudence have been examined and rejected. Each has provided insights into legal phenomena but each ignored other insights or distorted its own. Similar criticisms of existing systems theories are common enough but are normally mounted as 'clearing operations' to make room for the theorist to propound his own theory of legal system. The standard response to the failure of each theory of legal system is the propounding of a new theory of legal system based on the omitted insight or a different angle on the distorted insight. This book will not follow that path. It does maintains not that the above theories have looked for the wrong kind of legal or social system but that they were wrong to look for system at all. It sees society as essentially disordered and unsystematic. It claims that society cannot satisfactorily be understood from the social observer's standpoint if seen in systematic or orderly terms, but that it can be comprehended only if the disorder in it is highlighted. Law, which is seen as comprising several institutions within society, is infected by this. However, the belief that law must be a system is, as we have seen, remarkably persistent. It is illustrated by an objection some make that I have not *proved* that no systematic theory of law is possible, and not proved that no systematic theory could succeed from the point of view either of the theorist or of the social observer.

But justifying this alternative path requires neither proof. Where one kind of approach to a problem persistently fails, it is not necessary to prove that it will necessarily fail; instead, it is quite rational to try another approach.

Imagine yourself at a desert oasis looking for a way back to 'civilization'. There are a number of well-worn tracks that you can see ending at the waterhole. You explore these, hoping that one of them will lead you to a town. But, as you do so, you find that they either branch and peter out, or take you back to the waterhole. There may be several more paths still to explore, but you start to guess that none of these paths are going to take you out of the place and you are developing some very good reasons to believe so – for example you suspect that the tracks are either those of animals who come in from the surrounding areas to drink, or are those of other lost souls who have slavishly followed in the paths of their predecessors. At this point it may well be a rational induction to adopt a different approach, striking out with a compass rather than following the tracks which you once hoped might lead you home.

However, the attractiveness of the new approach is enhanced if two conditions precedent and one condition subsequent are met. First, reasons or factors should be adduced to indicate why the traditional systematic approach has continued to fail and is likely to go on failing. Secondly, reasons should be offered why people nonetheless persist with the traditional approach. Third, the alternative approach should work in the sense that a nonsystematic theory of law is shown to be attractive and useful. If it can incorporate the insights which inform systems theorists, and if it can draw from other nonsystematic traditions such as deconstruction, post-structuralism and some parts of CLS, it is further strengthened. Meeting the condition subsequent is one of the aims of the following two chapters, the first two conditions are addressed in the following two sections.

6.2 Some Reasons Why Legal Systems Theories Fail

Many of the reasons for the failure of systems theories are peculiar to the individual theories. But there is one reason common to all. Each involved the creation of a system to incorporate the achievements of many minds in a system, whether for the derivation of rules, the content of principles or the functions of institutions. Creating such a system is a natural aspiration as we attempt to order our ideas and perceptions of the world for our own purposes. Success in creating a system may be a considerable intellectual feat. It may also be of great value to the individual – allowing a judge to derive judgments in the same way, relate their contents, or provide an ideal society for which a politically minded sociologist might strive. But this occurs only in one individual's mind and in the minds of those (s)he can convert and educate to use or realize that system. Most of those involved in the activities or institutions sought to be systematized are untouched by this system. Most are not trying to build or enforce any system at all and are just pursuing their normal day-to-day goals. It would be quite extraordinary if those actions conformed to a system by either good luck or good design (which, as there is no designer, is indeed the very height of good fortune). But, ironically, there is an even greater problem where they do attempt to realize systems, because those systems will tend to be *different* ones. Each system will have the imprint of the mind and purposes of its creator. Thus positivist systems theorists who see law in terms of a single system of authorizing relations have the greatest difficulty with those who are using different sets of authorizing relations. Dworkin has greatest difficulty with the variety in the systems of consistent principles that judges would use if they could and did create them. Finally, sociological theories have to face the difficulty caused by those who see different functions and systems of functions for the institutions of law and society. Although each theorist creates or attempts to create a system of sorts in his or her mind, this could not represent the range of activity produced by other minds. That activity could not be represented as systematic despite the fact that many were attempting to realize a system – indeed the attempts by so many to realize their own *different* systems is instrumental in making the overall result of their activity, law as we know it, unsystematic.

All systems are created initially in the mind of an individual, an idea about how the world is arranged – the problem with all these legal systems is that they have remained there. They are not, as Dewey (1901) put it, 'worked over into the facts', either by making the system fit the facts or by changing the facts until they fit the system. Consequently, the facts themselves cannot be regarded as systematically organized.

We may query whether we should expect the world to be systematically ordered. Order and system are properties of human minds, for it is only there that the elements of legal systems can be created with sufficient precision to be tightly related into structures. Order and system are natural properties of persons. But they are not necessarily natural properties of peoples where the elements, if formed at all, so easily differ. We can see this in our discussions of social rules in Hart, practical reason in Raz, social roles in Parsons. Only Dworkin emphasizes the extent of human variability, on whose rock so many theories have fallen, and which provides central themes of a theory of society without order (chapter 7). The other theories have too readily assumed that different minds share the same ideas, especially normative ones, and that the products of many minds can be ordered in the same way as the products of one.

6.3 Some Reasons Why Legal Systems Theories Persist

Although a full explanation of the persistence of attempts to find system in law would require an extensive excursion into social psychology and the sociology of 'knowledge', several reasons can be suggested. In chapter 1 we saw the comfort that the belief in system may engender and the Quinean view that deeply entrenched beliefs will be protected from recalcitrant experiences. But what are the reasons for this deep entrenchment of the belief in law's systematic quality? Some of these reasons will not become apparent until chapter 8. But at this stage we can look at the support the belief receives from three popular and powerful beliefs (that only an ordered society can provide social peace; that theorizing necessarily involves systematization of knowledge and that this is the model provided by science; that predictability is an aim that can be met only by scientific theories) and the way legal academia developed.

Two Kinds of Order

Some theorists seek systematic models of law and society, because they believe that only such models can explain how social life can exist at all. The spectre that haunts them is a Hobbesian 'state of nature' – a war of all against all, where life would be 'solitary, poor, nasty, brutish and short' (Hobbes, 1929). The question they ask is: how could we have been spared this living hell (although the sparing is relative, given the terror imposed on some by the state and private organizations: Helmer, 1974; Friedenberg, 1971)? This is, for Parsons, the Hobbesian 'problem of order' (1949).

Such a question refers to 'order' in a sense different from that used so far. Although there can be an almost infinite number of meanings which the different writers find in words, their uses of 'order' cluster around two basic notions. 'Order' in one sense refers to systems where 'everything is in its proper place and performs its proper function' (OED, definition number 13b) where there is 'orderliness'. In another sense, 'order' is merely 'an absence of insurrection, riot, turbulence, unruliness or crimes of violence' (OED, 19) – what I shall call 'social peace'.

Thus the 'problem of order' involves questioning how it is that there is order in the second sense (social peace). Most of the solutions consist of claims that society is at least partly characterized by order in the first sense (orderliness). Indeed it would seem that many think that this is the *only* solution. This provides the impetus for a search for order – a search for some orderly feature of society that explains its relative peacefulness.

Such a search is specifically undertaken by Parsons, who was the first to put the Hobbesian problem of order in this empirical form (cf. Hobbes, who posed a normative question – *why* should citizens obey the commands of a sovereign?). He offers his vertically and horizontally structured social system as the answer.

Curiously, Marxists seem to be asking the same kind of question and giving the same kind of answer – they just get less joy from it! Why is it that capitalist society has survived the challenges of war, depression and *The Communist Manifesto*? The answers given by Marxist systems theorists are that, through an ordered system of repressive and/or ideological institutions, the dominant class has had defence in depth against the challenge. The problem of order is also highlighted by Unger. All social structures engender dissatisfaction which leads to social tension, eventually erupting into the violence which destroys social order in both senses. To him the problem of social order will be solved only when social structures are self-justifying, removing the tension within society and providing true harmony between its parts.

Despite the popularity of offering social order in the sense of system as an answer to the problem of social order in the sense of social peace, there is no necessity in the relation. Such necessity will occur only where the two concepts of social order have been so confused as to reduce the question to a tautology. There could be many answers to the question why we do not beat each other's brains out. Only some of them involve social systems. However, it is strange that we should be so concerned to ask ourselves why we do not have a state of affairs that never occurred. Hobbes calls his eternal war the 'state of nature', yet humans in their 'natural' state were tribal animals, having descended from tribal primates. Indeed the very image of 'war' is provided by an activity characteristic of socialized humanity and intensified with greater degrees of social organization.

The worst episodes of human-inflicted suffering have occurred when men have been organized around a simple set of ideas or a single loyalty to batter those who have different ideas or loyalties. Social order (in the sense of social peace) is threatened by social order (in the sense of social system). This is what Dahrendorf called the 'unsociable sociability' of man (1985). Hobbes's and Parsons's answer is that we need more order (system). As we shall see in the next chapter, the answer in modern western society is less order (system). In fact, we are saved from the Hobbesian problem of order by our 'sociable *un*sociability'.

Theories Must Be Systems

For some it may seem that theory-building is necessarily *system*-building. This is supposedly the only kind of account we can comprehend and the only kind of account that is of any use. Some take as a model the supposedly systematic nature of scientific theory. Some of those who do not see society and law as systematically ordered accept these assumptions and accordingly eschew theory completely. Such notions will hopefully be dispelled by the next two chapters.

However, the model of the physical sciences will be addressed squarely, because it provides no analogy for the kind of systems theorized for law. The image that science offers of the world is orderly in two different senses. There is a very limited number of related forces and those forces interact in a limited number of ways. There is, however, little order in the result of these forces. Combinations of those interactions rarely form structures to cover the phenomena investigated. Physics may tell us that a gas is composed of a limited number of molecule types subject to specific forces. They may interact in known ways but the gas is not systematically ordered. The key to understanding the gas is the randomness of the interactions and we do not feel cheated if the theory tells us so. Similarly legal theory can discuss the kinds of participants and the interactions between them and find reasons why no structures emerge.

Systems and Predictions

The scientific analogy is also associated with another hope of some social theorists. Once social science has 'progressed' as far as the physical sciences, predictions will be possible. However, the link between structure and prediction is not a necessary one. The behaviour of unstructured bodies can be predicted – as in the laws covering gases. And the reverse can be true. Giddens proposes a structured theory of society but he maintains that prediction is made impossible by the extent of unintended consequences and has eschewed prediction as a goal for social theory (1984, p. 285).

In any case, physical sciences rarely aim for predictions on the scale of legal institutions or whole societies. Ryan's view is that the laws, explanations and predictions in science can deal only with the constituent elements of the world rather than with the world as a whole (1987).

Even if society could be conceived according to some Newtonian paradigm – like thousands of billiard balls all with their own velocities and masses on a very large table – the physical-science analogy does not suggest that Newtonian laws would seek to tell us where those billiard balls were at any one time. With precise information about the original positions and with a great deal of calculation such a prediction might be possible. But it would not be very illuminating and it is not the point of Newtonian physics. The point is that physical laws cover the interactions; they tell us not how the physical world will end up but how it will get there.

Academic History

Goodrich offers a historical explanation for the beliefs that law is a system of sources and a system of content. He traces these errors to the first law school in eleventh-century Bologna. That school studied not feudal law but the code of Justinian and portrayed it as a content system, 'a universal, comprehensive, authoritative and self-consistent body of statute law.... A monumental design for a whole society.... A complete statement of a way of life' (Goodrich, 1986, p. 97). This study of Roman law spread throughout Europe and was seen, and used, as a superior law. The spread was aided politically because the idea of a single source for law suited the Holy Roman Emperor's claims. In eighteenth-century England, Blackstone (1979) made similar claims about English common law and in the nineteenth-century Savigny (1975) and other scholars did the same for the law of the emerging nation state. In all cases these claims to system were made to resist the influence of Roman law and had a strong political basis in the desire to assert national identity and sovereign power against the universalizing tendency of Roman law (Goodrich, 1986, p. 104). The assumption of system became even more entrenched in academic practice with the writing of legal textbooks which sought to show whole areas of law as systematically organized around a few key principles.

Goodrich's location of the systematic folly in the practice of law schools is a major insight. It helps explain why the view of law as a system has persisted despite the fact that judges and practising lawyers do not seem to treat it as such and despite Goodrich's own view that judicial and professional practice is pragmatic and result-oriented. It also helps explain why it is only within academia that surprise is expressed at the author's arguments that law is not systematic. Practitioners not only agree, but many seem to regard it as obvious. This sits uneasily with the view that this academic folly is an 'ideology' which has extended to the profession.

Goodrich's account suggests one of the reasons for the persistence of attempts by academics to find system (or at least one kind of system) in law. However, he also suggests some of the tendencies which are increasingly undermining systematic theories and which may support non-systematic theories including post-modernism, deconstruction and CLS and the ideas behind the theory that follows. His identification of the source of systematic notions within the university, and of the fact that it does not really extend much beyond it, offers some hope that a nonsystematic theory may ultimately succeed.

PART II

A Non-systematic Theory of Law and Society

7

The Social Mêlée

7.1 Introduction

In this chapter a sketch of society in nonsystematic terms will be provided. In the following chapter law will be pictured as a part of that sketch, constructed from the same building blocks, suffering the same centripetal and disorganizing influences as society. Within that sketch will be recognized many of the insights of positivist, content and sociological theories of law which, stripped of the distortions involved in incorporating them into a theory of legal system, will be singly more acceptable and collectively more compatible than in their original form. It can also include the insights of theorists who have tended to eschew any theories about society and law, including many conflict theorists, ethnomethodologists, post-structuralists, deconstructionists and critical legal scholars.

These chapters are essentially constructive, but they also add to the critical enterprise because the theories sketched help to explain how something so disordered may seem, or at least be hoped to be, systematic.

The theories sketched are not intended to be the definitive theory of social and legal disorder. First, in a single chapter it can only offer a sketch. Second, it represents the stage the author's theory has reached in late 1987 after eleven years of intermittent development. But it is also hoped that it will be but one such theory out of many. Some theorists who have been propounding less and less systematic theories of legal system may take their arguments and insights to what this book claims to be their natural conclusion. Other theorists who have eschewed general theories may return to the field. Some may adopt this theory or a variation of it or take such a theory in quite different directions. These chapters are intended to show that theories of law need not be theories of legal system, and that it is among theories of legal disorder that answers to jurisprudential questions should be sought. Some variation is almost inevitable because of the range of questions to which theories are addressed and the variation in standpoints of those who create and adopt those theories. As will be indicated at the end of chapter 8 and in chapter 9, this theory offers answers to many of the questions asked in jurisprudence and does so from the standpoints of judge, practitioner, academic and citizen. As the theory is perceived by some to have both right- and left-wing possibilities, it has considerable 'transferability'. But for some questions and from many standpoints, other theories will inevitably be preferred. The author has a natural preference for his own theory, but even among those who cannot endorse this theory it is hoped that debate will shift from the current competition between different legal systems theories to competition between theories of legal disorder.

The sketch of a disordered society outlined in this chapter begins with the social interactions and relations between its members. These can be divided into power relations (which include authority relations), unintended effects and value effect relations (based on 'normative' beliefs). The relations between any two individuals are likely to be a mixture of types and the variation of the mixtures between ostensibly similar pairs of individuals may not be readily apparent. Furthermore a typical feature of all social relations is this 'asymmetry' – they are perceived differently by the interacting parties. The varied mixtures and the asymmetric perceptions of those mixtures helped to explain several important social phenomena; the formation of individual minds, the identification of the range of possible actions for individuals, the formation of practices, the generation and transmission of ideology and the nature of the relations of production. From here we move to the larger picture, to concepts of institutions (concentrations of more intensive interaction), groups (those at either end of key social relations) and classes. The overall vision of society is as a social mêlée in which conflict within social institutions, classes and groups mutes the conflict between them and provides an explanation of both relative social peace and the mechanism of social change.

There are several reasons for starting, as this theory does, with social relations. First, all social theories must include some description of the interaction between social members, whereas the collective concepts are contingent on these. Unger's view of the social relations between individuals as the core of social description (1982, p. 587) and Hunt's call for a relational theory of law starting from 'social relations' (1987, p. 16) are shared. Second, theories which begin with the larger picture and work down to social relations often distort the latter in order to fit them into their larger picture (as happens so often with systematic theories). Third, as Ryan would argue (1987), larger social phenomena can be explained only in terms of aggregations of actions and interactions between individuals.

7.2 Power

The importance of power relations between individuals has rarely been doubted and has been re-emphasized by Foucault's work (1980). Foucault does not create a theory of power and is critical of such theories, which he sees as based on a uniform model of power relation that is built into a system. But not all theories of power have such defects. Dennis Wrong's categorization is capable of generating many insights and, with some very important variations, is adopted here.

Wrong sees power as the 'capacity of some person or persons to produce intended and foreseen effects on others' (1979, p. 2). Power is sometimes seen to include the ability to affect physical objects. These are not *social* relations unless they have effects on others (Arthur's ability to pull the sword from the stone was only social in that others took this as a sign of his legitimate authority).

Power involves the *capacity* to produce, or *probability* of producing, effects rather than the actual production of effects. The latter amounts to an instance of the *exercise* of power. It is the distinction that is important rather than the side to which the word 'power' is allocated. The distinction could be put in the following terms. An exercise of power involves a social *interaction* in which effects are actually produced. *Power*, the capacity to produce these effects, is a social *relation* referring to the possibility or probability, pregnant within the positions of the power-holder and power-subject in society, that such interactions will occur (Weber, 1982, p. 56).

Wrong sees power as the capacity to produce effects *intentionally*, including the production of anticipated though undesired effects among exercises of power. It is a social relation of which at least the power-holder is conscious. Wider definitions of power have been suggested, usually to take account of the fact that the powerful often affect others (Oppenheim, 1961) in unconscious ways and may benefit from collective forces, social arrangements and norms (Lukes, 1974). There is definitely a place for concepts to describe such effects. But it is preferred to use separate concepts for them which can be usefully compared with and related to power, rather than encompassing them in an all-embracing concept of power which strays too far from its paradigm.

Wrong distinguishes various types of power on the basis of the manner in which the power-holder affects the power-subject.

Force is found where the power-holder directly affects the power-

162   *A Non-systematic Theory of Law and Society*

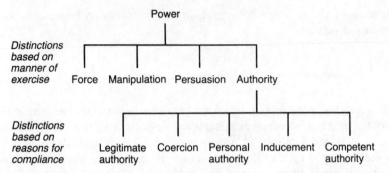

Figure 7.1 Wrong's typology of power (After Wrong, 1979, p. 24, © Dennis Wrong)

subject's body, and what that body can do, without relying on a conscious response. It can be used to affect behaviour by physically forcing the relevant bodily movements or by direct interference with the subject's thought processes (hypnosis, brainwashing and subliminal advertising). More often it can be used to prevent behaviour by physical restraint, confinement or by acting on the subject's environment (e.g. 'sitting-in' to prevent an office functioning, confiscation of a printing press or, drastically, by the deprivation of basic bodily needs like food and sleep). But force is distinguished from the *threat* of force which operates in a psychological rather than a physical manner (through the choice of the power-subject to avoid unpleasant consequences).

In *persuasion* the power-subject chooses to act as the power-holder wishes because the latter's arguments appeal to the power-subject's own values. In *manipulation* a similar response is induced because the power-holder deliberately restricts or falsifies the information reaching the power-subject.

Authority is found where the power-holder issues commands and the power-subject complies because of the *source* of the command (cf. persuasion in which the power-subject acts because of the *content* of the communication). Authority operates via the power-subject's beliefs about the power-holder (and the power-holder's likely actions) which the power-subject treats as reasons for action. Five types of authority are distinguished on the basis of various beliefs that provide reasons for compliance:

1   Inducement (the offer of material and social rewards).
2   Coercion (the issue of threats. If coercion is unsuccessful and the threat is fulfilled then force is exercised).
3   Competent authority (the belief by the power-subject in the superior knowledge or skill of the power-holder).

4 Personal authority (the power-holder's personal significance to the power-subject, e.g. love, charisma).
5 Legitimate authority (the power-subject believes that the power-holder has a right to issue commands and that (s)he has an obligation to obey).

Wrong requires that these normative beliefs be shared by power-holder and power-subject. But it is not necessary that the power-holder and power-subject adhere to the *same* norm – indeed the problem with interpersonal variation in the meaning of norms would make that difficult. All that is necessary is that the power-subject holds a belief that makes compliance for *that* power-subject a matter of obligation rather than self-interest. It is not even necessary (though it is usually the case) that the power-holder believes his power to be legitimate.

Wrong makes the issuing of and obedience to commands the paradigmatic case of authority. This opens him to Foucault's criticism that theories of power are based on an inadequate 'juridico-discursive' model (1980, p. 93) – in fact the outmoded Austinian notion of command. It also concedes and restricts the usefulness of the concept. Wrong has sketched one of the most significant kinds of social relations: where one person reacts in the manner desired by another because of beliefs the former holds about the latter. Yet the actions of such power-holders do not usually, or perhaps even frequently, resemble commands. They may involve the intimation of a desire or belief that is held, the statement of a rule to be followed or merely the statement of a definition. They will not necessarily involve speech (there are many kinds of communication), or even an overt action (in the case of anticipatory reactions by the power-subject noted above). The intended effect on the power-subject will also vary. It may involve the performance of an action or the adoption of a normative or factual belief. The conception of authority adopted in this book is a broad one – where the action of a power-holder intentionally affects the actions of power-subjects and the effect is achieved because of the beliefs the power-subject has about the power-holder and the power-holder's capabilities.

Resources

One of the consequences of the intentionality of power is that power, the probability that one person will affect the action of another, must be distinguished from the 'resources' (Dahl, 1963, p. 226; Giddens, 1984, p. 16) which make it possible. The possession of power requires knowledge that the resources can be used and a willingness to use them (cf. Turk, 1980, p. 108).

Some resources are attributes of the power-holder – physical strength, intelligence and knowledge. The first makes coercion possible, the last two make persuasion possible. Other resources include the money and goods (s)he controls which can serve as a basis for inducement. The power-subject's beliefs and perceptions of the power-holder can constitute other important resources. Reputation, social standing, charisma, popularity, and/or belief in their legitimacy allow power-holders to exercise personal, competent and legitimate authority. Beliefs held by power-subjects that the power-holder possesses other categories of resources can themselves constitute resources; for example, the belief that someone can carry out a threat is as effective a basis for coercion as the actual ability.

Some of the most important resources involve the ability to exercise other forms of power – e.g. the ability to induce a third party (whether police or bully-boy) to harm the power-subject. Indeed, to be effective, some resources, like the control of money or goods, require power or other social relations.

Power-mixes

Power relations involve the ability to affect intentionally the actions of others. But the scale of those effects is usually limited along one of three 'dimensions' noted by Wrong (1979, p. 14): extensiveness (the number of power-subjects), comprehensiveness (the areas of the power-subjects' activity that can be affected), intensiveness (how far the power-holder can affect the power-subject's behaviour). Two more dimensions should be added: cost (the resources which must be consumed in exercising power) and sufficiency (many exercises of power are incapable by themselves of producing the desired effect but can contribute to it). Force is limited in the first four dimensions, few persons can be affected at the one time and, although very effective in preventing undesired action, it is of little use in securing positive action, and is costly. Personal authority can be highly comprehensive, intensive and cheap, but, except for some charismatic personalities, it is rarely very extensive. Coercion in large populations cannot be very comprehensive because of difficulties in detecting non-compliance. Legitimate authority is not costly but is limited in all other dimensions by the necessity for the power-subject to hold congruent values.

However, the exercise of one form of power can be used to acquire other forms of power with the requisite dimensions. An individual may induce another to act as a bully-boy, someone who frequently persuades another may soon become regarded by the latter as a competent authority, and coercive regimes seek to gain legitimacy by manipulation.

Where a power-holder exercises a combination of power relations, different power-subjects will be affected for different reasons. Some might obey a command out of fear, others out of respect for the competence or personal qualities of the leader, others out of a belief that such a person's commands ought to be obeyed. Thus the greater the number, and especially the heterogeneity, of people sought to be affected, the greater the difficulty encountered by a power-holder possessing only one form of power.

All this is reasonably obvious, so we should expect power-holders to regularly avail themselves of the opportunities for acquiring other forms of power out of self-interest and the tendency for the powerful to want legitimate authority. Thus power-holders will tend to possess several forms of power, i.e. a range of means by which they can produce intended effects in others. Nowhere is this clearer than the personal wielder of state-power who will have, over large numbers of people, coercive, legitimate (over those holding relevant norms), competent (as a military leader or economic manager) and, for a limited number of officials, personal authority. They have popular control over goods to offer induce- ment and the means to manipulate the information supply and physically to prevent some acts of non-compliance. Yet nowhere is this range of power more necessary than in the case of the state where the population of power-subjects is large, varied and variable.

The extra forms of power gained will usually not merely cover new power-subjects but extend to power-subjects of the original power rela- tion – e.g. power-subjects may be threatened with sanctions for disobedi- ence to orders they regard as legitimate. To the power-subject, these multiple exercises of power appear as multiple reasons for compliance. If the power-subject finds these reasons sufficient then the resulting com- pliance will be for a mixture of reasons (not always clearly distinguished in his own mind) and the power relation will be neither coercive nor legitimate but a mixture of both. The capacity to deal with such mixtures is a major virtue of Wrong's categorization.

Exercises of power may be mixed in a further important way. They may be indirect (Law, 1986, p. 17), affecting the power-subject via the actions of other persons. A whole chain of different power relations could be involved: A induces B to coerce C to restrain D by force. However pure the relations of inducement, coercion and force may be, the chain as a whole is not one of inducement but is a mixture.

Even more important than the mixture of reasons within any one power-subject is the *variety* of mixes that will be found in different sub- jects of the one power-holder (Wrong, 1979, p. 114). The strength of the reasons provided by the original power relation varies from subject to subject as do the additional reasons provided by the additional power relations. Herein lies another advantage of possessing several forms of power, they can 'top up' the reasons for compliance felt by power-subjects until they are sufficient to provide compliance with the power-holder's wishes. Of course, single power relations will not always be insufficient for all power-subjects. In these cases the exercise of multiple power relations will lead to what the social observer sees as '*overdetermination*' (Lukes, 1974, p. 39) of the power-subject's response, or what the power-subject sees as an oversufficiency of reasons for compliance.

7.3 Asymmetry

All this makes it highly possible that the two persons involved in a power relations may have quite different perceptions of that relation. Following Weber (1982, p. 56), such power relations may be described as *asymmetrical*. This is implicit in the nature of manipulation where the ignorance of the power-subject is part of the very nature of the power relationship. But the phenomenon of differing perceptions does not stop there. The holder of authority may make his/her wishes known but be ignorant of the reason for compliance. If (s)he holds different forms of authority over the one power-subject (s)he may be unaware of how strong the various forms are and the actual mix of reasons that lead the power-subject to comply. Indeed, there may be very strong psychological forces which lead him into error. The above-mentioned desire of the powerful to feel their power to be legitimate may lead to the self-delusion that the dominant reason for compliance is the shared belief of their power-subjects in norms legitimating their commands, exaggerating both the strength of these norms for individual power-subjects and the number of power-subjects who hold them at all. Thus the same power relationship may be seen as essentially one of legitimate authority from one end, yet essentially one of coercion from the other. Similarly, someone with the resources to coerce attempts to control others by propaganda (manipulation). The power-subjects 'see through' the latter, yet comply with the power-holder's wishes from fear of the former.

The sources of this asymmetry are worth examining. First, one action may produce a large number of intentional social interactions (e.g. an order may be addressed to several persons, an 'offer' to several employees, and propaganda to whole populations). The mix of power relations activated may vary from power-subject to power-subject, yet the power-holder will not examine each relation but rather make general assumptions about the operation of his power relations. These generalizations will undoubtedly be wrong in respect of his relations with some power-subjects. Second, there are the tendencies to self-delusion mentioned above. Third, many social interactions do not involve face-to-face contact, making differing perception easier. Fourth, even in the most visible case of social interaction, where the two parties come face-to-face and the action of one leads the other to act, the two parties may have quite different perceptions of those actions. It may be described differently by the power-holder and power-subject and these different descriptions may read quite different meanings into the act (White, 1968, p. 12). Where these actions involve words these different meanings are even more likely. For all these reasons, asymmetry should be regarded as a normal part of regular social relations.

This asymmetric view of power relations is a Weberian insight that is not widely discussed. It has some support in literature,[1] social theory[2] and some of the comments of legal theorists discussed in earlier chapters.[3] But the tendencies run headlong into the strongly entrenched view that human interactions have 'common', 'shared', 'agreed', or 'cultural' meaning (or indeed 'mutual knowledge', Giddens, 1984, p. 332) and that interaction is impossible without it. The idea may be an old one but much of its current popularity among social philosophers is bolstered by hermeneutics, structuralism and even some symbolic interactionism and ethnomethodology. In England it was given a strong impetus by Winch's application of Wittgenstein's views on language to social theory. However these traditions should be critically examined to see whether they really support such asymmetric view of social relations. Hermeneutics seeks to understand texts according to the meaning attributed to them at the time the texts were written (in historical or religious applications) or in the author/group/community in which the texts are read (in sociological applications, e.g. Gadamer, 1975; Habermas, 1979). Traditionally hermeneutics assumed single cultural meanings at the time of writing or the time of reading. It has become more common, especially among deconstructionists, to emphasize interpretive *sub*-communities where the different meanings are based on the interests of its members (Bloor, 1983). Because such approaches only look for common meanings between interacting parties and do not consider such interaction possible without it, they are blind to asymmetrical interactions. However, asymmetry is initially guaranteed if members of two different interpretive communities interact and use terms or actions which have different meanings for their respective communities. Such interactions are far from rare, especially in law, which claims and even attempts to exercise comprehensive powers over all citizens regardless of the community of which they are a part.

Winch and Wittgenstein are particularly worthy of reconsideration. Wittgenstein saw people learning rules about the use of language through participation in 'language-games' in which words were used and actions performed. The latter helped the learning process by indicating what actions were associated with the use of the words and what actions counted as 'mistakes'. Winch extended this to the understanding of social interactions through learning shared rules about their 'meaning'. But the central idea that shared rules could emerge from such language-games is too optimistic. It suffers a problem similar to one already noted for Hart's notion of a social rule: the same action may be a mistake under several rules between which Wittgenstein's 'mistake test' does not distinguish. So the rule learned may not be the same as the rule taught and neither rule is shared. No solution is provided by suggesting that the shared rule can be directly communicated. It must first pass an 'interpersonal communication barrier'. The mental events we call ideas must be formed in one mind and processed by it into words, the words formed into speech, and speech must be heard and then processed by the listener's mind. Thus an idea in one mind affects the production of an idea in a second mind; but because it does not pass directly from one to the other, and must pass through the interpersonal barrier by means of speech, those ideas will frequently vary. That a degree of communication occurs is due to the fact that language is not used in isolation but in the context of action – in language-games. The other verbal and physical stimuli in these language-games aid this process of communication and the repeated use in slightly different circumstances results in the original and received ideas being drawn closer together. The similarity between the ideas is a mark that communication has occurred; but the frequent variation between them indicates the crudity of the process.

This is not the kind of language-game that Wittgenstein had in mind, but it does help to explain how communication occurs. The action context in which speech acts are made helps the communication that the speech acts are at least partially intended to achieve (language has many other uses than mere communication). Much of the success is due to the fact that people know what is going to happen next.

As it is for language, so it is for social interaction, not least that within law. The word 'theft' is used by a draughtsman to a politician. Later a judge uses it in front of a barrister, twelve jurymen and the accused. It conjures up quite different images and meanings for each. Yet such regular interactions recur because the participants know, if not the meaning of the word for each, the actions that accompany it.[4]

Cultural meanings do not determine and shape actions. It is rather that the actions enable some communication of meaning though not successfully enough for the meanings to be shared by the two parties involved in the communication (let alone all those who are part of the 'culture'). But most importantly of all, the action-contexts of language mean that we can still interact *despite* this imperfection of communication because, though the interacting parties give the words different meanings, they have some idea of the sorts of actions that accompany or follow the use of various words. Where the above concept of a language game indicates how this is *possible*, asymmetric power relations provide specific examples both of how such different meanings of words can be generated and sustained, and of how interaction is nevertheless a continuing possibility. Furthermore, to the extent that such power relations do not involve language we can see how the same asymmetric appreciation of the meaning of an interaction can be generated and sustained without prejudicing the continuity of such interaction within a stable social relationship.

Winch and others who saw language as a model for social interaction were quite right to do so – it is just that the most appropriate model is one based not on shared rules and perceptions but on interaction between people whose perceptions of the interaction run from complete congruence, through diametric opposition, to the complete ignorance by one or both parties that any interaction has occurred at all.

Power relations cannot be understood without recourse to the standpoints of both power-holder and power-subject. If they are viewed solely from the former: (1) the power-holder cannot know the mix of reasons for the power-subject's compliance with his wishes, (2) where (s)he tries to affect the action of an unseen person (s)he will not know whether the effect has been achieved and thus whether this is even a case of power at all, and (3) (s)he cannot even be sure which form of power is being exercised. If power relations are viewed solely from the power-subject's point of view, as some conflict and compliance theorists do (e.g. Krislov, 1972), some forms of power disappear completely (e.g. manipulation and some forms of force).

This leads us to refine the model of a social *interaction* offered here. A social interaction occurs when some thought, action, inaction or attribute of A (a person) affects the body thoughts or actions of B (another person). Put most simply, something about what A is or does affects what B is or does. A social *relation* between two people is the tendency or *probability* that such interactions will occur. A *power* relation occurs if A *intends* the effect. Other types of relation will be discussed below. This model is a 'causal' one. Sociological causes are rarely either necessary or sufficient, so that most social relations are by themselves insufficient to cause a change in B's action, and are effective only in combination with several other social relations. The interaction is rarely purely physical. It is part of the nature of social causality that most causes are instigated, and effects realized, by the processes of the human mind. In all cases involving a thought or an action and most involving inaction, A's action has to be observed by B and processed by his brain before B changes his thoughts or actions. Thus B's perception of the interaction is an essential part of the social relationship. This is so whether or not the perception is accurate. It is so even if the perception is not of a social relationship but of something else (as in manipulation, where B does not see the action of the other person upon him but sees only the 'facts' he is intended to see). A's perception is equally important, and equally a part of the relation, for without that perception the interaction would generally not take place. And without it we would be unable to comprehend his action and distinguish between quite different social relationships.

7.4 Unintended Effects

That power relations are not the only social relations is indicated by the variety of situations described by other theorists of power who adopt broader definitions (chapter 7.2). These are excluded as instances of power not to deny their importance but to provide a better understanding of them and to enable comparisons with other categories of social relation.

The first type of non-power relation may simply be called 'unintended effects'. Wrong regards 'unintended influence' as a larger category than the 'intended influence' (power) his book covered (1979, p. 4). Both Merton (1957) and Giddens (1984) regarded their study as one of the major tasks of the social sciences (although both, remarkably, argue that they help structure society). Environmentalists will provide any number of fearsome anecdotes, but such evidence is available in all spheres of life. Companies may seek greater profit by competition but merely ruin themselves and others. Road accidents are, by definition, unintended and have the most widespread and devastating effects.

There are good reasons for assigning unintended effects such importance. Human behaviour is not completely calculative so we inevitably produce more effects than intended. Indeed, it might be added, many actions are performed without *any* thought for their consequences because they are routine, instinctive, reflexive or amount to small ill-considered choices in response to low-level environmental stimuli (e.g. 'choosing' a toothpaste from a supermarket shelf). Even when we consider the effects of an action we may not calculate its effects on others (the action may be entirely self-centred) or on those outside our immediate circle. Even when we do attempt to calculate the broad effects of our actions or else calculate what actions will produce desired effects, we may be quite wrong. Such calculations will involve little more than a guess – theories of social prediction tend to be very weak. Indeed, considering the past difficulties with social theory and bearing in mind that it is probably not advancing in sophistication as quickly as society is developing in complexity, it might be a good rule of thumb to ignore the remote consequences of our actions, removing them from our calculations and intentions altogether (a position some would take on moral grounds).

Even when we do anticipate effects we are often completely wrong about their extent. Foucault emphasizes how effects are often very different from those intended because people are a 'resistant' medium (1980, p. 141). It may be said that ignorance about the nature and extent of the effect of our actions is a key part of social interaction, especially in a society as complex as ours.

Unintended effects have the same form as other social relations, i.e. a causal relation between one person's attitudes, ideas, actions or inaction and the ideas, actions or position of another. But in contrast to power relations the person who is the cause of those effects is not aware of the relation. There are two important categories. The first is the category of *anticipatory reactions* (Friedrich, 1963, p. 199), where one person (B) *modifies* his/her action because of an anticipated reaction by another person (A) but A is ignorant of the fact. Something about A has led B to assume that A possesses resources and a willingness to react in certain circumstances; B is anticipating a power-act by A. (These power-acts would presumably include force, inducement, coercion and the exercise of legitimate or personal authority, but not manipulation and only very rarely persuasion and competent authority.) A could be dubbed the *reactor* and B the *anticipator*. Depending on whether the reaction is desired or not, this will either be a reason for or against the anticipator's performance of the relevant action.

Anticipants will sometimes be wrong about the capacity or willingness of the reactor to react but the anticipatory reactions are still important. Over time these errors will generally be discovered. If several people are in the same position of the anticipator their perceptions will vary and some may not anticipate a reaction or, for various reasons, welcome it. Consequently they will act and the reaction will not occur. Knowledge of this might initially be known only to that actor but one would expect word to spread to others so that they no longer anticipate a reaction and cease to modify their behaviour accordingly. But all this will take time. During the interval the circumstances may change and the capacity and/or willingness may develop. Although it may be wrongly assumed that the reactor has the specific resources for the anticipated reaction, the assumption is normally based on the possession of other resources. For example, it may be assumed that a large corporation has the ear of government. This assumption may be quite wrong but is based on the possession of resources that are often found with, and may over time lead to, the relevant power relation. Willingness to act may be assumed because it appears to the anticipator that the self-interest of the reactor is served in doing so. In fact the reactor might feel that reaction is not in his best interests or feel morally constrained from so reacting. The misperception of a reactor's willingness or resources to react may cover a period when that willingness or those resources are absent, effectively protecting the reactor against the actions of the anticipator until the willingness emerges or the resources are acquired.

Even if the willingness or resources do not emerge, the effect is still important. Many factors affect our estimations of the willingness and resources of others to act. There is a tendency to overestimate the power and capacity of others vis-à-vis oneself. One is more likely to know the costs and difficulties of exercising power over others than of the same costs and difficulties of one's opponents exercising power over oneself. This would explain how it is possible for two opposing groups simultaneously to wring their hands at their own powerlessness (e.g. business and unions). Even if overestimates of an opponent's strength are no more likely than underestimates, wrongly assumed weakness is soon disproved, but wrongly assumed strength is rarely challenged and thus rarely disproved.

The second important category of unintended effects could be called 'unforeseen' effects. In this, one person (the *affector*) acts and expects the act to have *some* effects but not those that result. The person affected in this way might be called the '*affectee*'. Unforeseen effects vary in nature, extent or target, but can be divided on the basis of how the error occurs:

1   The affector fails to consider the remote effects of his/her action or is unable to calculate them.
2   The effects are contingent on whether others act similarly and the affector is unaware of whether they will or not. Selling sterling will only lead to a sterling crisis if many others do the same. (This assumes that there is no conspiracy, a case of power, involved.)
3   The affector exercises power, but the effects are much greater than expected because of the (again, non-conspiratorial) action of others. This would cover cases like the above where the affector deliberately sells sterling to affect the exchange rate but is unaware that others are doing the same.

Even more than power relations, relations of unintended effect are asymmetrical. In relations of anticipated reactions, the reactor is ignorant of the relation. In relations of unforeseen effect, the affector will at best find out afterwards. In some cases, the relationship will not be discernible to either party although its effect may be.

7.5   Value–Effect Relations

The earlier criticisms of various normative theories of legal system should not lead us to ignore the fact that the values held by individuals significantly influence their actions and the effects they have on others. These are particularly significant where many hold identical or similar values. Many writers tend to concentrate on values that lead people to refrain from certain actions and hence the effects on those who benefit from such restraint (Lukes, 1974, p. 22). But values also induce action. Values which condemn non-believers and outsiders lead to their persecution and ostracism, and the values placed on wealth accumulation have had significant effects on those who accumulate it, on those who do not and on our physical and social environment in general.

This points to a different kind of social relation – a *value–effect relation*. In this relation, the attitude of one person (the *value-holder*) tends to lead him/her to act in a manner different from the way (s)he would act if (s)he did not hold the value, and another person (the *value-beneficiary* or the *value-sufferer*) is affected in some way by this difference. For example, if the value-holder believes that certain desirable material things should be regarded as another's and should not be removed from his proximity, then, to the extent that the value-holder could have removed them, the latter person's enjoyment of those material things is more secure. This raises an important feature of such value–effect relations. They frequently operate to *neutralize* power (Thompson, 1975). In other examples, values lead their holders to act rather than refrain from acting, in which cases the values *direct* the exercise of power. Finally, some value–effect relations create power for others. If the value-holder believes (s)he ought to obey commands or follow the rules laid down by another, then, provided the latter is aware of this, the latter has the power of legitimate authority.

Several people may hold similar values. Indeed the social significance of values will not be great unless the value-holders are either numerous or very powerful. The word 'norm' itself may be used to announce the fact that many people do hold such similar values. It should be stressed that this notion of norms involves *similar* values. As argued in chapter 3.10, values are entirely internal mental phenomena. Even if their content is identical, values in different minds remain separate phenomena. But the vagaries of interpersonal communication and the variety of meanings given to words in normative discourse make identity unlikely and approximation the best possible result. Yet this variation in norms does not destroy their effectiveness. As noted in discussing Hart's social rules, different ideas may lead to the 'same' actions and hence to the same effects. Consequently, insistence that people share the same normative beliefs (or 'internal aspects') leads us to miss what is socially relevant in those cases where they are *sufficiently similar* to produce the same effects (see chapter 3.3).

Like other social relations, value–effect relations are frequently asymmetrical. Indeed, they rarely appear as a relation from either end. To the value-holder the relation does not appear so much as a *relation* as an *obligation*, something quite outside the self. It is a nice irony that, seen from the external point of view, values are phenomena internal to the mind, but from the internal point of view they seem to be external ones. Where power is neutralized, the value-beneficiary may also be quite unaware of the relationship, viewing only the effects (e.g. the objects that the value-beneficiary continues to enjoy because of the value-holder's beliefs about property rights). Where value–effect relations create legitimate authority, this complete asymmetry of mutual ignorance is impossible. But the value under which the power-subject considers he has an obligation to obey may be different from the value (if any) under which the power-holder considers he has a right to be obeyed (chapter 7.2). This asymmetry will be particularly likely if several people consider the power-holder to have legitimate authority. Where there are several values under which the value-holders/power-subjects consider themselves obligated, the value-beneficiary/power-holder can hardly share them all. To do so would be inconvenient and, to the extent that the power-subjects' values contradict each other, morally inconsistent. If (s)he holds any value legitimizing the authority, then it will at best correspond to that of *some* of the value-holders/power-subjects, making value–effect relations with *them* symmetrical but relations with the rest asymmetrical.

7.6 Some Interrelationships and Combinations

Just as different forms of power relation are interrelated, combined and shade into one another, so do social relations in general.

Power relations tend to produce relations of unintended effect because (1) not all the effects of their exercise can be foreseen, and (2) power-holders are likely to have the capacity to react and power-subjects are likely to anticipate such reaction.

Power relations also produce norms. A classic example is the parent/child relationship, where coercion is used to prompt adherence to values. Another is where legitimate authority commands obedience to a rule of conduct which is then internalized.

An individual may be subject to a combination of social relations each of which is insufficient to determine behaviour but which together are more than sufficient. (S)he may be subject to the power of one and to unintended effects from a second and hold certain values that retard his or her willingness to act against a third. It is the combination of social relations that determines an individual's actions rather than any single one.

Just as power relations may be mixed and the mix perceived differently from each end, so may social relations. A manager may tell employees that the company cannot continue to pay current wages and that a wage-cut would be best for all. Even if (s)he does not imply a threat, the employees may anticipate that (s)he would sack them if they refused. If so, there is a mix of persuasion and anticipated reaction. But there may not even be any mix. The employees may find the manager totally unpersuasive yet still fear that the anticipated sacking will follow a refusal to accept. Here the social interaction is totally effective – but from one end it appears to be through the activation of a relation that is, in fact, totally ineffective, and from the other end it is seen as a relation of which the other party is, in fact, totally unaware.

Different social relations shade into each other. Where power is exercised, power-holders often have a clear idea of some of the desired effects, and hazier ideas of the remoter effects. The actual dividing line between intended and unintended effects is blurred – a problem not unknown to lawyers. Power and value-effects will tend to merge when a legitimate authority restates a rule that is already held as a value by the power-subject. However, the typology is useful in all these boundary situations analysing the *extent* to which the relation is one of power, value-effects or unintended effect.

Role

One concept that can usefully be analysed as a combination of social relations is the problematic one of 'role'. The distinctions between role-expectation, role-orientation and role-behaviour have already been noted and any undifferentiated conception rejected. Naturally enough, the three are interrelated and the social relations listed above can be used to indicate how. Role-orientations (what the role-occupant thinks (s)he should do) affect role-behaviour in the same ways as any other personal normative beliefs affect action. Role-expectations (what others think the role-occupant should do) affect role-behaviour. If the person with a role-expectation is power-holder in a relation of persuasion, manipulation or legitimate authority, (s)he can affect the role-orientation of a power-subject and, through that, role-behaviour. Alternatively, if the role-expectation is held by an anticipator or power-holder (in relations of force, coercion, manipulation and inducement) the role-occupant will have a reason to behave as expected, with or without a corresponding role-orientation.

Note that these power relations and anticipatory reactions must be expressed in the plural. Conflicting role-expectations about the same role-occupant will be held by different people (indeed, conflicting expectations are often held by the *same* person). Thus the same action may receive a critical reaction from some and a positive reaction from others, and in many cases a role-occupant can anticipate that *any* action will receive some critical reaction. The individual role-occupant need consider not so much a uniform communal reaction to role-performance or role-deviance as the variety of pressures on, and reactions to, any action (s)he takes.

7.7   Mind and Environment

That someone's social environment is crucial in the moulding of that person's perceptions, ideas, values and action is accepted by all social theorists. Disagreements are about the extent of the effect, the part(s) of the environment that have the greatest effect on consciousness, and the manner in which they produce these effects.

The theory outlined here treats the environment of any individual as all that surrounds him or her – whether objects or interactions or other persons. The *social* environment of any individual is that part of society that surrounds, and interacts with, him or her. The social observer will see that environment in terms of the social interactions and relations (s)he has with others, and the objects and ideas with which (s)he thereby has contact (objects are applied to the individual in force, threatened in coercion, offered as inducement or left in that individual's possession by value-effect relations: ideas are thrust forward in manipulation, persuasion, competent authority and legitimate authority). When (s)he acts, the effects become a part of his or her environment, and also of the environment of those whose actions (s)he affects.

Point of View

The individual's view of the environment will not be the same as the social observer's – it may not even be similar. (S)he may be ignorant of the nature of the social relations that affect him or her (e.g. seeing manipulation as persuasion) or that there is a social relation at all (e.g. many value-effect relations). Moreover, past interactions with other people will have set the terms in which (s)he can describe the world. The meanings of the words (s)he uses to describe the environment may be different to the social observer's because of the different contexts, language-games, in which they were learned. These words, and the meanings, images and ideas of the world they create in the mind, are used to analyse the environment. They are a part of the mind/brain's methods of processing the incoming signals from it. Furthermore, this mechanism is selectively focused on that part of the environment to which the individual's attention is directed. *For an individual*, the environment does not contain all the physical objects and movements within sensory range, but *some* of those things as processed by the brain using the mechanisms at its disposal.

Of course, these word-meanings/ideas are not static. Experiences of the environment, though filtered and selected, are continually coming in, and some of them do not sit easily with pre-existing ideas and beliefs – thus providing Quinean 'recalcitrant experiences' (chapter 1.1). Such experiences lead us to question, modify or reject one or more of our beliefs, ideas or word-meanings, including the understanding or, in drastic cases, the memory of the experience. Consequently an individual's ideas of the world are the result of a constant interaction between pre-existing ideas and his experience as interpreted by these ideas.

It should be noted that what is being discussed is a person's view of his environment or at best view of the world. The term 'world view' is deliberately avoided because it has connotations of something that few, if any, possess: a unified, coherent, consistent and systematic set of concepts, values, ideas or perceptions. One reason for this could be the disorder in the social world itself. But this is neither necessary nor sufficient to produce a disordered view of it in the mind of one of its inhabitants. The lack of consistency and system in an individual's ideas and perceptions lies in the fact that they are generated in and for different situations and activities in which the individual participates. The words learned vary, as do the people from whom, and the contexts in which, they are learned. In quieter moments an individual may try to take out the key ideas and order them into a consistent whole. But few, if any, would have the ability or the time. Even if it were possible to systematize an individual's ideas, it would be that individual's structure, that individual's system, and, as we have seen in relation to all three systems theories, the different systems of those who participate make it even more difficult to find system in their product. And even if we could confine ourselves to the individual's created system, how would (s)he deal with changes in his or her ideas generated by different experiences? Would an entirely new system need to be devised? Would the systematization mean that each belief was so strongly supported by other beliefs as to be unchallengeable by experience? Or would the new experiences lead to rejection or modification of ideas so that the set of ideas quickly becomes as disordered as this book claims it always was? These were problems for Hercules in systematizing his view of the law, they are exacerbated in systematizing any view of the world.

An individual's ideas are not seen as systematic or unified, but part of a Quinean 'web of belief'. Some ideas are connected, and this provides a source of strength for each because rejecting one would usually mean doubting the other. There are contradictions, but these may not emerge because we are not called upon to consider both ideas in one context. When this happens through experience (or, sometimes, reflection), the contradiction becomes apparent and is dealt with by taking on new ideas or modifying or rejecting old ones.

The views that different individuals have of the world will differ because of variations in (1) physical position in relation to other persons (and objects), (2) social relations, (3) asymmetric perception of those relations, (4) the words/meanings/ideas/concepts with which (s)he interprets what (s)he senses, (5) what the individuals sensory interpretative mechanisms are directed at, (6) practices and (7) values (for 6 and 7 see *infra*). These variations are interrelated and are themselves the results of previous interactions with the individuals' environment through social relations with others. People who are similar on any one of those variables tend to have similar perceptions of their environments. Accordingly many writers have written of the 'point of view' of persons who share such a similarity. Jurisprudence has especially concentrated on the hoped-for similarity between the points of view of those engaged in the same 'legal' activity (based on 6 and sometimes, controversially, 7). This hope has been confounded not only by the many activities within law, but by these other factors listed which affect the point of view of those engaged in legal activities.

Practical Reason

An individual's social environment does not merely affect the view taken of it. It affects the individual's actions, which in turn affect the environment. Both sorts of effects are mapped out in the social relations of which (s)he is a part. But to understand how these effects are achieved requires an understanding of the way the mind processes the sensory information about the environment into actions that affect it. This constitutes the most dynamic aspect of the interaction between mind and the environment. The interaction operates at several levels.

Conscious choice of action is based upon brain processes which appear from the internal point of view as reasons – practical reasons. Values held (themselves the result of a complex interaction between mind, practice and environment – see *infra*) provide reasons. Beliefs about how the world works (which are perceptions about the environment) provide reasons because they give an indication of the consequences that will flow from considered actions and hence what values will be realized by performing them. But environment also provides reasons more directly. From the standpoint of the power-subject, the social relations of which (s)he is a part provide reasons for and against action. Force, where (s)he is physically prevented from doing something, provides a reason to give up any hope of doing it (*pace* Raz, this is one of the few 'complete reasons'). Persuasion provides reasons in which the persuader points to certain of the power-subject's values that provide reasons to do as the persuader suggests; in manipulation, the same *appears* to be so. Authority relations provide various reasons for conforming to the dictates of the power-holder. These reasons may be because of the respect in which the subject holds the power-holder (personal authority) or the power-holder's expertise (competent authority) or the power-holder's capacity to provide or deprive him or her of objects or feelings (s)he values (inducement and coercion). Further reasons are provided by desired or undesired reactions of others that the reasoner anticipates will follow certain actions. Yet more reasons are provided by the norms or values that make certain outcomes preferable or make certain actions appear obligatory. Finally, reasons are provided by the resources at the disposal of the practical reasoner. These will take the form of physical objects within the practical reasoner's environment, or power relations in which (s)he is the power-holder, that (s)he can direct to the achievement of that reasoner's purposes. These resources provide opportunities, but the lack of such opportunities provides the strongest of all reasons for not acting – impossibility! Even where the action is possible and the desired effect achievable, the cost involved and the alternative uses to which those resources could be put constitute reasons against the action.

This long list shows both the large number and disparate nature of the reasons that may be provided by the environment of physical objects and social relations as seen from the individual actor's point of view. Frequently several such reasons combine and reinforce each other – the *over-determination* of action seen by the social observer becomes an *over-abundance of reasons* from the point of view of the actor. All too often, the power and other social relations to which (s)he is subject effectively reduce an individual to a single course of action: practical reason merely identifies this fact.

But this is not always the case. No single action is overdetermined and the reasons all point in different directions, providing reasons for and against a range of actions. The actor appears to have a *range of choice*.

How does the brain process the profusion of reasons to make that 'choice'? Raz's model, as qualified in chapter 3.10, provides an excellent starting point. First-order reasons are direct reasons for action provided by the values it is likely to realize. Their weight is determined by the probability and value the reasoner places on the expected outcome. Conflicts between first-order reasons are resolved by balancing their weights. Second-order reasons are reasons for acting on, or ignoring, certain first-order reasons – positive and negative second-order reasons respectively. The latter are *suppressory* reasons because they suppress consideration of first-order reasons, so only first-order reasons of sufficient weight to overcome the suppression will be considered. They are *protected* reasons if they are, at the same time, a reason for acting themselves.

Raz saw the statements made by those the actor regarded as having 'authority' over him/her as protected reasons. Raz's discussion seemed to cover only legitimate authority and it can easily be extended to cover personal and competent authority, but the concept is far more useful that that. Other kinds of authority can also provide such reasons. Although a single interaction of inducement or coercion will provide a first-order reason for doing as the power-holder requires, the regular or probable interactions within power relations of those kinds may lead us to create a 'rule of thumb' that those requirements be adhered to. In the many cases of mixed authority relations these reasons will usually not be considered separately but compounded into a more powerful composite reason for following the dictates of the power-holder.

The mixture of reasons for according someone or something authority has a further consequence. The reasons people have for obeying the law are classically a mixture of the possibility of sanction, inducement (rewards include social approval and protection of transactions), belief in its legitimacy and the correctness of its content. These may be jointly sufficient to create a suppressory reason of great strength. But if one or more of those reasons is not perceived the effectiveness of the overall reason may drop enormously. Take Raz's example of someone passing through a red light on a deserted road with a clear view in all directions (1979, ch. 1). It is not that the value placed on breaking the law is so great that the authority of law is not regarded as a sufficient reason for disregarding it. Rather it is that the loss of coercive and inducement-related reasons for according the law authority has reduced its suppressory capacity. Consequently it is not sufficient to suppress the first-order reason that the convenience of crossing the road provides.

Other social relations also provide reasons. Relations of anticipatory reaction produce the same kinds of suppressory reasons as authority relations and value–effect relations may produce either first- or second-order reasons depending on how formalized the value-beliefs are. Persuasion and manipulation provide only first-order reasons. No secondary reasons could be provided by manipulation because it operates through the ignorance of the power-subject. Nor could they be provided by *persuasion* which operates via the content of the advice not its source. If a power-subject does make rules about following the persuader's advice (s)he has created a power relation of *competent authority*. These reasons take their place in an individual's practical reasoning alongside those provided by the authority relations that Raz considers. All the second-order reasons will complement and conflict on the basis of their weight vis-à-vis other second-order reasons. Because even legitimate authority relations provide merely suppressory reasons, first-order reasons have new importance. Strong ones can overcome the suppressory effect of other relations and, if they do, bring others into play. This image of practical reasoning does not permit the construction of elaborate systems of practical reasoning and structures of authority relations that Raz is so good at. Indeed it should be emphasized that for most individuals practical reasoning will not be a unified or structured affair. In the different areas of their life they will have different procedures for dealing with decisions over actions. These procedures ('skills') will have emerged in response to situations calling for action on the spot and reflection afterwards on how they might have handled the decision better. In any case, they would be hampered in the construction of any elaborate system of reasoning by the very factors that prevented their having a unified world view – lack of time, lack of ability, the need to deal with changing and unforeseen circumstances and the lack of a consistent world view itself.

Action is rarely preceded by full-blown exercises of practical reason with considered and conscious choice analysing the many reasons our values, beliefs and especially social relations give us. Much of our action is conscious at a much lower level and few if any reasons are considered. This may not make much difference. Frequently the same reasons and reasoning processes work at a less conscious level (which makes the rather formal model provided above a useful representation of the brain processes involved). Searching for them is rightly called 'rationalization'. It is common to seek a simple explanation and search for a single reason in our mind (mirroring our search for necessary and sufficient causes in the world). Yet if we were asked, or asked ourselves, for twenty reasons we could probably provide them. In fact the truth is likely to be somewhere in between. When we are not consciously searching out and analysing all the reasons for an action, it is unlikely that the unconscious brain is fully engaged on the same enterprise or that the influences will operate as if they were well-defined reasons. Instead of beliefs about the world and our interactions with it, there will be semi-conscious or unconscious feelings for what will work, and instead of values there will be unconscious motivations. 'Rationalizing' may produce apparent reasoning that was not in fact operative.

Practices

Regularities of behaviour may result from interaction between the mind and environment at all levels. The independent reasoning processes of individuals may bring them to act in a similar fashion.

Reasons and reasoning processes will vary from person to person.

Values, beliefs, experiences, social relations and all the mixes within them vary. Consequently the reasons for acting and perceptions of the act itself vary too. Yet power-subjects in similar situations often act in what appear to be identical ways – both physical actions and the effects are similar – yet be doing it for quite dissimilar reasons and perceive it in quite dissimilar ways. Indeed, if they are subject to the same power-holder, who will not detect the difference in internal perception, the same physical actions will produce the same response and are just as suitable for each. Thus it is quite unnecessary to postulate common perception, common meaning, shared norms or shared reasons for action to explain and understand how behaviour is regular and hence predictable. As has been maintained throughout, we should delve inside the minds of the social actors, but we should not presume to find the same ideas and processes just because the same movements are being performed.

Much regularity of behaviour results from lower levels of interaction between mind and environment and at lower levels of consciousness. We are constantly making decisions about what action to perform next; crossing the road, watching television, buying goods. These mobilize little of our conscious brain or bring into play few of our attitudes, ideas and values. If the behaviour has an 'internal' aspect, it is a very muted one (Giddens calls this the 'durée' of social life, which is more 'monitored' than consciously directed by the higher processes of practical reason, 1984, p. 3). To the extent that we are aware of making choices about such mundane matters, it is common to note how others around us choose and do as they do to save mental effort.

If the action that results from either conscious or unconscious choice does not produce known consequences undesirable to the actor, and if the conditions of the earlier choice (the same social relations and obser-vations of others' practices) are repeated, then the action is likely to be repeated as well. In fact, the likelihood of a repetition is enhanced because our earlier action will be a more impressive example than the actions of others. Indeed, however conscious the *initial* action, later ones are likely to become less a matter of conscious choice and more a matter of unconscious 'habit'.

Sometimes our practical reasoning is used to decide not merely single actions but practices to be followed deliberately because, given our values and knowledge of the world, we consider them suitable. Within that pro-cess of practical reasoning, rules laid down by others play a role through the relations of persuasion, manipulation and personal, competent and legitimate authority and the reasons for those relations. Sometimes in-dividuals model themselves on others, placing a value on being like them or on what they have gained. This effectively gives the other person per-sonal, competent or legitimate authority to affect the individual's behaviour by example (although to the individual it will appear as a reason to do something 'because so-and-so does it'). But, as in the choice of single actions, the choice of practices involves all the other reasons arising from social relations and available resources. These frequently narrow choice to a very limited range of practices in which others have successfully engaged and impose heavy costs on apparent alternatives.

There may well be more alternatives but unless they have been successfully pursued by role-models, practical reasoners may not be conscious of them and, if they are, their untried nature provides a reason for caution. Of course, following role-models is no guarantee of success. The role-model may have simply been lucky, or the role-follower may not have the resources or perceived attributes that lead others to enter the kind of social relations which were necessary for the role-model's success. Note that this concept of role-model is rather different from that of a role in functionalist theory. 'Trail-blazer' would perhaps be more apt. But it is also rather more individual than the depersonalized concept of role in structural functionalism. Most people in choosing their practices (and, indeed, whole career paths) are likely to take *particular* individuals rather than abstract roles as examples to follow (and, even if they do follow abstract roles, they are abstracted from examples known to them). Thus each participant's view of a 'role' is abstracted from a diverse set of examples. Despite the generally greater knowledge of the model by the role-follower, the follower is less likely to have the same internal conception of the role as the model. They know the person sufficiently well to separate that individual from other 'role-occupants' and from themselves. They may say that they do not share the model's views but they will still follow in their footsteps. It is really a matter of following some of the *actions* of others, but interpreting those actions in their own way. The point is that the role is not necessarily interpreted in the same way by those past whom the trail is blazed, the trail-blazers and those who would follow.

Practices common within groups show the same diversity of origin. In unconscious or semi-conscious reasoning, the examples set by one can be adopted by many others. This may result from similar values or from any other social relations that provide reasons to indulge in externally similar practices. In many cases the members of the group are subject to a mixture of social relations linking them to the same person(s). The mix will vary from subject to subject and with them the reasons. But each has sufficient reason for adopting the same practice. Thus those who adopt common practices may, for different reasons, have little choice or find the costs of some actions out of the question.

At other times we adopt practices because there is something we would like to do and there is only one way to do it. An example was the success of 'Bankcard' (an Australian equivalent to 'Access'). Many swore not to use it or to use it only in an emergency because of the temptation to overspend and because of the manner of its introduction (it was sent unsolicited to everyone with a cheque account). Although usage started slowly, it rose steadily and many of its detractors became regular users. Dr Hugh MacKay (Centre for Communications Studies, Bathurst) has suggested that this was a classic case of practices being formed by simple environmental conditions. Some situation would arise where a fairly simple desire to buy a particular object could not be fulfilled by the familiar means (no chequebook or cash in the pocket) but could be bought by Bankcard. Once this happened a few times it became a practice and the users justified their use on the basis of convenience, ready credit, etc. and declared Bankcard a 'good thing'.

Values

The last example tells us something about the relationship between attitudes and practices. The practice changed the attitude rather than *vice versa*. Many of our practices are the result of low-level choices in which we do not invoke any of the values we regard as important. When it comes to justifying or rationalizing our practices, we select from the ideas known to us (most of which would have been presented to us as arguments and were therefore themselves part of our environment) one that fits our practice. Of course, we may decide after such reflection to reject the practice – but, because it is normal to believe that most of our actions are justified, we do not come to such personal value questions as neutrals. More often than not we adopt values congruent with our actions. In more major matters we are likely to bring into consideration more of our values before taking action. But, because we tend to have less time to consider action beforehand than justify it afterwards, we usually mobilize fewer beliefs and values in choosing than in justifying. Thus, although values and practices interact, key values will tend to be determined by practice rather than *vice versa*. Even where there is time for value-choice to precede action, the environment plays a key role, because such choices are usually thrown up by concrete situations people encounter in their social environment. Thus the value-choice is defined and delimited by the experiences that led to the need for a choice, and by the environment in which the actor will have to live after his choice has been made and acted upon.

Once these supportive attitudes and values have been formed, they provide reasons for continuing the practice and create a value-effect relation(s). Where practices are adopted not out of carelessness but out of lack of choice, then the newly created value will reinforce the practice by adding a new social relation and a new reason for following it.

Furthermore, the fact that the practice can *precede* the attitude means that it can exist without it (*pace* Winch, Althusser, Parsons et al.). Indeed, if the social relations that provide reasons for the practice are strong, or if the individual cannot or does not think of any reasons against it, then the practice can survive a long time without such attitudes – perhaps even long enough for those attitudes to develop!

Ideology

In the above there lurks a bare-bones Marxist theory of ideology. From the ideas available to them, individuals choose those that suit their practices and experience. The key determinants of their final ideas become their practices and experience on the one hand and the supply of ideas on the other. The latter is not a random matter. As Hunt puts it (1985), there are sites that produce ideology and sites that transmit it. Some, especially 'opinion leaders' quoted in the mass media, so-called 'think tanks', private economic advice bureaux, universities and, sometimes, those in the mass media themselves, play a greater part than others in providing and disseminating the pool of ideas from which individuals choose to fit their behaviour. These people and institutions have power – one or more out of manipulation, persuasion, competent and personal authority. There are some cases of manipulation. But, on the whole, the ideas they promulgate are the ones they hold. The problem is that such ideas will be related to *their* experiences and will tend to justify *their* practices rather than those of the people to whom they communicate their ideas. This obviates the need to assume either a conspiracy of the powerful or wholesale manipulation to explain the convenient correspondence between the interests of the powerful and the bulk of ideas generated and disseminated. Wishful thinking is a common failing. Statements that moral value or community interest coincide with the accretion of power, wealth and privilege to certain individuals are never rigorously scrutinized by those individuals who benefit, but are more likely to be accepted by them as obviously true. The wealthy and privileged are usually strong on wishing and, even if they are weak on thinking, there are usually enough intellectuals and 'opinion leaders' prepared to do their thinking for them. Those who generate the most plausible ideas justifying wealth and privilege will be applauded and they and their institutions will be well supported.

This should not lead us to imagine that individuals are likely to accept *any* ideas that are transmitted to them. The ideas individuals accept will be the ones from those presented, and to which they are given sufficient exposure, that sit most easily with *their* experiences and practices and fit best into their web of belief. There is a balance between exposure and fit. Individuals are unlikely to adopt views of which they are only dimly aware, but for most there is a level of exposure at which they are capable of taking on ideas that fit better than other ideas to which they are more frequently and forcefully exposed. On the other hand, truth is only indirectly relevant (many who transmit ideas have scruples against transmitting ideas they *know* to be false and false ideas may be found not to fit in practice). This approach integrates recent Marxist insights into the (at least) partially institutional nature of ideology with the more traditional Marxist insight that practices provide a material basis of intellectual life (Larrain, 1979, p. 59; Sumner, 1979), without having to assume that individuals will soak up any labels by which they are exposed (*pace* Althusser). The ideas involved in practice *may* be changed by devising and disseminating new ideas that will fit *better* with their experience of the world than those currently held. But for further modifications of belief, material practices and conditions have to change, or clearly appear to change, as well.[5] This is why Marx and others believed socialist ideals could be accepted by the working classes and would gradually become more acceptable as those ideals were disseminated (thereby supplanting the ideologies that had best fitted their material conditions until then, e.g. those of the Chartists) and conditions changed as they predicted. But they believed that those ideals would never be adopted by the peasantry because their environments and practices were so different.

So far the argument has been that an individual's environment shapes his or her ideas which shape his or her view of environment, and the combination of his or her ideas and environmental perceptions determines his or her action. This might appear to provide the 'last chance' for a theory that in any one society the ideas, perceptions and practices will be the same for all because they all share the same environment or because only one acceptable set of ideas is presented. Neither condition is fulfilled.

The supply of ideas is never so limited or constant. At the very least every ideology at least suggests its opposite (Luhmann, 1985, p. 96) and the key symbols of an ideology can usually be used to generate new ideologies (Sumner, 1979, p. 216). But human minds, especially when subjected to a variety of experiences and social relations, are usually far more inventive than that, and new ideas that fit travel quickly.[6] This is aided by the variety of sites for the production of ideology, and the variety of practices and experience of those who occupy them mean that a single set of views are unlikely to be produced. This is increasingly acknowledged by ideology theorists (chapter 5.9), who tend now to talk of ideologies (Sumner, 1979; Hunt, 1985) rather than dominant or hegemonic ideology and of ideological mechanisms which operate within particular processes, practices and relations rather than as a society-wide whole (Sumner, 1979, p. 218). Finally, the methods of transmission do not distribute the ideas evenly, so some may receive different ideas in different forms and in widely different dosages.

The 'last chance' theory also requires that we really do share the same environment. The word 'environment' itself should make us suspicious of such assumptions, for an environment is that which surrounds something. My environment is what surrounds me, your environment is what surrounds you. The above discussion provides substantial reasons to back the suspicion that the view which one person has of his or her environment will be different from those which others have of their environments. First, in purely physical terms, the view from one place in the social milieu will vary. Different objects will be in view; and, even when the same object is viewed, it will be from at least a slightly different angle. Second, what is seen depends on the direction in which the individual's sensory and brain mechanisms for observing the environment are focused. Third, these mechanisms vary from person to person, involving different ideas and word-meanings which are applied to processing the sensory inputs and creating an image of his or her environment within his or her brain. The differences between individuals' experiences may well magnify the differences in the ways that an otherwise identical experience are seen because the earlier experiences have led to differences in the ways the two individuals appreciate and define those experiences. Finally, and probably most importantly, social relations, which are a key part of anyone's social environment, can look quite different from their respective ends, so producing a variation in their environments.

Thus two individuals who regularly act with each other may consciously or otherwise adopt different ideas to explain and/or justify the practices they engage in at their end of the relationship because the relationship appears different from each end.

There are clear consequences in this for any theory of ideology. Such a theory may tell us how these ideas are generated. It may help explain the content of an individual's ideas – given adequate knowledge of their practices, social relations and the opinion leaders and idea-disseminating institutions with which they come into contact. But it is unlikely to uncover a uniform ideology of shared beliefs. Indeed it gives good reasons why key beliefs will vary within society and even between those who are interacting regularly with each other in (asymmetric) relations. But the view outlined here, of practices being developed and supported by social relations without the benefit of shared values and perceptions, indicates that we could get by without them. So that which makes these shared values and perceptions unlikely also makes them unnecessary.

The Individual, Self and Personality

This view of the interaction of people with environments sheds light on how personality and an individual's own concept of 'self' are generated and the problems with it.

1   It captures the very deep sense in which self and social context are inseparable. In a sense the social relation *includes* a part of each person, i.e. that part of each person's mind which contains the view which that person has of the social relationship. For it is by and through those mental elements that one person affects the other. The social relation is both a part of each person and a part of the society. Much of each individual is bound up in that person's 'end' of the many social relations of which an individual is a part (cf. Gramsci, 1971; De Michiel, 1983, p. 34).

2   It also captures the view that self and society are mutual products as individuals are formed by their social relations and society is constituted of the relations between individuals (Holland, 1977). However, there is an important difference. It is not society as a whole, as a totality, or even its institutions and/or sub-cultures that produce or constitute individuals but the particular relations of which the individual becomes a part.

3   The uniqueness and individuality of persons, though partly determined by genetic factors, has ample explanation in the infinite combinations and permutations of social relations of which individuals can form a part. This justifies and reinforces the criticism, so often levelled at systems theories of all three kinds, that they ignore the individuality of the people who had to fit into their systems. A disordered society and an infinite variety of unique individuals mutually produce and explain each other. An Althusserian system would produce the individuals who can reproduce that social system. A disordered society produces the varied individuals who produce a society that remains disordered.

4   It also explains the experience of individuality – an acute sense of uniqueness. Despite being a part of society through the social relations of which we are a part, our experience is of our 'end' of those social relations and, sitting on our side of the interpersonal communications barrier, is unique. We are also acutely aware of the processes going on in our own minds, so we have a conception of agency and free will. Agency may amount to no more than the active operation of our unique brains as uniqely constituted, reacting to the perception of external social relations by generating thought or action. Free will may be no more than our

experience of the range of 'choice' of action left open by those social relations from which the practical reasoning of our brain selects. It admits of as much variability as a free will and something which, as it represents our unique self created by our unique experience, is something to which we can remain strongly attached.

5   Self and personality are not entirely internal matters but are usually seen as concerned with the way an individual is related to others (Holland, 1977, p. 38). This feature is certainly provided by this model. Part of each individual's personality is tied up with each social relation, and (s)he usually sees part of the 'self' involved in each. But the way this theory accounts for this feature of self and personality also accounts for the tension within them. The social relations that drive an individual's actions this way and that (partly consciously and partly unconsciously) also drive the personality and self (e.g. the manipulation, coercion and inducement relations a businessman engages in present a tough-minded image which may conflict with his self-image deriving from the personal authority and persuasive relations of which he is both power-holder and power-subject with his own family). The construction (partly conscious and partly unconscious) of a unified image of 'self' from these conflicting glimpses is very difficult. Some of the relations will appear very important and (s)he will try to build his or her concept of self around the glimpses of it provided by those relations. Some relations provide glimpses of the self but do not lie well with the above – if possible the individual will try to change the relations to those which suit the self-image or withdraw from such relations to remove this image of self those relations supply. If this is not possible then the result maybe a feeling of 'alienation' from the part of self contained in that relation, or a self-hate reaction against that part of the self. A Freudian model would suggest that the latter is particularly common where the conflicting relations are strong and involve the one person. For example, in the 'anal stage' there is a conflict between the relationship in which the mother provides all the baby's needs on demand and that in which the mother coerces the baby into controlling its instinctual impulses. This leads to a conflict within the 'self' between the *id, ego* and *superego* that remains throughout life. Another possibility is that the individual does not complete the process of unification of self-image but has related the distinct and sometimes conflicting images of self in different situations (i.e. at the end of the social relations of which (s)he is a part). Thus the view of sociologists who see individuals acting through roles contains a grain of truth and Selznick's criticism that people act as whole persons rather than role-occupants goes too far (chapter 5.3). The unification is not so poor that individuals act only on their images of self involved in the batch of social relations connected with the role; they are affected by their images of self generated in other relations. Nor is it so

good that they do not present conflicting images of themselves to themselves and the world at large.

Micro- to macro-theory

So far the bare-bones theory being sketched in this chapter has covered the variety of interactions and relations between individual members of a society and the way they perceive them, the way individual actions are performed and practices are entered and the way values, 'ideologies' and the individual itself are generated from them. It has provided the 'micro' part of the theory and in doing so it has pointed to answers to some of the questions social theorists may be expected to ask of a theory. But there are other questions that macro-sociological theories have attempted to answer – questions about the overall picture of society, how one kind of society can be differentiated from another, how a loss of social peace is avoided, how change occurs, into what intermediate entities society can be divided, how they interact with each other, and how these macrosociological phenomena produce different environments, practices, relations, experiences, for those in different societies. As suggested in chapter 5.2, macro-theory has traditionally been systematic and has been separated from micro-theory. It is thus fairly easy for microsociologists who saw their subject matter as nonsystematic to go no further. As this chapter moves into its sketch of macro-theory, the nonsystematic image will be maintained but the dividing line will not be so clear-cut because the larger picture will be of the aggregation of those phenomena. Indeed the next issue deals with the subject matter which lies in both fields: the most significant relations in society. This may help the macro-theory to provide 'criteria of similarity and difference'. Depending on whether they are asymmetric or not it will also help explain the extent to which the experiences and environments of different people vary (and with that their ideas, values and points of view).

7.8   Relations of Production

The Marxist insight into the significance of the way goods are produced for understanding the nature of society and the way societies change has not been lost on later generations, although it has been watered down by Marxist and non-Marxist alike.

All Marxist theories assert the paramount importance of the *social relations of production* – the set of social relations between members of a community when engaged in the production of goods (most would, and all should, include services too). It is this *set* of social relations that constitute the 'mode of production'. Much of the variation in Marxist theories is due to the different ways in which these social relations are described – from what can come close to a pure empiricist description of the manufacturing process (Shaw, 1976, p. 28) to what amounts to a set of legal norms (Collins, 1982, p. 85). Naturally enough, the description adopted here sees those relations of production as a species of social relation. Like all social relations they have the general form that what one man is or does affects what another is or does. The relations are mostly power relations, predominantly authority relations. Consider a simple case where a 'capitalist' power-holder gives an order about how the 'worker' power-subject is to act towards certain physical objects – processing them as, and handing them to those to whom, the capitalist directs. The reasons for obeying the order are mixed because, like any other group of power-holders, capitalists have, deliberately and otherwise, extended the range of power relations they can exercise over employees. Initially the relation may be one of inducement – landlords, merchants or skilled artisans may have resources with which they can induce another to work for them. In addition, they may have forged personal links with the workers (giving them personal authority), gained a reputation as efficient users of economic resources (competent authority), or persuaded or manipulated workers to think that this is the best way to work. Finally, norms which treat the capitalist's control of what goes on in 'his' or 'her' factory as legitimate may have spread. They have also acquired the ability to make threats, sometimes of the crudest kind, but more often via political and legal institutions. The actual powers held and their sequence of acquisition are a matter of history. The general processes by which these further forms of power are acquired are a matter for the theory of social change (*infra*). There are other relations too: unintended effects (e.g. the capitalist seeking profits may impoverish his/her employees) and anticipatory reactions (e.g. the owner of the small plant who doesn't even conceive of the 'loyal' workers wanting to strike whereas they all know that (s)he would sack them all if they did).

The relations of production, in any mode of production, are a *set* of social relations involving different levels within the same production enterprise. These relations point in both directions. The manufacturer may be the power-holder in several power relations involving his workers but in other areas of activity they may have power over him. They may enjoy the power of the strike weapon (seen as coercion by management and many others) and what Veblen (1925) calls the 'conscientious withdrawal of efficiency' (a form of either coercion or manipulation). Just as capitalists seek to extend the forms of power exercised over workers, so will workers over capitalists. The workers may also cause many unintended effects and there may be normative relations in which one side or the other is inhibited from action because of similar values held by its members. The ratio of power to other social relations may be higher than in other sets of social relations because the constant conflicts will make each side less likely to feel constrained from actions in their perceived interests, but all types of social relations will still be present.

It is axiomatic in Marxist theory that the environments of workers and capitalists are radically different, and when the relations of production are put in the above terms we can clearly see why. These relations look quite different from each end (Hirst, 1979, p. 103), and the *effects* of these relations on the environments of 'capitalists' and 'workers' are very different, providing an abundance of material goods to the former and far fewer to the latter. These environmental differences lead to the generation of different ideas, values and attitudes which lead to different perceptions of those environments and the tendency to adopt different 'ideologies' from those available. *Classes* are defined in terms of the relations of production – a class includes all those at one end of the same type of relation of production. The similarities in their environments mean that they are likely to have similar values, ideas, perceptions of the world and 'point of view' and to act in similar ways. However, the variations in the environments of different capitalists (the sort of enterprise they are in, their wealth, other social relations and especially the particular mix of relations they have with their workers) will ensure differences in those values, ideas, perceptions and points of view. The same will be true of different sets of workers.

Marx dealt in detail with only one set of relations of production. Many have taken this to imply that there is only one set in any society, or that one set is so dominant that the rest of society can be explained by its effects (e.g. the hegemony of the class that drew surplus from those relations, or the ideas adopted by participants in those relations). The problem with such systematic totalizing theories led many to seek insights into society from other phenomena before full value could be extracted from Marx's insights into productive relations. The Marxist theory of history deals with the rise and fall of relations of production and their attendant classes. Thus at any one time there could easily be four classes – the two defined by the new mode of production and the two defined by the old. Indeed there may be what some call 'survivals' (Collins, 1982) of even earlier modes of production. These may provide better explanations of the nature and origins of some current relations. For example, it could be argued that the relations within most professions do not conform to the capitalist mode but are variants of the distinctive productive relations of guilds (differences being due to the different environments and consequent characteristics of the participants). Likewise, the role of women engaged in unpaid domestic labour has little similarity to serfs or wage-labourers. However, it is more than reminiscent of the place of the wife in the old 'familial' relations of production[7] in which (male) heads of families directed the productive activities of family members and the product was distributed largely on the basis of his (rather biased) perceptions of need. Such relations of production once accounted for most of the goods and services produced and consumed, although most of any surplus was skimmed by local lords in feudal relations. 'Survival' may not be the best term for such a mode of production: it may be taken to imply something residual that remains today only because it was there before. As Delphy (1984) rightly argues, the domestic mode of production currently accounts for a large proportion of the goods and services produced and it exists today because of current, not historical, forces. On the other hand, seeing it as a continuation of a pre-existing mode of production is no less useful than seeing capitalist relations of production developing from the twelfth century; and given the ways in which existing productive practices are repeated and supported by relations of production, any pre-existing relations *will* be entrenched (see *infra*). The real problem with the term 'survival' (and 'dominant mode of production') is that it obscures the number and significance of modes of production.

If we look at relations of production which produce services and the relations of distribution and exchange (which formed Marx's trinity of key relations) we see the possibilities of yet more classes, all with their own sets of values, perceptions and point of view. In the notes which formed the basis of the last two pages of *Capital* Marx listed ten classes (1967, p. 862) in nineteenth-century England. It is not clear whether this was his final tally or was just where he wearily put down his pen. However, the fruitfulness of a view of society involving multiple relations of production, the multiple classes and ideas that result, and the complex interaction between them,[8] was indicated in some of Marx's best descriptions of contemporary politics and by some later Marxists (e.g. Poulantzas, 1975) and commentators (e.g. Avineri, 1968; Craib, 1984) and those who use Marxist methods of analysis (e.g. Delphy, 1984, with feminism, and Fitzpatrick, 1983, with third-world societies). Marxist views of relations of production and the classes at each end can become a potent part of the description of a disordered society rather than the core of an unbelievable description of a systematic one that was rejected in chapter 5. It will be a key part of the description given below.

7.9 Institutions

Society consists of the individuals within it and the social relations between them. However, we cannot understand society by looking at all of these separately – we would never have time to do it and we would be none the wiser for it once we had. Fortunately the social relations between individual members of the society are not completely haphazard. Some sets of relations can usefully be distinguished and, as such, recognized as institutions.

There are two common uses of the word 'institution' and both are useful in social description. The first is a set of particular social relations, often found between pairs of people. Capitalist relations of production constitute such a set – the institution of 'wage labour'. Another favourite example is the 'institution' of marriage, consisting of the set of social relations commonly found between husband and wife, although these may be seen as partly productive relations too (*supra*). As such, they can be a significant part of the environment of each person and can go a long way towards explaining how each thinks and acts. Of course, the most commonly found combination of relations between husbands and wives do not determine the *actual* relations between particular husbands and wives. Given this rider, it can be useful to look on all those who stand at one end of such a set of relations as a group or class (chapter 5.10).

The second use of the word 'institution', and the use adopted in this book, is the web or matrix of social relations between a set of persons in closer, more frequent and more intense interaction with other members of the set than with nonmembers (cf. Eisenstadt, 1968). Corporations, government departments, courts, prisons, trade unions, political parties and individual families are examples. On such a definition the boundaries are vague – each institution is likely to be a part of another institution and include parts or all of several other institutions. But this is true of any of the examples we come to ponder. The constellation of relations between a set of persons that is called an institution will be based on descriptive utility on one or more of the following criteria: (1) the relations between the members are particularly strong or numerous, (2) the relations between members of this group and outsiders tend to take on a particular characteristic, (3) the relations between the members enable some members to act with greater strength or power against or upon outsiders because the actions of, or the resources held by, other members can be mobilized against those outsiders. We might loosely say that the institution's existence places greater power in the hands of some of its members or that they act through these persons.

The last is the most common reason for the identification of institutions. It is a consequence of the internal social relations implied by the definition. The web of relations will include a number of chains of relations; some of the most common are 'chains of command', a series of authority relations by which one man acts and affects others with whom he has no direct relationship. These are common in corporations; some positivists thought they had found them in law. Other chains become evident only as effects pass through them. In response to outside circumstances a set of intra-institutional social relations is activated. The social relations that constitute the institution and the chains of relations within it have all the characteristics of social relations discussed above. They will be as mixed and varied as social relations in general rather than purely coercive (Etzioni, 1971) or legitimate. The environments of the parties to these relations will tend to differ, as will their perceptions and points of view. Because much of the members' social interaction is with others in the institution, and ideas will flow more freely between members in such constant interaction, there will tend to be more similarity of environments, perceptions and points of view among members than between members and outsiders. These similarities will lead to talk of the 'institutional point of view' and are part of the explanation for the pursuit of 'institutional interests' (chapter 5.6). However, the differences are sufficient to explain why institutions can be understood in those terms.

Individual members of an institution will also be linked by social relations to others *outside* the institution. It is through those social relations in which members of the institution are power-subjects, anticipators and value-holders that the institution is affected by those outside it: and it is through those social relations in which the members are power-holders, reactors and value–beneficiaries that the institution has its effects. Not all the effects achieved through the latter relations could be called 'institutional'; the relationship of a policeman to his wife is not an external relation of the police force, and if Constable P beats Mrs P it will not usually be seen as an effect of that institution – although contrary argument may often be possible (figure 7.2a). The effects of an institution typically involve the activation of a chain of relations between members of an institution before the effect is achieved on an outsider. If Chief Commissioner A orders B (his or her senior officer on the spot) to disperse a demonstration, and if the same Constable P hits a demonstrator, then *that* is one of the affects of the institution. The effect is gained through the activation of two mixed authority relations within the institution and a pure relation of force between P and the demonstrator (figure 7.2b). Even in an apparently isolated interaction involving a member of the institution and an outsider, the effect can still be seen as an institutional one if it is largely caused by social relations within the institution (e.g. when an off-duty policeman sees someone breaking into a store and arrests him, the action is the result of his police training and his standing orders, both received through intra-institutional, social relations (figure 7.2c).

Of course, in none of these cases will the chain of interaction have 'originated' with A (in a world of continuous and mixed causation, such

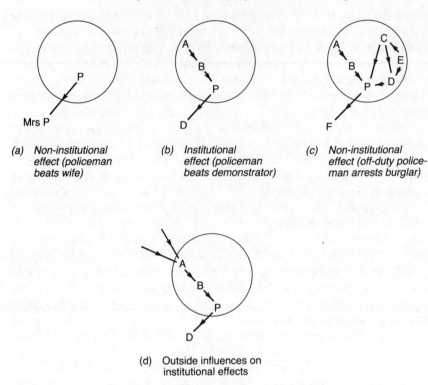

(a) Non-institutional
    effect (policeman
    beats wife)

(b) Institutional
    effect (policeman
    beats demonstrator)

(c) Non-institutional
    effect (off-duty police-
    man arrests burglar)

(d) Outside influences on
    institutional effects

Figure 7.2 Institutional effects and interpersonal interactions

original causes are best left to metaphysics). (S)he will probably have been affected by social relations such as the anticipated unfavourable reaction of politicians or ratepayers if the demonstration appears out of hand (figure 7.2d).

This raises an important point about officials. Holding a key institutional position may greatly increase the strength and number of the social relations in which they are power-holder, affector or value-beneficiary. But they are also subject to, and limited by, a large number of social relations with people, both inside and outside the institution, which impose practical limitations on their action. They are rarely free to use their powers as they choose and, to the extent that others have sufficient power over them to direct their use of that power, it is not really *their* power at all. But they are still usually left with a significant *range* of actions to choose from. By making a choice from within that range an official can *shift the overall effect* of the institution on its social environment. It is for this reason that conflict over such positions is an endemic factor of social institutions.

This image of institutions as made up of these social relations seems to accommodate the paradigmatic examples of institutions listed earlier. But it also helps to explain why they do not possess the supposedly key characteristic of other conceptions of institutions – a purpose, function or goal.

The conception of legal institutions in terms of their *function* was rejected in chapter 5.6. The same sorts of arguments can be applied to institutions in general, especially when they are seen in terms of webs of social relations. However clear any initial goals of founders or members may be, those of new members will not necessarily be the same and cannot be ensured to be the same. They join for their own reasons, usually provided by the inducements offered, favourable reactions antici- pated, or the power relations they hope to exercise through the institu- tion. Even if institutions are created within a group holding common goals, the creation of social relations within the institution and external social relations with non-members changes their environments. These factors give most (though not all) a reason for strengthening the external relations of the institution through which it affects the outside world (although the fact that these relations will be through individuals intro- duces a conflict – those individuals will want to maximize their range of choice in the exercise of those relations while others will want to mini- mize it). But as the internal relations of an institution multiply, they provide a greater diversity of environments for the members, and make the sharing of goals and interests less likely.

This matrix of internal social relations, which provides the source of an institution's strength, is also the source of its weakness in carrying out its goals. It makes possible the pooling of resources to magnify the action of individual officials through whom the institution affects its social environ- ment. But this must be done through chains of relations that include several members whose perceptions and purposes vary, and who are subject to social relations emanating from outside the institution that limit the effect of the chains of relations on the above officials. Furthermore, in a matrix of social relations, different chains of relations pass through the same person, some pushing one way, some the other. Finally, the institu- tion's resources, though considerable, are in the hands of its members (partly because of the impossibility of complete concentration and partly because subordinate members have to be given resources in order to achieve the effects expected of them). But these very same resources are the basis of some of the social relations in which subordinate members are power-holders, reactors, etc., and their superiors are power-subjects, anticipators, etc. – these give subordinates the ability to resist their superiors' attempts to control their behaviour. Thus relations in a chain will be, like all social relations, only *partially* effective. By the time we reach the end of an internal chain of relations where effects on the environment are supposed to be achieved, the individuals concerned may be achieving quite different effects from those intended. Sometimes the chain of relations breaks down and no effects are achieved at all. Furthermore, where the institutional effect must be achieved through several such persons acting on the institutional environment, they may be acting at cross-purposes (Trubek, 1977, p. 539). Thus the overall effect the institution has is likely to be rather crude. Institutions are powerful but very blunt and unwieldy instruments. It is not always clear *whose* instruments they are and for what purpose, if any, they are wielded.

Structural-functionalists may choose to look at *some* of the effects they claim the institution has and dub them the 'function' of the institution. But the lack of common purpose makes the fulfilment of that function problematic; and the disparate nature of institutional effects makes the selection of one such function a distortion of how the institution affects society.

Another justification for treating institutions as having a purpose is offered by Honoré (he uses the term 'group', but it covers the same sort of phenomena as 'institution' in this book). He rejects the idea that the purpose will be consensually held but considers co-ordination of action as conclusive evidence of a common purpose (1975, p. 169). The meaning of co-ordination is, in his own words, 'liberal' – one action following another as in a game of tennis. This is a little too liberal. It is in the nature of causality that events follow each other. What is clearly meant is that the nature of the activity (or, as this book puts it, the relations between the people engaged in it) leads to a sequence of actions. But the same could be said of a street-fight, in which one punch follows another. One action follows another because of the nature of the activity and the relations between the parties, yet no one could find a common purpose. There is not even a desire for the interaction to continue as each action is intended to *stop* the interaction. Honoré's next example is of workers on a building site who co-ordinate their action to erect a building although they have a variety of reasons for taking part in the activity and conflicting interests in how and at what speed it is completed. This shifts the emphasis on to the result, or *effects*, of the activity rather than the way in which one action follows another. But if the institution concerned is a construction company it will continue after the completion of the building. If it is merely a group of workers employed solely for the job then they may have a real, felt and actively pursued common purpose of delaying the completion indefinitely. More fundamentally, in either case the completion of the building is only one of the effects and results of the activities within the institution. Other effects include the employment of the construction workers (this may be the principal effect and, in 'job creation' schemes, that which is primarily intended), pay is handed out, taxes are paid, dividends are given, materials are diverted to private use. Just as in functionalist theories, the purpose chosen is only one of the institution's many effects, and looking only at how that one effect is produced by interrelated actions distorts the image of interaction within the institution.

Honoré argues that the achievement of a common purpose requires and stimulates the co-ordination of action (1975, p. 177). But this does not mean we can infer a common purpose wherever there is 'co-ordination', for that co-ordination may result from other factors. First and foremost, it may merely involve a sequence of actions, each of which affects the next. The subsequent action may, in turn, affect the initial actor (as in the tennis match or street-fight) or may go on to affect other actors through a chain of social relations. It may be co-ordination imposed by a third party who uses power relations to affect the behaviour of each (e.g. a slave-driver coerces two members of the chain-gang to throw rocks to each other, or a foreman induces site-workers to do the same). Finally, actions may be co-ordinated because various factors lead one person to engage in a practice of which another becomes aware and takes advantage.

Even when members do co-ordinate their actions to achieve common purposes they will not necessarily be common to the institution. Much organization theory is concerned with the strength of sub-groups in institutions and their tendency to conflict with each other and prevent the achievement of institutional purposes. These are especially prevalent in large permanent organizations with low staff-turnover, low technology and a differentiated social setting (Froman, 1980) – virtually a blueprint for major legal and social institutions.

The beliefs that members hold about the functions or common purposes of the institution are important and may be one of the key factors affecting their actions and interactions with other members. But this will happen even if they have different beliefs about those functions and purposes. In such cases the institution will probably not fulfil *either* function or achieve *either* supposedly common purpose. But this is no bar to the continuation of either interaction or institution. People also have beliefs about the existence of institutions and what they can get or achieve by interacting with them. This leads to an increase in interaction among members of institutions. This is borne out by Finnis's archetypical institution) – a family. There is intense and frequent interaction within families that live under the same roof. The belief its members have that they constitute a family is an important stimulus to interaction. Yet its members would find it extraordinarily difficult to agree what common purpose a family has.

Institutions involve both more and less than actions co-ordinated to achieving purposes. They involve more because the purposes are so many and the institution continues even when a purpose is achieved. They involve less because those purposes, if achieved at all, are so ambiguously and partially achieved.

The objection might be taken that, despite all the above, people do link institutions to ideas, functions, goals and purposes. This *could* be partly due to manipulation as key officials justify their positions and the resources the institution extracts from others. But it is due more to the fact that individuals are concerned with only some of the effects of institutions – generally the effects the institution has on them or those they hope to achieve through the institution. This selectivity is natural for individuals indulging in their own practical reasoning in pursuit of their activity. But it cannot be justified for the social observer who must notice the variety of such practical reasoning and activities within each institution and the consequences it has for its operation.

For the social observer, the importance of institutions is not the allegedly shared purposes of its members but the fact that they typically involve interaction between those with differing purposes for the institution and different purposes, norms, even expectations and interpretations of the interactions between themselves.

Likewise, for the social observer, the importance of institutions is *not* their ability to fulfil goals, purposes or functions. Their importance lies in their ability to concentrate, albeit partially, via their internal social relations, the resources of their members into the hands of a few members who interact with the outside world. These individuals cannot exercise those resources as they please; they are subject to internal social relations, especially the chains of such relations that link them to key officials. They are also subject to the social relations they have with others, especially officials in similar positions in other institutions. It is a useful shorthand to say that society consists of a network of institutions. But it should be remembered that those institutions are not black boxes with arrows coming in and out. They act through individuals who do not experience institutions as such, but as social relations with other individuals. Institutions inject *some* organization into social life, but only *some* and, as we will see in the next two sections, they provide a good deal of the *disorganization* and *disorder* of social life too.

7.10   Groups

A group was defined earlier as a set of people at one end of a type of social relation. Unlike members of an institution, there will not necessarily be any social relations between members of such groups. Indeed, groups are defined in terms of the relations members have with persons different from themselves. These groups can be very important socially because they are likely to share certain characteristics on which could be founded common subjective interests and other values (chapter 5.7). But different groups are likely to have subjective interests that are antagonistic to those of other groups (in the sense that their subjective interests cannot be realized simultaneously). This is essentially because the asymmetry of the social relations between men are a source of difference rather than similarity. Most social relations appear different from each end, they affect each individual differently, so that the environments of the two people involved in a social relation are made more, rather than less, different because of the interaction. These environmental differences lead to different perceptions of that environment and to different values and ideas generally. The various relations of production are especially important because of the part work plays in the lives of most and because they usually lead to a differential distribution of the social product. This differential distribution produces clashes of subjective interest, not only via its effects on the resources and environments of the classes at either end of the relations of production, but also quite directly. There will always be someone who proposes alternative social arrangements that would reduce the differential distribution and those who believe they would benefit under them have a subjective interest in their introduction. It may or may not be true that in the proposed alternative the poorest classes would be better off. Dr Pangloss might claim that we have reached a maximum distribution of social benefits, but the acceptance of that argument by the 'worst-off' is problematic. This conflict of interest does not cease with the aspirations of the worst-off. If someone does accept the existence of inequality, there is every chance that (s)he will want to be one of the beneficiaries of that inequality. Even the wealthiest classes are subject to a desire for more: first, because of the general tendency of all people to make comparisons with those better off rather than worse off than themselves; and second, because, once someone believes (s)he is entitled to, or is prepared to seek, more goods than others, there is no logical point at which the desired superiority of possessions should stop.

If members of a group come to *see* these subjective interests as common interests based on common characteristics they become *subjectively* a group, they have 'group consciousness'. Where they *mobilize* their resources (e.g. votes, money, labour, skills or time) towards the realization of those subjective interests, they can provide a significant social force. This may occur spontaneously – the individuals become aware of a subjective interest and act independently to achieve it. But such action will be uncoordinated and unlikely to enjoy much success.

Far more effective is the mobilization of groups by institutions. Frequently it is an institution that *arouses* the group to awareness of common characteristics and subjective interests. The institution may be specifically set up to do so or may be an opportunist institution (especially a political party) which sees the potential for mobilizing a group. Once mobilized, the subjective group may then be said to exercise power through that institution, although all the caveats about achieving purposes through institutions should be inserted here – *especially* in the latter case. Indeed, sometimes such mobilization may do more to increase the institutions' resources than to extend the power of groups.

In all cases only some of the group's resources will be mobilized, and among different groups there can be wide variation in the degree of mobilization. There are many reasons for this (Olsen, 1971). However, the more directly the position of a group is threatened, the more likely it is to become a subjective group and mobilize or be mobilized against the persons or institutions threatening its interests. Any ensuing conflict strengthens the group's cohesion and organization (Coser, 1956). This is so well known that other persons and institutions will frequently modify their actions in order to avoid these anticipated reactions. If the group is unaware of this then it is a social relation of anticipatory reaction: if it is aware then it is a case of power. These constitute important social relations and strong practical reasons for the anticipators.

These relations include cases where actions are modified because of the anticipated reaction of as yet unformed groups as well as existing ones. In such cases the anticipating group is reacting to perceived resources and willingness to mobilize them for action. The anticipation is merely of a two-stage rather than a one-stage process. An example can be found in Hough and Fainsod's book on the USSR (1979): they argue that much government policy was based on avoiding action that will mobilize the as yet disorganized and passive population against them. It is also common for institutions and groups under threat from another to attempt to limit the latter's effectiveness by making it more difficult to mobilize or by affecting the form the mobilization takes (e.g. compulsory strike ballots).

Yet members of a group whose interests would be threatened by the mobilization of other groups frequently do *not* anticipate the threat that such mobilization poses. Consequently, they and 'their' institutions may unwittingly act in such a way as to provoke it. The relative lack of organization of groups, *especially* those not subject to immediately perceived threat (Coser, 1956), means that, even if most members of the group perceive the threat, the few who do not may act independently to promote it unwittingly.

Thus the form and extent of group mobilization is affected by the action of other groups and institutions as well as by the characteristics and interests of the group itself. And whether mobilized or not, social groups are important components of any social description.

7.11 An Overall View: The Social Mêlée

Society is composed of individuals and the interactions between them. Macrosociological theory must provide an overall model or picture of those interactions. Parts of that picture are provided by the relations that have the greatest effects on individual's values, beliefs and environments and the similarity of those effects which produce groups and classes. Other parts of the picture are provided by the institutional webs of relations which partially mobilize resources and magnify the effects of their officials' action. Descriptions of society in terms of systems of commonly held norms or systems of institutions with interlocking and complementary functions have already been rejected.

The nonsystematic picture to be drawn in their place is naturally complex but the single word that most captures it is 'mêlée': a fluid, constantly changing set of interactions in a complex struggle between a large number of groups and institutions. The members of those groups and institutions will have conflicting subjective interests and other values which they will pursue and defend, sometimes individually but usually through institutions.

Institutions will be in conflict with each other because of the conflicting interests, not only between members of different institutions, but also between members of the various groups whom the institutions have mobilized. Their resources and power will vary, but something like Humean conditions (Hart, 1961, p. 190) apply. No institution is so powerful that its key decision-makers can ignore other institutions in choosing how to act. (In the only apparent exceptions, where 'totalitarian' states are regarded as single institutions, the same Humean conditions apply to the powerful sub-institutional groupings within it.) The mêlée is not a Hobbesian war of all against all. There is only a degree of organization of persons into institutions. More importantly, there is not all-out 'war'. Nor is there any likelihood or generally any apprehension of it. Indeed the nature of institutions would make it very difficult for them to take part in one. First, there are all the difficulties of directing the activity of institutions towards singular purposes. The basic problem for any institution is that, being a web of mixed relations between different persons with different environments and values, there is rarely a consensus or unity of purpose within that institution. Those in key positions can influence the action of other members by exercising the power that they have over them, but the range of actions they can demand is limited. Second, though the total resources held by a group's members may be quite massive, these resources are rarely, if ever, fully mobilized. There are many reasons for this:

1   Individuals may not realize that there are many like-minded individuals to mobilize.
2   Commitment of resources to the mobilizing institution means that the group members will have to forego the benefits of alternative uses for those resources.
3   Even if greater benefits could be achieved by pushing resources, there is always the temptation to be a 'free rider'.
4   Even if individuals are prepared to put their resources at the disposal of a mobilizing institution, there may be several such institutions for each group and they may see themselves as members of several groups with conflicting demands on their resources.
5   The inability of institutions to achieve intended purposes and their tendency to pursue their own interests is well enough known to inhibit the size and number of contributions.
6   Mobilization of large groups itself requires resources.
7   Many resources involve the activation of power relations over others; these may be effective in normal times but not at times of extreme conflict.

The actual degree of mobilization will vary for different groups and at different times. Conflict tends to increase mobilization of any group. If a perceived threat develops the group will, unless its members believe that the threat cannot be met, probably become more mobilized. This is a factor that parties who seek to mobilize the working class must remember. The privileged groups are by no means fully mobilized against them. Mobilization of one side's resources is pointless if it provokes the other side to mobilize even more (especially if it stimulates coalitions of subjectively threatened groups – *infra*). Also important is the rate of mobilization of resources and the capacity to switch them to different purposes. This may enable an apparently weaker group to pursue its own interests successfully to the prejudice of a stronger group. But neither even approaches full mobilization, which would entail the complete commitment of all resources to the conflict.

Thus the intensity of conflict is reduced by the disorder within the combatant groups and institutions. This is the complete reverse of those social theories which postulate that social peace must be the result of order and common values. Here we see that social peace is *not* aided by common values (which are found in the groups of persons with conflicting interests) or order (which is found in the institutions that mobilize these groups). Instead, social peace is preserved by the *disorder* which hampers the combatants in their struggle. This is what I call the 'sociable unsociability' of people and it is more central than their 'unsociable sociability', the propensity to organize for conflict, that Dahrendorf needlessly laments (chapter 6.3).

The mêlée is not a conflict between two sides. It is not simply a 'class' war. It is a disorganized struggle between many different institutions and groups with the frequently noted limitations that this imposes on the extent and decisiveness of conflict (Cotterrell, 1984, p. 81; Foucault, 1980; Stone, 1966; Eisenstadt, 1985; cf. Unger, 1976). The first reason for the large number of combatants is the number of social relations which are significant enough to produce pairs of important subjective groups – workers and capitalists, consumers and retailers, husbands and wives. Following Marx, the relations of production are regarded as the *most* significant but there are likely to be several relations of production in any one society (chapter 7.9). Some may claim other relations are as significant (e.g. race and sex). To the extent that such distinctions are not essentially economic (thereby representing versions of the above relations of production), these relations add more groups to the mêlée. The second reason for the number of combatants is the divisions of interest within those groups at either end of a social relation. A third reason is the tendency of institutions to perceive and pursue their own interests. Whatever purposes or interest groups that institutions are created to serve, there is the tendency for them to develop institutional interests of their own. Even institutions that are founded to mobilize the resources and further the interests of the same group frequently develop their own interests and values to the point that they conflict with each other as well as other institutions (e.g. trade unions and the Labour Party).

The numerous combatants are involved not in a general conflagration but in diverse and specific struggles (Foucault, 1980, p. 123; Craib, 1984, p. 154), each threatening or defending the subjective interests of one or more institutions or groups. Some of these struggles are over the distribution of spoils from a common activity. Some are over attempts to influence the actions of officials with the power to make decisions affecting group interests. Other struggles are over attempts to influence the filling of key (official) positions. As we saw in chapter 7.9, officials cannot do just as they please but, within the limitations imposed by the external and internal social relations to which they are subject, they have a range of choice, making the attempt to influence appointments to such positions worthwhile. The outcomes of such attempts depend not only on the size of, and speed with which, resources can be applied to the struggle, but also on the internal power relations within the target institution. These battles are fought out within the institution and the results are naturally affected by the terrain over which they are fought. Institutions that are, in general, weak may have special advantages in certain target institutions and may succeed where generally stronger institutions fail. Of course, the network of social relations in which each institution is immersed will include some relations by which it can bring other institutions to its aid to create conditions in defence and promotion of some of their interests. This is a matter of *cross*-institutional or intra-group mobilization. But it will be hampered by all the problems of the latter and, unless the interests of the members of the other institution are affected, these problems will be magnified because it is at one further remove. The mobilization is likely to become weaker the further it moves from the few institutions or groups whose members' interests are directly affected by the outcome of that particular struggle. Thus the shockwaves of conflict tend to be damped as they pass through the social mêlée. In the rare cases where this is not so, and mobilization of resources to the struggle runs right through society, the conflict will polarize the society into two rival camps in a civil war (or perhaps a civil version of the 'cold war'). But in most cases the relative disinterest of citizens in such conflict prevents this, and turns the disinterest of citizens from a 'problem' for society (Luhmann, 1985) into a factor that preserves it.

The image of society outlined above has similarities to a view of group conflict common among American political scientists. In this view, conflicting parties fight for political power by attempting to mobilize the votes and other resources of various social groups, this conflict being regulated by, and subject to, commonly held rules and conventions about its conduct (Dahl, 1961; Coser, 1956, p. 121). But even this minimum liberal consensus about the 'rules of the game' is rejected. Although political scientists may lecture and write about them, they are certainly not much discussed by the politicians who supposedly practise them. When they are discussed, members of different political institutions tend to refer to different ones. The opposition will emphasize full disclosure and discussion in the house, the government will emphasize the confidentiality of ministerial discussions. Conservatives will emphasize claimed constitutional restraints on the exercise of power, reformists the principles of parliamentary sovereignty. Even when the same rule or convention is referred to, it will often be formulated differently or given a different meaning (e.g. ministerial responsibility). This is another example of how the same norm may appear different to different people: and we see again that if beliefs restrain action, they tend to be different beliefs for different people.

But let us assume that there *were* such commonly held rules. Such rules would be unlikely to hold a key place in the value systems of politicians. The goals of personal power, or of advancing the cause in which they believe, are likely to be valued more highly than the goal of 'doing it the right way'. People are not participants in the political process because of their belief in political rules (*pace* Winch, 1958, p. 131; in an ironically Winchean way, that would be to miss the 'point' of the activity for each side, which is conflict!). They are participants because of what can be achieved by political action. Such single-minded determination is possibly even a prerequisite for political success. Thus any rules would be likely to lose in choices between following them and achieving personal or party goals.

These rules would also figure minimally in the consciousness of ordinary citizens. Public discussion about rules and conventions is generally subdued. Politicians do not like to use the media time they have agreeing with their opponents. Alleged rules and conventions are usually raised only when one side accuses the other of a breach; hence they come to the public eye as partisan issues (Sampford, 1980, 1987a). Since those who lean towards one party rather than the other normally do so because they give it more attention and have greater trust and respect for it and its aims, they are more likely to adopt that party's view on the issue. Therefore, the loss of votes will not be a significant restraint on unconventional action. In other areas of social conflict, we will expect even fewer rules governing conflict, and that those who support a person or institution on substantive issues will also adopt their interpretation of the rules governing their pursuit.

Commonly held rules would act not as internal constraints on social action so much as weapons that can be used against someone who can be accused of breaching them. If, as argued here, there is no such consensus then we are left with the fact that individuals have values which affect their actions, but those values vary from person to person and are no more likely to lead to co-operation or mutual limitation than conflict. Conflict is not limited by commonly held rules. It is limited by each party's perception of how far conflict can successfully be pursued before their interests would be prejudiced by the anticipated reactions of others (whether directly or via other institutions, like courts, and unions, that they can mobilize).

The complex interaction between such heterogeneous entities that constitutes the social mêlée is hard to picture. Most analogies will be poor because they will be taken from the lower levels of social life, which tend to be more organised – clubs, organizations, games like chess and cricket and, the perennial favorite, ships at sea. One image that may be enlightening is of a football game in which all the different codes are being played at once. There are many sides of differing sizes whose players have different abilities. Some play as individuals, although most try to join or start teams. There are no rules to cover the overall game but some teams have their own rules to which they generally adhere until they can clearly see the advantage of not doing so. The teams themselves do not play very well together because, although there are often captains, the 'organization' of teams is complex and several vice-captains may pass on instructions to ordinary players that bear little relation to the instructions they received from the captains. Players are usually involved in several teams at once, which limits the extent to which they can devote their time or effort to any one of them. They are taking part for a variety of (usually personal) reasons, and some did not want to play in that team or play that code of football at all.

The objects of the players vary considerably within, but especially between teams. Several want to put the ball between certain posts (or a different part of those posts). But most others have targets of varying size and shape all around the field. Some are playing with different balls. Whatever their object, players must take note of the actions of other players and teams. In dribbling a soccer ball, it would be foolish not to watch for the line of rugby players coming down the field. The rugby players may make it obvious to the soccer players that they had better move out of the way. But usually the soccer players will move by themselves without the rugby players ever realizing that they were there. Players may take notice for a different reason. If a player has threaded his/her way through the packs to score the kind of goals other players desire, (s)he may be taken as a 'role-model' or 'trail-blazer'. Players who follow his or her path may score similar goals if they have similar resources and if the state of play is sufficiently unchanged. They may find the beaten track easier to follow because others have adjusted their own play to assist or at least steer clear of those coming along it. They may find the track harder if those who do not share those goals are lying in wait to tackle them.

There may be co-operation between the teams but each team eventually goes its own way. There are umpires but it is very hard for them to decide what rules to use or even what it is to be an umpire. They are often ignored. To be more effective the umpires may be partially organized into teams, but invariably they get involved in the play. There are several scoreboards manned by historians and sociologists, but they have a nightmare in deciding what to record. Their team affiliations make it difficult for them to decide what it is that they should be recording and those who try to write down everything contract writer's cramp and terminal confusion. In any case there are no boundaries to the game so the scoring is a part of what is being scored – social life can never be a purely a spectator sport. One could continue: the more complex the picture becomes, the more like society it seems, but such is the nature of society.

The social mêlée is seen as disordered conflict. *The disorganizing influences that produce the conflict* (the asymmetry of social relations, the indeterminacy of language, the variety of environments that produce differing values and interests among the members of different groups and institutions) *also operate to frustrate and mute it* (producing the relative inability of groups to mobilize the resources of their members and of institutions to concentrate their effect). The inconclusiveness of the struggle over the short term leads to a *social inertia* in which certain interests of groups tend to become *entrenched* because of the inability of others to dislodge them (Riesman, 1951, p. 244).

To state that a person's or group's interest is entrenched is to sum the effects of all the relevant social relations on one aspect of their fortunes. Interests are entrenched either if they can be successfully defended or if they will not be attacked. The strength of both attack and defence will be largely determined by the resources of the attacking/defending party, the resources of those on whose support it can call in such a conflict, the extent and speed of their mobilization, and the power relations in which they can be deployed.

Interests are being defended all the time but few will be under attack at any one time. A common reason for this is that those who are in key positions in the institutions whose members would benefit from a successful attack have considered the question and concluded that the interest could, in fact, be defended. Here we see relations of power or anticipated reactions at work. The calculations may be right or wrong but they have the same effect in restraining the attack. As indicated in chapter 7.4, it is easy to overestimate the strength of others because you do not take account of the fact that *their* ability to mobilize their members' resources may be just as limited as *yours*. Wrongly assumed strength is not disproved and provides another source of interest entrenchment. However, it is not suggested that this is a major determinant. Those in key positions on either side usually do have a fair idea of each other's strength because one of the results of conflict is that the parties establish each other's power (Coser, 1956, p. 137).

The discussion in chapter 7.7 indicates other reasons for the non-challenge of interests. First, there are all the practices generated by the social relations in which those with the entrenched interest are power-holders, reactors and value–beneficiaries. These will tend to generate practices that do not challenge the interest. Many potential challengers will adopt these practices either because *they* are subject to the relations themselves (and hence have little choice), or because they adopt the practices of *others* who are so subject. Second, these practices have the effects on values noted in chapter 7.7 which produce value-effect relations that may prevent action challenging certain interests. If previous practices had left the relevant interest unaffected, values will have been adopted justifying these practices which are, if not supportive, at least not inimical to the interest. Third, perceptions depend partly on experiences. Someone who has not had any experiences in which (s)he was affected by the entrenched interest may not even be aware of his/her conflicting interest. Fourth, there are 'ideological' limitations – the potential challengers may not have been exposed to ideas congruent with or conducive to the challenge of the relevant interest. The ideas that are actually disseminated are those of certain 'ideological' institutions and individual opinion leaders, many of whom may actually have the relevant interest and who would not conceive of, let alone disseminate, the ideas facilitating its challenge.

Finally, even among those who are individually opposed to the interest (or rule, institution, state, etc.) ignorance of how many others are opposed and a presumption that they are not opposed can prevent challenges that would be successful (Luhmann, 1985, p. 202). This entrenchment of interests exists for the weak as well as the strong. Although the weak have, by definition, few resources and little power to defend their interests, they also have few resources for more powerful groups to plunder. The taking of those resources and the attack of the weak group's interests may not be worth the costs involved. (There is the 'opportunity cost', using the resources for that rather than another purpose, and the costs imposed by the weak in the resistance they put up.) A point would normally be reached, even for very weak groups, where attacks on their interests would fail. These attacks would be so prejudicial to what little they have left that most of their resources would be mobilized to its defence; whereas few members of any resource-rich group could be mobilized for so unlucrative a challenge. In such cases a greater proportion of the weaker group's fewer resources outweighs a lower proportion of the potential challenger's greater resources. Thus even where there is a great disparity of power and resources the social mêlée can produce social inertia.

7.12 Social Change

The last section depicted society as a mêlée of conflicting groups and institutions. Social peace and stability are the result of frustrated or inconclusive conflict endemic in such a society. This explanation does not suffer the problem posed by some strong theories of social order – how is social change possible? If stability is related to the balance of forces mobilized by the parties to these conflicts, change results from alterations in that balance. To the extent that interests are not successfully challenged there is social inertia. But the converse of this is that where officials of institutions or members of groups do see that it is possible successfully to challenge an interest to their own or their members' benefit, then that interest will usually be challenged (value-constraints being rarely sufficient to stop this by themselves). When such challenges occur there will be conflict, adding to the social mêlée, and if the challengers are right, social change will occur. Such challenges and changes are happening all the time. What a theory of social change needs is a criterion for distinguishing more and less significant ones (simultaneously providing 'criteria of similarity and difference' between societies, Unger, 1976, p. 37). Some of the more ambitious will claim that changes in the criteria they establish will be accompanied by changes in just about everything else that anyone could regard as important. However, the chosen criterion will generally be a matter of value – a matter of which differences are important to the theorist. A theory of social change also needs to provide some explanation of the mechanism(s) by which such significant changes occur; and why those changes follow the direction, if any, postulated by the theory.

The theory adopted here uses Marx's criterion of difference between societies – the relations of production. However, where he looked almost exclusively to the 'dominant' mode of production, the one by which the greatest proportion of the social product is produced, I look to all the relations of production to distinguish societies. Marx's 'dominant' or, more accurately, 'pre-eminent' mode is given first but not sole place among criteria of similarity and difference. Second place and several subsequent places will be given to other modes of production. The importance placed on the relations of production is not solely because work takes up so much of our lives. They will affect a much wider range of human activity. This is partly because of the way such relations affect our environments and ideas. But it is also because the power-holders in these relations, like all power-holders, have a tendency to extend the range of power relations that they exercise over their power-subjects. This diversification is made particularly easy by the differential distribution of economic resources produced by the exploitation inherent in most relations of production. These resources make it possible for the 'pre-eminent' class (that which benefits most from the pre-eminent relations of production) to have greater success in the social mêlée than the class they 'exploit' and classes based on other modes of production. They are more likely to be able to set up, take over, hold and limit the actions of institutions so that their interests are furthered rather than challenged. It is highly probable that such changes will alter other outputs of these institutions so that those who define social change in other ways will find society altered according to *their* criteria as well. For them, change in relations of production would *cause* rather than define social change. The Marxist advice to them is 'watch this space'.

This account also demystifies the base/superstructure relation. The social relations of production constitute the base, though as an aggregation of social relations involving multiple modes of production it should not be imagined as systematic. The relations involved in the institutions not primarily engaged in production constitute the superstructure. The base does not determine the superstructure. The relations within it provide the resources that can be, at least partially, mobilized for attempts to create and influence noneconomic institutions in order to provide outputs favourable to the interests of classes created by the relations of the production in the base.

The second requirement of a theory of social change, a *mechanism*, is provided by the development of 'productive forces'. This potentially nebulous concept is unpacked neatly by Shaw (1976) to include 'labour power' (skills and technology) and the 'means of production' (tools and raw materials). Marx sees their development as initially aided but later 'fettered' by the relations of production (Feuer, 1969, p. 84). The optional extra for a theory of social change, an explanation of the direction of historical development, is provided by the claim that productive forces have a tendency to increase. This is not adopted here. Continuous improvement of productive forces is *not* inevitable. They declined in late Roman and immediately post-Roman Europe, and might again if mineral and energy resources ran low or a nuclear war were to destroy most of the North's means of production. In such cases the relations of production may well change, but in response to a *decline* in productive forces rather than a rise. Historical change is not unidirectional (Habermas, 1979, p. 138; Giddens, 1984, p. 229).

Where this theory differs significantly from that of most Marxists is in its emphasis on the slow rise and fall of modes of production and the multiple modes of production current at any one time. New relations emerge and grow while the old decline, rather than the old spontaneously disintegrating under the weight of their own contradictions and the new emerging from the wreckage (Larrain, 1979, p. 62; Shaw, 1976, p. 142). Although this theory criticizes Marxist pictures of instantaneous change, it attempts to construct a coherent picture of gradual social change using the same theoretical building blocks as Marxist theory.

Productive forces do change – skills are developed, science and technology improved, machinery invented, minerals discovered. In the opposite direction, skills can be forgotten or deteriorate, or the number of people trained in them decline; science and technology may suffer waves of reaction; minerals can be used up and machinery destroyed. Increasing productive forces will often lead to increased production using the *existing*

The Social Mêlée   213

relations of production but the ingenuity that improved the productive
forces may also conceive of new ways of producing things. (Although the
ideas held by most people are a result of practices copied from others and
the ideas adopted to justify them, the range of experience is usually
sufficient to *generate* these new ideas.) The realization that more can be
produced by engaging in new practices and entering new relations by
doing things differently will be a first-order reason of very great strength
for doing so, appealing to rich and poor alike.

If sufficiently different, these new ways of doing things will constitute
new relations of production. Most relations of production include power
relations, anticipated reactions and various value-effect relations (chapter
7.8). But they will usually begin as power relations: their newness means
that others will not be used to considering the reactions of those involved,
and norms and values are likely to be congruent with the old rather than
new practices. The power-holder in these new relations will be using
resources that (s)he possesses to ensure that the power-subjects involved
produce goods in the new way. For this (s)he will require resources to
induce, or coerce, compliance. The resources need not be great. New
relations of production are likely to start in a small way and the power-
subjects are likely to come from the very weakest members of the society
(many early factory workers were women and many early townspeople
runaway serfs). But the need is still there, and as the resources predate
the social relations, those resources must have been acquired under old
relations of production. Therefore the new class of power-holders is not
likely to be the least powerful under the old relations. Capitalists are
unlikely to come from the peasantry (although wage labourers might).
They will come from the still pre-eminent class or, more usually, from
classes based on other relations of production (e.g. guildsman) or on
relations of distribution and exchange (e.g. merchants).

Not only is the new way of producing things unlikely to be congruent
with many pre-existing values, but there will be many institutions unsym-
pathetic or antagonistic to it. Key personnel will hold the old values and
their actions will be influenced by those groups most powerful under the
still pre-eminent old relations of production. So (*pace* Cohen, 1978, p.
226) legal rules supportive of the new relations will not be made quickly.
However, such rules are frequently unnecessary to support the practices
of economic agents (chapter 5.10). Far from supporting the new relations
of production, legal institutions may treat them as illegal. There may be
limits on the number of workers a 'master weaver' may employ (Hamerow, 1958), or the serfs, who made up the population of the towns, may be
regarded as still bonded to their lords (Tigar and Levy, 1977, p. 83). But
such restrictions will frequently have little effect. The new relations of
production may be set up outside the jurisdiction of those legal institu-

tions (Pirenne, 1936, p. 211). The law may be hard to enforce, as in the case of runaway serfs. Loopholes may be found, as in the prohibitions on usury (Tigar and Levy, 1977, p. 38). Alternatively old legal forms may be very flexible, as in the case of UK land-tenure (turning old concepts to new uses is a traditional legal skill).

More often, legal institutions will have simply failed to consider the new relations. Indeed, restrictive laws are likely to be reactions by those legal institutions to the new relations of production and are a part of the fight put up by the groups adversely affected by their spread. Consequently, such restrictive law will not be enacted or decided until conflicts of interests have been recognized and legal institutions have been successfully influenced by adversely affected members of the pre-eminent class of the outgoing mode of production (Collins, 1982, p. 79). Even then the new laws may be circumvented or may impede the new class only marginally.

If the new relations really do produce valued goods more efficiently and in greater quantity, there is a good chance of their spreading. Others who can change existing relations of production or set up new ones along the same model will see the practices of other power-holders in the new relations of production as models for their own action. With the spread of these relations, the class of power-holders in them grow in size and strength. As these new relations become established, the forms of power exercised by that class also grow, and the activities of those involved in these relations become practices with all the consequences for value-generation outlined in chapter 7.7. Most importantly, as these new relations of production are more efficient, the power-holders gain disproportionately more resources than would be indicated by the proportion of labour (and even the proportion of social product) created by those social relations. If mobilized, these resources can be a potent force for creating new institutions and taking over old ones.

There is no inevitability about what happens next (*pace*, Cohen, 1978). Although the emergent class is growing and powerful for its size, it is still weak in relation to the pre-eminent class in the still pre-eminent mode of production. In terms of pure economic resources the latter will still be stronger because so much of social production will still be under the old relations of production. They are likely to be even more favourably placed to influence institutional action. They are more likely to have influenced the filling of key positions with suitable personnel, often with former members of their own class, and their general power would limit the institutions to actions broadly favourable to them. The still pre-eminent class would clearly have the resources to crush the emergent new class. Certainly some attempts will be made to mobilize their resources to that end: most legal restrictions on trade and industry dated from the period of the rise of capitalist modes of production rather than from early mediaeval times when they had not even been conceived. Should these attempts be successful then social change would be halted, or even reversed, despite the increased production that would have been possible had the change continued. The new class has to fight with the resources currently, rather than ultimately, available to it. Such reactions might explain why some, 'Asiatic', societies appeared completely unable to change – a unified ruling class, based on one mode of production, could make the rise of new classes and relations of production impossible (Feuer, 1969, p. 84). But this class reaction may never occur. Members of the still pre-eminent class will be hard to mobilize, especially as the mobilization would be against an unfamiliar enemy. Ideology and experience attune them to conflict with the class of power-subjects of 'their' relations of production, the power-holders in even earlier relations of production or other groups in the society. Mobilization will later become harder as some members take part in the new relations of production and some of the emergent class gain positions within it (e.g. by buying bankrupt estates). The unfamiliarity of the situation will also increase the likelihood of error and unintended effects. But, most important of all, if society conforms to the rather disordered model sketched in the last section, then such a reaction is unlikely. The society in which new relations of production grow will be fragmented by old disputes and a significant variety of groups and classes. Some members of the old and still pre-eminent class will be unprepared to join the necessary coalition. The mere fact that small quantities of certain goods are produced in a different way does not appear immediately threatening, especially in a society with several modes of production. Indeed, if those goods are produced more profitably, the new ways may even be inviting to members of the old class. Many such members will benefit from the changes (e.g. landowners from increased ground rents in new towns, and improved markets for agricultural produce). Furthermore, the emergent class provides useful new allies in the old disputes. Initially, they will be seen as minor newcomers whose resources can be mobilized to tip the balance in old struggles. They will rarely be seen as the ultimate threat which will make all the old struggles redundant, and against whom the old and still pre-eminent class must unify to retain their position. In mediaeval Europe the nobility was split by rivalries between great landlords and princes. Merchants and towns provided allies for the princes against the great landlords, providing loans and taxes in return for economic concessions and independence from the nobility (Tigar and Levy, 1977). If not 'nipped in the bud' the new relations of production will spread further – their greater efficiency leading more people to adopt them as a model and increasing the proportion of the social product produced within them.

The size and resources of the emergent class will grow. This constitutes significant change in itself but will also provide the motive force for further, 'superstructural', social change. Members of the new class will develop ideas as justifications of their practice which will challenge the old ideas and make the new class into a subjective group.

The emergent class will be mobilized by new institutions. They will also be mobilized into attempts to 'take over' existing institutions – or at least to shift the range of choice open to key personnel within them. As the resources of the groups and institutions involved in the social mêlée change, so also do the successfully challengeable interests of those groups and institutions. Challenges will be made and succeed, further weakening the old (and now declining class) and strengthening the new. The institutions which once acted so much in the interests of the old class will now act more in the interests of the new (e.g. the changing decisions of the courts) or lose out to the institutions that do act in the new class's interests and hence receive their support (e.g. the decline of the House of Lords and the rise of the Commons). In time, it will be the new class, rather than the old, whose position is bolstered by noneconomic forms of power. Naturally, this will be a gradual process. Different institutions will 'fall' earlier than others, depending on their internal social relations and personnel (e.g. the judiciary was controlled by capitalist sympathizers long before the army).

The ideological struggle will also shift in favour of the new class. Ideas favouring it will be given wider circulation both because sites for the generation and transmission of ideology will come under the increasing influence of institutions sympathetic to the new class and because opinion leaders will increasingly come from it. As the spread of the new relations of production affects the practices and the environments of more people, these new ideas will seem to fit more than those which appeared to fit the old practices best. It is not that the liberal conceptions of political democracy *best* fit the lives of wage-labourers, but they fit *better* than the old aristocratic ideas of status and feudal privilege. Furthermore, whereas the new practices could be, with some mental agility, squeezed into conformity with old ideas (e.g. interest and usury rules), they could be practised more self-confidently and comprehensively under later ideas more favourable to them (e.g. interest is justified by risk).

Thus the increasing resources derived from an ever growing share of the social product is reinforced by support from 'ideological' institutions. The new class may achieve undoubted pre-eminence supplanting all or most of the previously pre-eminent mode of production and sometimes parts of the other modes of production as well (e.g. more capitalist relations may sometimes supplant guild-type relations of production in law firms and McDonald's may perform some of the cooking previously done in familial relations of production).

But victory is never total. Long before such victory is even possible, the new class will find that mobilization, always limited, is harder to maintain, further victories against some groups and classes are too costly, internal divisions multiply, and cross-cutting loyalties and interests make some members of the now pre-eminent class resist the extension of the now pre-eminent mode of production (e.g. especially, few capitalists or managers want the end of familial relations of production). Finally, the next relations of production with attendant classes may have already emerged.

The actual place of political revolutions in this process is relatively minor, even if occasionally spectacular. Taking over the state is merely a matter of taking over one of society's institutions. It is a very powerful institution and one that can be used to create and take over other institutions. But it is still an institution with all the difficulties that institutions have in mobilizing resources to achieve desired goals. Controlling the state (to the extent that it is possible to control it) may be sufficient to tip the balance of power between the old and new classes. But it cannot be the sole or prime instrument of social transformation.

If there is to be a successful political revolution in which institutions (whether or not aided by other groups which are mobilized against the pre-existing class) sympathetic to the new class take over the state by force, it will come late in the process of social change. It cannot predate the social changes for two reasons. First, for there to be a class war there must be a class and the class can have emerged only if the new relations of production already exist. Second, for the revolution to succeed the institutions fighting it must be able to mobilize sufficient resources to overcome those of the old class and, more than anything else, such an overt challenge is likely to mobilize those old classes. Even if the new and still weak class could be quickly mobilized to launch a pre-emptive strike to take over the state, and withstand the almost inevitable reaction of the old class, production of goods must, and will, continue. Indeed, the damage a revolution generally does to the means of production – destroyed machinery, lost labour-power of dead workers, and liquidated or uncooperative·experts – will provide great urgency. (This is a particular problem for those Marxists who see new relations of production arising naturally or inevitably from greater productive power of labour – if productivity reaches the point which triggers the revolution, the revolution will push productivity back through the threshold.) The new relations of production will not emerge spontaneously, nor will they suddenly grow from next to nothing to provide the bulk of the social product. In fact, people will produce things as they know how, according to existing practices even if they do not value them. If the existing practices are those congruent with the old relations of production then the old relations will continue (e.g. the NEP after the Soviet revolution) although sometimes slightly modified (e.g. it could be argued that the removal of the Russian capitalists left most productive relations unchanged and merely eliminated the relations between managers and owners). This is why the victorious new class must be based on new relations of production – victory by an exploited class does not change the relations of production. If the relations of production change little then, according to this theory's criteria, neither does society. It is only if the new relations of production have reached a point where they can provide the largest portion of the social product in the post-revolutionary period that social change will accompany the revolution. But if the new relations of production have reached this point, then significant social change has *already* occurred and the revolution merely quickens the pace, putting the final touches to the victory of the new class. This is not to deny that social change may occur in the period following a revolution, but this will be in the nature of the gradual change outlined above in which the state is one of several institutional actors in the social mêlée.

There may not even be a political revolution or any particularly violent change. The corollary of the tendency not to attack interests that can be defended is that interests that can be successfully attacked are rarely defended. Challenges will lead to violent conflict only if members of one side miscalculate the resources they can mobilize and hence the power they can wield, thereby wrongly believing they can win, or if they decide to fight despite this. Where some institutions of the new class believe they have grown strong enough to take over the target institutions or act to prejudice the relevant interests, and some institutions of the old and declining class believe they can resist the challenge, there will be mobilization of resources on each side. If one side does not realize its miscalculation, conflict will increase and more resources will be mobilized, including, sooner or later, the capacities of both sides to apply physical force. But the calculations will be made by several people in several positions in several institutions. They will not all make the same miscalculation. The mobilization that is weak in theory becomes doubly weak in practice. Thus the too early revolutionary attempts of a new class are weakly supported; and at the other end of the process of change the old class may finally go under with the spasmodic kick of its more foolish members. Of course, miscalculations could be made on the stronger side too (Luhmann, 1985, p. 202). If sufficiently more on the stronger side than the weaker side underestimate their strength, then a potentially successful revolution or reaction will fail. But the most likely result of the multitude of individual calculations and miscalculations is that the overall level of conflict will be less, involving those on each side who think they can win along with those members of other groups and classes they can mobilize. If any tendential law is to be offered, it is probable that more declining classes will make miscalculations than emergent ones because perceptions of strength are strongly influenced by experiences of the past (when the declining classes and their supporting institutions really *were* stronger) than accurate calculations of the future.

It should be emphasized that the above process is one of *gradual* change during which there will be *several classes* involved in struggle carried on through conflict within and between *different* institutions. The institutions 'fall' at different times, revolutions merely making the passing of state institutions more rapid and violent. A society in the process of social change is a disordered one, with different institutions emerging both as the battleground for the interests of rising and falling classes and, once won, as attempted instruments for one class to use against others. Even if I am wrong and social change is not simply the ebb and flow of class fortunes within a disordered mêlée but change from one kind of order to another, slow social change will still produce disorder in the interim. Furthermore, slow change will make this interim period very long so that many, probably most, societies will be in the process of change with its concurrent disorder. Our society is surely one of these. It has long since passed the high point of capitalism (Avineri, 1968, p. 158) and although we do not know to what other type of society it is changing, we can be fairly certain it has not yet done so. If I am right, it will not be ordered even when it has. The view of social change by conflict reinforces the view of society as disordered by conflict. Rather than requiring separate theories to explain each phenomenon, conflict is used to explain both social stability and social change. Conflict always seemed the most suitable explanation for change, but that very suitability seemed to disqualify it from explaining social peace or stability. But as this chapter has attempted to demonstrate, it can do this if conflict is seen as disordered and unsystematic in a disordered and unsystematic society.

7.13 Key Disordering Influences Within Society

A useful way of summarizing this chapter is to list the key disordering influences within society that it has elucidated. As some of these are also the factors which others had hoped would provide the basis for social order, it also helps to explain the failure of systematic theories of society and, to the extent that it is conceived as part of society, law.

1 *Language.* Despite that fact that members of the same society often use the same language, this is not necessarily a source of order and unity. Members of different groups within society will tend to use different words in describing the same situation, and even when they do use the same terms the meaning will vary.

2 *Social interaction and interrelations.* Just as language and a form of communication is possible without commonly held meanings, so interaction is possible without it. Social relations are asymmetric because those at either end of them tend to see them differently or not at all. This is compounded by the variety and mixture of social relations between any two people and the asymmetric perception of the mix. The variety of social relations also means that social interaction within them is as likely to produce antagonism as feelings of solidarity.

3 *Social environment.* Social relations produce different environments for those at either end of them. This is particularly true of the social relations of production and the social relations within institutions.

4 *Values, ideas and subjective interests.* Rather than common values arising from a common cultural environment, the *different* environments and practices found at either end of relations of production generate different ideas, values and subjective interests.

5 *Norms.* These do not provide order because of the irreducibly individual nature of value-judgments.

6 *Groups.* Far from laying the basis of social solidarity, groups are formed from those at either end of social relations who are likely to have antagonistic subjective interests, ideas and values.

7 *Social institutions* are composed of these social relations. These leave members of institutions with different interests and frequently the resources to pursue them, providing centripetal tendencies within institutions. These, in turn, make it difficult for them to co-operate in achieving institutional or *trans*-institutional goals or purposes (thus systems of functioning institutions are not supportable).

8 *Social conflict.* Although social relations produce conflicting groups, the nature of institutions, and the limited extent to which they can mobilize and direct the resources of the members of antagonistic groups, mutes the conflict.

9 *Social change.* Rather than being sudden and producing pure types of societies which can exist between revolutions, social change is gradual, in the course of which societies change and the balance of forces within the social mêlée changes.

In addition, the disordered picture of a society that results from the above influences can explain some of the features of society that some might think could be explained only by a social system. Social peace is the result of the incomplete mobilization of forces into conflict. Social predictability is the result of social inertia and the relative stability of social relations – value-effect relations will continue as long as there is a value, coercion as long as one party has the ability to inflict undesirable effects on another, etc. At no point need any reliance be placed on the commonality of values, norms or internally held views of practices. Indeed the view of social relations showed that these are likely to be anything but common. Yet the social relations could explain social practices, the co-ordination of action and relations of production (chapter 7.7 and 7.8 respectively) that some have regarded as inexplicable without such common values, norms and practices.

Notes

1 E.g. Fowles (1971) writing about the same relationship from the point of view of both parties.

2 Symbolic interactionists, phenomenologists and ethnomethodologists recognize the role individuals have in giving their own meaning to their environment and the interactions within it (Craib, 1984, p. 90). However, many theories that recognize the sources of asymmetry still end up describing social relations in symmetric terms. Symbolic interactionists believe that the parties to relations which might otherwise be asymmetric 'negotiate' a shared meaning. They seem to share with Parsonians the belief that such common meanings are necessary for continued interaction. Yet if the interaction could occur once without it, perhaps it could occur again. And if the parties must, for one reason or another, continue to interact, it might be better for them to keep their differences to themselves. If they are going to negotiate about anything, surely they are more likely to negotiate about what is actually done rather than the meaning that should be given to it.

3 E.g. Dworkin sees different participants in the same practice giving that practice different meanings (1986, pp. 63, 199).

4 *Other language-games.* The same problems and the same solution are to be found in other kinds of language-games where the use of language has different effects. Consider language-games involving performatives in the special sense that use of the word indicates a change of state of something which involves changes in the future behaviour of at least some persons (MacCormick, 1981, p. 14). This would seem to necessitate common agreement on what change that performative achieved. Yet consider these performatives: by Captain Cook, 'I claim this land in the name of King George III,' and by a policeman to a suspect, 'You are under arrest.' Those words may have different meanings to the speakers and listeners. But the words have achieved an important effect which is due less to commonly held meanings than to an awareness of some of the differences in people's actions surrounding, and at least partially resulting from, the making of the statement.

5 Some argue that *ideas can themselves change material conditions*. Of course ideas can lead power-holders to change physical conditions. But they can also change the most important social conditions directly: by changing the way a social relation is viewed from one end and hence how it operates to produce effects. Changes in the beliefs of power-subjects may wipe out some relations completely (e.g. if a power-subject of legitimate authority no longer thinks the power-holder ought to be obeyed) or make them less effective, more costly or

more difficult to exercise (e.g. if the power-subject decides he no longer values or fears what a power-holder can offer or threaten, inducement and coercion become ineffective). However, such changes in ideas will not easily be produced. Changes in values are difficult to achieve, especially where they fit in well with practices and other values. Changes in the inducement value of desperately needed goods and services or the coercive value of threats to life and limb are not readily achieved.

6 Sumner at some points rubbishes the idea of the great pluralism and inventiveness of even academic minds. He points out that in the conditions of the 1970s he and several other left-wing academics started working on theories of ideology, consciousness, etc. But this is hardly a convincing argument for the lack of ideological diversity within universities given that at the same time monetarist economics also passed through universities. More seriously he also suggests that certain ideas are necessitated – they will necessarily be thrown up by the social relations and the social relations will not continue without them. In Dworkinian terms only one set of ideas fits. One example he gives is of authoritarian lecture-room relationships (which necessitate deference). But, as always, there is an alternative 'ideology', an alternative way of explaining the relationship and justifying the practices of those at either end of the relationship. Sumner's lecturer may not see himself as an authority or see student/staff relationships as deferential. Yet he may still adopt the practices of authoritarian lecturers because students are more familiar with them or because these are good ways of getting out the material his senior colleagues require to be presented in exams. The students may not have a deferential attitude to the lecturer and may similarly not regard him as being an authoritative fount of wisdom yet may adopt the same practices as deferential students – careful note-taking, asking about the lecturer's ideas, not volunteering their own – because they see the knowledge of what the lecturer thinks is most useful for the examination success necessary for their credentials.

7 This is the term I have used since the first draft of this work (1981). Fitzpatrick uses the term 'family relations of production' (1983). Delphy's term 'domestic mode of production' to which Richard Ingleby subsequently directed me is not used as she insists it only applies to contemporary society.

8 For example, the familial relations of production make possible a greater degree of exploitation in feudal relations because there is more product to extract from the male head and greater exploitation in at least some stages of capitalism because so much of the sustenance of wage-labourers is due to the unpaid work of women.

8

The Legal Mêlée

8.1 Introduction

The last chapter sketched a nonsystematic theory of society. This chapter will do the same for law. It is not necessary to accept the picture of society outlined in the last chapter in order to see law as unsystematic and disordered. It would be theoretically possible to find a legal system within a disordered society and even an unsystematic law in an otherwise ordered society. But the two disordered images of law and society sit easily together, draw on each other for plausibility and rest on similar theoretical positions and empirical claims.

This chapter envisages law as a part of society as depicted in the previous chapter and uses the same concepts and images. First, it sees law as made from the same building blocks – social relations between individuals in all their variety and complexity (chapter 8.2) and especially asymmetric tendencies. Many, especially persuasive, legitimate authority and value-effect relations involve rules which provide reasons for action at one or both 'ends'. But the rules will not necessarily be shared between those at the same ends of similar relations or at the two ends of a single relation. Second, it sees law as subject to the same forces and tendencies as other parts of society, showing the same centripetal tendency to become partially organized into institutions, the same centrifugal tendencies to conflict and disorder. Third, law, as part of the social mêlée, is both disordered by its conflicting relations with other institutions and adds to that disorder (where functionalists saw the legal sub-system as a microcosm of the larger social system, the legal mêlée is seen as a microcosm of the social mêlée). As such, it reinforces the image of law as disordered. It appears as evidence that a part of society is disordered – and also a further reason why the rest of society is likely to be disordered (because the effects of law will tend to make it so).

The overall image is of a vast web of relations (or perhaps a multi-dimensional maze) which link directly and indirectly vast numbers of legal officials to each other and to the citizens they affect and by whom they are affected.

The theory attempts to provide an understanding of legal phenomena from the standpoint of the social observer. But as we shall see in the final section of this chapter it can serve to provide theoretical answers to many other jurisprudential problems as well, including a new problem that the theory has created – why do so many people see such a disordered phenomenon as systematic?

This 'legal' web is only a part of the larger web of society. The next question comes naturally – *what* part of the larger web is 'law'? There are no natural boundaries, indeed the whole concept of a boundary is problematical given that anything within any such boundary interacts with that outside and the very concept of a social interaction incorporates parts of those persons at either end of the interaction. But the institutions do provide foci of attention because of the way they concentrate interaction and magnify (as well as dilute, deflect and distort) the effects which individual officials and those who influence them can have on others. A theory of law will centre on certain institutions within society including some or all of: courts, legislatures, police, bureaucrats, prisons, the bar and firms of solicitors. These institutions will seem to many as 'legal' for several reasons.

1   They contain many social relations involving language-games in which the word 'law' is used; many in which one or more of the actors would associate the word 'law' with the relation and that association affects the interaction (the fact that frequently only one of the actors involved will regard these interactions as part of law demonstrates both the asymmetry of much social interaction and the impossibility of distinguishing between legal and non-legal institutions, shared rules or meanings); and many which involve a use of rules which actors attempt to derive from institutional sources and apply to themselves and others.
2   They involve the creation and interpretation of texts for the purpose of affecting the actions of others.
3   The effects achieved are among those seen as characteristically legal.
4   The ways in which effects are achieved are characteristically legal because actors attempt to derive rules from institutional sources (and especially their textual output) and apply these rules to themselves and others.

The institutions included within the theory of law will depend on the purposes of the theorist. The theorist may be interested in certain kinds of activity or effects that are more common in some institutions than others. The theorist may be interested in the effects certain institutions have on him/her or on those in whom the theorist is interested. For the social observer, the division is not vitally important. Some might wish to exclude from 'law' some of the aforementioned institutions and the social relations that constitute them. But a decision to exclude some only divides the social relations that are a part of the operation of law into the internal social relations of law (between members of legal institutions) and the external relations of law (between members of legal institutions and outsiders). The theory outlined here will include the full list of institutions nominated above – partly to show that the range of relations, the kinds of processes and the essential dynamics are similar in all these institutions, and partly because of the distortions and inadequacies we have seen in trying to confine theories to judges and courts.

8.2 The Range of Social Relations in Law

Social interactions and relations in law take the form outlined in chapter 7.2: some thought, attribute or action of one person affects the thoughts, attributes and actions of another. These social interactions are the instances of social relationships between those persons. These include the full range of interactions and relations discussed in the last chapter.

The power relations that most epitomize law are authority relations, in which officials indicate, verbally or otherwise, what lower officials or citizens are expected to do and they comply. These indications are often non-verbal (as in the hand gestures of policemen directing traffic) or in the consciously aggressive body language of a cross-examining council or sentencing judge. However, the method of affecting the actions of others that is characteristic of law and by which the effect of legal institutions can be magnified and extended to the furthest reaches of society is the creation of texts – statutes, by-laws, judgments, wills, standard-form contracts, writs and so on. The intended response is, in most general terms, that the power-subject will take the power-holder's action as a reason for his/her own action. Sometimes this will involve a reason for acting in a single case – a writ is generally intended to induce an offer or a better settlement offer, a policeman's raised hand is even more strongly directed towards a single and simple response. But the most common response intended is the generation of a rule or standard to guide the power-subject's action. This is not merely a matter of internalizing a rule stated by the power-holder. Often the power-holder's actions are not in the form of language (e.g. a policeman's raised hand). Even if they are, they may be in an indicative rather than imperative mood and may not be in a form that can be immediately applied to the power-subject's situation. They may be directed to slightly different circumstances or be phrased in an unfamiliar or awkward way that needs to be translated to fit into the power-subject's thinking patterns. The text may be a collection of appellate judgments or the recorded compromises of parliamentary majorities. There may be no rule in the power-holder's mind. If there are several power-holders, there may be different rules in their minds, or rather a range of normative phenomena that provided the power-holders with reasons to create the text. In all cases, the power-holder's text or action must be interpreted by the power-subject and the rule, or other reasons, generated for the power-subject's use. The power-subject's rule will be separate and unique in two senses. First, it is generated by and for that person whose rule it is. Secondly, the variation in the way rules are generated from the interpretation of text and the different intellectual houses in which they must rest mean that each rule generated is likely to be different in some respects from others generated, even in similar circumstances. The positivists' insight is that from the power-subject's point of view the action of the power-holder is a source of texts and the rules that come with them. Earlier positivists spoke as if the text contained a rule – Raz and later positivists talked of reasons rather than rules without concluding that this located the reason/rule firmly in the mind of the power-subject. MacCormick rightly identifies the emphasis on the elements of law as practical reasons to be the greatest advance in contemporary analytical jurisprudence (1983). Although this moved attention away from texts, most theorists still attempted to give the reasons a wider existence than the contents of individual minds. Finnis claimed objective standards for some of the reasons (principals of practical reasonableness), whereas MacCormick, Weinberger and Raz saw legal reasons as parts of a system of reasons shared by those with a legal point of view. They tried to avoid the conclusion that, as *reasons*, legal rules were phenomena within the minds of those who derived and used them. Some Scandinavian realists took this view of legal rules but positivists tend to dismiss such notions because they made legal rules more transient phenomena, which died when the reasoner's mind passed on to something else and the rule was forgotten. Surely law was more stable than this. The solution adopted here is that both were right. Legal rules are transient phenomena as reasons for action in a particular case or transaction. But there is something more – social relations by which power-holders affect power-subjects and the texts by which this effect is generally achieved.

Among authority relations, most writers have concentrated on legitimate authority. But other authority relations are also abundant. Coercion has always been a part of law, threatened sanctions being commonplace if not universal. Evidence of fairly simple coercive relations is seen when police give warnings and judges issue suspended sentences. Personal authority may appear in its most dramatic form in the sway held by a charismatic dictator, but it is more often found in relations between members of institutions in fairly close contact with each other – especially within units of the bureaucracy or police force and in such small groups as the members of an appellate court (Paterson, 1982, p. 120) or cabinet.

Competent authority is a vital part of the operation of law. The belief in judicial competence to resolve disputes was the basis on which many disputants took their grievances to courts when there was a choice between courts and between courts and self-help. To some extent this choice is still there. Habermas has pointed to the importance of belief in governmental competence to 'manage' the problems of modern society (1979). In lesser cases, competent authority is seen in the testimony of regular expert witnesses and in the expertise of some officials. Inducement is not only found in tax concessions and government grants but also in contracts and wills (nullity may not be a sanction but enforcement is certainly an inducement).

Other authority relations are also important. Direct force is exercised by prison officials over prisoners and by bailiffs over some unsuccessful litigants. Persuasion is exercised by successful counsel over judges. More generally, Goodrich (1986) and Katz (1986) see legal activity centred around the persuasive interpretation of texts to induce desired responses from judges, other lawyers and their clients.

Value-effect relations are as important in law as in the rest of society. The values that individuals hold are vital in affecting the content of their actions, in creating relations of legitimate authority and in limiting the power of certain key actors (e.g. most policemen could easily 'verbal' suspects and many judges could indulge their whims in decision-making – but many believe they should not).

Unintended effects are inevitable in anything so complex as law. In fact it is riddled with them. In 1979 the Conservative government changed the tax-mix to stimulate investment and raised interest rates to reduce inflation: in fact the changed tax-mix raised inflation and the interest rates killed investment. In the courts, consideration of the general effects of decisions is often deliberately excluded. If Dworkin were right and decisions were made purely on principle then their unintended effects would be even greater. Some attempts are made to reduce these unintended effects – there are debates in parliament over the effects of legislation, there are reports from specially appointed commissions, 'judicial notice' is taken in English courts and the 'Brandeis brief' is used in American ones. But it would be rash to claim that the ability of officials to predict the effects of law is improving more quickly than an increasingly complex society makes such prediction problematic. Indeed, little is done to increase official ability to predict. The amateur sociology contained in 'judicial notice' is not subject to argument and if a judgment is reached on the basis of its expected effects, the failure of those expectations is not accepted as a reason for reversing the decision.

Anticipatory reactions occupy a particularly important place in law. The behaviour of many citizens is much modified by what they or their lawyers anticipate judges' reactions will be in circumstances those judges have not considered. Such occasions are particularly common where legislation is new, where the members of a court have recently been appointed, or where no potential pair of litigants have had both the funds and the willingness to test a question in court. The anticipation of such judicial reaction is a part of lawyers' skill in filling the interstices of law and advising their clients on whether to settle or proceed. Anticipation of legislative reactions generally is not, but certainly ought to be, part of lawyers' skills too, especially when corporate structures are created. It is also part of the skill of a parliamentary draughtsman to anticipate judicial interpretation in choosing the wording of statutes (D'Amato, 1975, p. 197).

More generally, anticipation of the reaction of others is vital in persuasion. Not only must the persuader find arguments that appeal to the audience's values, but he or she must avoid those which will antagonize the audience or appear outside the range of expected interpretative techniques and outcomes. Many theorists have drawn attention to this last factor and have seen interpretations and interpretative conventions shared within interpretative communities (Fish, 1982). However, some deconstructionists (e.g. Norris, 1985) have come closer to the mark by emphasizing that it is not *interpretations* which are limited but the interpretations that will be recognized by others as possible (Fish, 1982). Some interpretations will be unacceptable either because the interpreter used different interpretative techniques or, more often, because similar techniques have produced conclusions that conflict with the judge's values. Consequently the judge feels it *must* be wrong and either rejects it out of hand or uses the familiar technique of getting rid of unwanted interpretations.

Interpretative communities limit not the interpretations that can be thought but merely those which can be *said*. Anticipation of the reaction to what cannot be said constitutes important relations in law, especially where the anticipator (e.g. barrister) is dependent on the reactor for the desired outcome.

Social relations in law are subject to all the same limitations and vagaries as social relations in general. First, they refer to a *probability* that one person will affect the behaviour of another in that the second person takes the action of the first (as it appears to him) as a reason for action. In particular instances the probability may not be realized. In many others the effect will be weak or swamped by other influences so that the second person modifies his/her action minimally, if at all. This limited effectiveness of legal relations leads directly to the oft-noted limited effectiveness of law. Law is a limited resource in the hands of legal officials and a limited weapon in the hands of those who would use it. Second, relations between officials of legal institutions and between officials and citizens tend to be a mixture of the different types of social relations. In authority relations the reasons for compliance will tend to be mixed and the mix will vary from individual to individual. This is uncontroversially true of citizens and has been shown to be true of officials by compliance theorists (chapter 5.6). Some respond more to the threats of sanctions for breaches (coercion), some respond more to a belief in the right of the institutions to require certain forms of behaviour (legitimate authority), and yet others respond more from a belief in the benefits of compliance (inducement and competent authority) or personal loyalty to the person issuing the statement (personal authority). The individual may independently believe in the correctness of a legal prescription missing authority and value-effect relations. To the extent that this belief was induced by honest arguments put, or false facts spread, by the power-holders, then the relation is also mixed with persuasion or manipulation respectively.

This mixture of reasons is not confined to citizens. When a lower-court judge interprets the text of a higher-court judgment as a source of rules to guide his or her decisions it will not necessarily be a simple case of legitimate authority. Several social relations will give him or her reasons for the action of so using the text: the legitimate authority of precedent, hope of promotion (inducement), belief in the ability of higher-court judges to resolve the issues involved (competent authority), fear of being 'overruled' (either anticipated reaction or coercion), or of criticism by colleagues and barristers (another example of anticipated reaction which, *pace* Paterson, 1982, is no weaker for the criticism being largely unvoiced). Even higher-court judges will take into account the anticipated reactions and sometimes even direct threats of executives and legislatures if they went 'too far' in constitutional interpretation (e.g. declaring parliament invalid: see chapter 3.4) and can never ignore the fact that some decisions could not, and other decisions would not, be enforced by state institutions (Stone, 1966, p. 590; Sampford, 1980; Galligan, 1987, p. 257). Another mixed relation between judges is that of 'persuasive authority'. The relation of persuasion is suggested by the name but is mixed with value-effect relations (especially stemming from the value of not changing or varying 'the law'), a competent authority and, generally, personal authority.

The pressures on judges over the content of their decisions are many – their study constitutes much of the sociology of law. These involve the social relations outside social groups and institutions have with judges – some may be power relations but they are more likely to be relations of persuasion, manipulation and especially anticipatory reactions (they may anticipate the influence of offended groups on parliament or a major strike that might follow the gaoling of some unionists). Even if we confine ourselves to the immediate relationship between the lawyer presenting the arguments and the judge hearing them, that relationship is a mixture of persuasion and manipulation, the latter being affected by the selection of cases and facts and the light in which they are presented.

This is not just a matter of confusion and variation in the minds of power-subjects about their reasons for action which they glean from law. The mixture of relations is created by power-holders' attempts to extend the types of power they exercise over a large and varied group of subjects. This is unsurprising, given that much legislative, bureaucratic and judicial official action is intended to control, channel and redirect the behaviour of so many subordinates and citizens, and given the limited effectiveness of some of those relations. These attempts are evidenced in the efforts of all regimes to claim legitimate authority, to claim competence in governing, to attempt to establish the charisma of key members of the ruling institutions and to persuade the public of the rightness of their edicts (though rarely hesitating to manipulate the flow of information in the process). These attempts are also seen in the way some courts use their coercive contempt powers to restrict unfavourable comment about them to bolster their personal authority, and in the way bureaucrats use bureaucratic secrecy (a form of manipulation) to bolster their competent authority.

This process of power extension can be seen in microcosm when a judge passes sentence. (S)he will usually not merely state the term of imprisonment (thereby exercising force over the accused and coercion over those who hear of it), but also emphasize the wickedness of the act (an attempt at persuasion), and claim the legitimacy of the state's rights to proscribe such activity. In a sense, law can be said to be 'hedging its bets'. Far from confining themselves to claims of legitimate authority to determine questions of law, officials in legal institutions attempt to exercise several forms of power in order to achieve the desired effects (*pace* Selznick, 1980, p. 7). For some subordinates and citizens some of the power relations will prove ineffective, but the hope is that, for most, at least one will not. Honoré has noted that laws are usually not phrased in normative terms (1977, p. 106) – they are usually expressed in the indicative mood. This reflects what was said above. Officials state what is to be done, the individual supplies the reason (or reasons) himself – it does not much worry the officials which ones they are.

8.3 Chains of Relations in Law

The relations between individuals made possible by law, especially those between higher officials and citizens, can be quite indirect. Even the power of a judge to incarcerate a convicted person and hence exercise force requires the activation of other relationships involving police and prison officials. The relation between a legislator or law lord and a citizen involves an even longer chain of intermediate relations. The complexity and variety of relations to be found in such chains can be exemplified by a crackdown on tax-evasion. Influential MPs persuade the relevant minister to act. (S)he presents legislation which is passed because of the government's majority and then instructs the Inland Revenue head to devote extra resources to catching evaders. Because (s)he believes ministers have the right to issue such directions the departmental head complies. Further instructions are passed down through the department – through some who act out of similar beliefs, some who act out of loyalty to their superiors, and some who act out of fear of losing their job. An investigator discovers facts about a tax-evader, and gives this information to the departmental lawyers. Trusting the investigator's reliability and information, they offer a fee to a barrister to act as prosecuting counsel. The barrister persuades the judge that the 'taxpayer's' income is higher than declared, and the judge issues an order under which the bailiffs descend upon the taxpayer's house and seize sufficient chattels to meet the taxpayer's debt to society. The effect of the influential legislators on the taxpayer is by way of a chain of power relations: persuasion, legitimate, personal and competent authority, inducement, persuasion again, and finally force.

The situation is further complicated by four factors. First, some of these intermediate relations may be weak, making the whole chain liable to break down. Second, these intermediate relations are likely to be mixed in the way seen in the last section rather than taking the pure forms described above. The relations throughout the bureaucracy that are activated will probably be mixed authority relations in which the mixes vary with the bureaucrats involved. The lawyer may take on such cases partly because (s)he believes that such persons should be prosecuted (value-effect relations), and we have already seen how the relations between lawyers and judges are mixed. Third, there may well be several chains of relations between the legislator and citizens, some involving essentially persuasion and some essentially coercion and force as above. The persuasive relations will operate through quite separate, and probably shorter, chains involving those who record and transmit speeches and interviews. Fourth, the relations between the legislator and citizen may take different paths for different citizens. Consider a second 'taxpayer' who pays up before prosecution so that several relations need not be activated. The final relation becomes one of coercion rather than force.

The relative shortness of the chains of relations in coercion is a common feature, especially in law. A power-holder may threaten a power-subject directly, but in order to carry out the threat (s)he must activate separate relations, often of a different type, to influence others to impose the force.

The creation and transmission of texts, a typically 'legal' method of long-distance influence on the behaviour of citizen, might been seen as a way of short-circuiting these chains of social relations. But even these will usually be indirect. The texts produced by the most powerful institutions and individuals in law are rarely directed at citizens. Despite the hopes of Napoleon (who hoped his code could be read by a *poilu* in his tent at night) and 'plain English' advocates in legislative drafting (who have similarly Napoleonic hopes for ordinary citizens), it is lawyers who read the textual output of legal institutions. Citizens are affected because their beliefs about the law provide reasons for them to act. But they get their knowledge indirectly. They may glean it from media reports of the political debates and their legislative outcomes. The politicians have induced or persuaded the reporters to write about the issue, the citizens may regard the reporters as competent authorities but the overall politician/ citizen relation is one of coercion and/or legitimacy. Alternatively, citizens gain beliefs about law from lawyers or bureaucrats who interpret the texts for them and frequently create new texts to encapsulate their interpretations. The relation between legislator and lawyer is one of legitimate or competent authority (lawyers may regard text-creators as competent authorities for predicting the behaviour of officials who use the text). The relation between lawyer and citizen is one of competent authority and inducement (which is usually necessary to get the lawyer to act at all). Some citizens will gain their beliefs about law at one further remove by their interpretations of what other citizens tell them about the law. In such cases, an extra relation of competent authority is added which carries the chain of relations between politician and citizen one stage further.

In the last two sections we have seen how varied are the social relations in the multi-institutional web of law. This contradicts those theories of law which picture that web of relations as a system of either coercive or legitimate authority relations. These theories are persistent because two factors appear to support them: (1) there is often at least *some* element of coercion or legitimate authority in the mix, and (2) so much human action is overdetermined that this element may be *sufficient* to produce it. But such theories should be rejected on several grounds. They distort the relevant social relations by overemphasizing the part that legitimate authority or coercion play in what is a variable mixture of both and much more besides. They also ignore other relevant power relations operative in law (usually and most importantly the one out of coercion and legitimate authority on which the system is *not* based). These theories also ignore the many power relations other than coercion and legitimate authority that are deliberately created by officials of legal institutions to increase their effectiveness. Systems based on one type of relation will not explain situations where a relationship between two legal actors is clearly operative despite the lack of the relevant relation: there will be inexplicable gaps in the chains where command and sanction theorists could not explain what sanctions were faced by judges (Hart, 1961, p. 30), or when legitimate authority theorists have to deal with those who accorded law no legitimacy at all (Hodson, 1976, p. 394). The reverse is also a problem: where the type of relation on which the system is based exists, yet people supposedly subject to that relation are quite unaffected by it (e.g. there is a sanction but the law is not observed, or people who see law as legitimate still break it). Thus the law operates where such systematizers do not suppose, and it does not operate where they do. Both puzzles are solved by seeing the social relations in law as mixed, so that sometimes the mixture is powerful enough to produce compliant action and sometimes not. This view cannot be as neat and systematic as some other theories: the claim is that it is more realistic.

8.4   Asymmetry in Legal Relations

Asymmetry, the differential perception of a social relation by those at either 'end', is an important property of many social relations in law.

This may, at first, seem a surprising claim. In the authority relations most typical of law, power-holders attempt to influence power-subjects to adopt certain rules for action and use texts couched in legal language to convey them. However, such texts and such language provide much scope for differential perception. Despite the fact that the language is often, though not always (Stone, 1968), intended to be very precise, and that it is generally intended to affect citizens' actions and reasons for action, it is notorious that the language used is very difficult for laymen to grasp. It may mean little or nothing to them or else may convey a quite distorted or different message. Thus if citizens attempt to read the text or otherwise come into direct contact with legal communications (e.g. as a witness being told to avoid 'hearsay') the interaction will appear differently from each end. The power-holder and creator of the text may see it as a legitimate authority relation which attempts to induce specific actions and reasons for action, but the citizen may see different actions and reasons intended or may see it as a generally hostile and unintelligible interference. Most citizens manage to avoid making court appearances and reading legal texts. As we saw in the last section, most use intermediate interpreters. This is no easy solution as citizens are not alone in drawing from texts and other legal communications different meanings from those perceived by the text-creator/communicator. Long before deconstructionists pointed to the multiple meanings that could be given to legal texts, Stone pointed to the 'categories of illusory reference' (1968, p. 242) which listed some of the ways in which legal communication may have several meanings (categories of concealed, multiple and competing reference) or those which have little meaning (categories of circular or indeterminate reference) or no meaning at all (categories of meaningless reference). In all such cases the meaning has to be chosen or inserted by someone and it is quite possible for the speaker/writer and the listener/reader to insert different ones. Thus, if a lawyer is retained to interpret official texts there will often be an asymmetric perception of the relation by both text-creator and lawyer. Even where a form of words is used in a statute and mouthed by many as their reason for acting, the internal workings of their minds either give the words different meanings or translate it into other words which they are more accustomed to use in the decision processes. This asymmetry will be compounded by the asymmetric perceptions of the lawyer/citizen relationship. In general, the longer the chain, the greater the asymmetry between the perceptions of those at either end of the chain.

The situations and social relations in which legal communication takes place are rife with potential sources of misinterpretation. The complex dynamics of the courtroom have been a fertile study for ethnomethodologists (Cotterrell, 1984; Craib, 1984). There is generally antagonism between the litigants and often between at least one of the litigants and the legal officials concerned: defendants may be unhappy with the way they have been treated or the fact that they are defendants at all, and all lay participants tend to be alienated by what they see as a meaningless process or as a process that is understood differently by laymen and lawyers. The legal representatives themselves do not come to litigation free from bias. Each will be looking for interpretations that suit the client's case and although each will attempt a mental somersault to look for opposing interpretations with which it may be necessary to contend, neither will see those interpretations in quite the same light as their opponents. Furthermore, several of the participants may have come from, and exist in, different environments and sub-cultures (Luhmann, 1985, p. 221), with all the consequences which that has for different interpretations of social relations. Whereas lawyers may share more similar backgrounds than police, legislators, bureaucrats, defendants and witnesses, they are not a homogeneous group. Different initial perspectives may lead them to seek different kinds of legal practice, separating them from lawyers in other kinds of practice and providing experiences which reinforce the original perspectives. At more exalted levels, Gottlieb (1982) refers to the different self-interpretations of constitutional rules by the institutions and their officials involved. Carracciolo points out that 'ideological discrepancies' between legislators and judges can lead to 'breakdowns in the process of linguistic communication' (1979, p. 464). These ideological discrepancies are made all the more likely by the differential rate at which the institutions of law will fall to the groups involved in the social mêlée.

The long chains of relations involved in law make the asymmetrical way in which they are viewed even more likely. There will be little or no direct contact between legislators or higher judges and the citizens who are subject to their indirect exercises of power – especially when the intermediate relations in the chain depend on individuals who hold yet other perspectives.

Although the creators of legal texts attempt to affect the behaviour of others by writing down rules they want citizens and officials to use as reasons for their action, those texts are passed down a chain of relations being constantly reinterpreted and used to generate different rules for the actors to use at each point in the chain. In the tax example given above, the same taxation statute may affect the actions of all the participants, activating separate relations between the legislator and bureaucrat, barrister, judge and so forth. But each such power-subject will be acting in his or her own context and interpreting the text in his or her own way from his or her point of view to produce rules or other reasons for their actions.

Examples of asymmetry will be found wherever the law includes social relations of anticipatory reaction, manipulation or attempted manipulation and most relations of unforeseen effect. Face-to-face relations may suffer from asymmetry too. A barrister putting an argument to a judge was earlier given as an example of persuasion. The judge may see it as either persuasion or a recitation of his duty, but the lawyer may see it as a form of manipulation. The different views of judges and defendants are the stuff of which criminology is made – judges see their warnings to defendants as examples of legitimate authority but the defendant will usually see them as some kind of force or coercion.

As most authority relations in law are mixed, there is always a good chance that the individuals at either end of a relation will pick a different reason for the perceived compliance and hence see the relation as a different type of power relation. Even if the relation is perceived as mixed, there is a good chance that a different mix will be presumed –

power-holders such as judges and legislators believing the legitimate authority part of the power relation to have greater weight than it really has with the citizen. They share the tendency of all power-holders to overestimate the extent of their legitimate authority (chapter 7.2). Judicial remoteness from their power-subjects (chapter 8.3) and general reluctance to consider the effects of their decisions (chapter 8.2) aggravate their ignorance of the citizen's reasons for compliance and hence of the very nature of the power relations in which they are power-holders.

The power-subject's understanding of the relation will likewise be incomplete. (S)he will be unaware of manipulation and of many of the value-effects his or her beliefs have on others, and uncertain of where some of the effects (s)he experiences originate. In cases where several social relations bear upon him or her, providing several reasons for action, (s)he may not have considered them all. This is especially so if *one* of the reasons provides sufficient justification for the action taken and that reason better accords with the subject's self-image. That image may be of a victim of society and hence driven by coercive authority relations, as a responsible citizen freely following legitimate authority. Once again, the overdetermination of action and the concomitant over-sufficiency of reasons for action provide a barrier to the perception of social relations.

Judges are no more immune than citizens from such processes, making their perceptions of the relations in which they are involved as power-subjects as faulty as those of the relations in which they are power-holders. Judges are subject to a wide range of social relations (chapter 8.2). The judge may not be aware of the exact nature of these social relations but only sense a vague 'pressure' on him/her. If a judge is under such pressure and accepts an argument from authority pointing in the same direction, (s)he may convince him/herself that the latter is the only reason and that there are no other social relations affecting the decision. But it would be wrong for the social observer to confine it to such terms.

8.5   Relations, Rules and Reasoners

The view of social relations in law provided from either end is inadequate because of the asymmetrical properties of those relations. This provides yet another justification for this book's continued rejection of the jurisprudential tradition among positivist and content theorists of taking the standpoint of a judge on a generalized legal point of view in considering such relations. This is not to deny the importance of views of such relations held by judges and other lawyers for understanding those relations. As we have seen, the effect of one party on the other is mostly achieved via the thought processes of the person affected. The rejected positivist and content theories of legal system offered many insights into those views. The problem was that those insights tended to be distorted or buried by the theorists' zeal to turn them into systems – systems which judges neither could nor even sought to construct.

Positivists emphasized the way judges and other lawyers generate rules for their own action from the actions of others (especially decisions written and statutes passed). This theory accounts for this as part of the way individuals view the social relations that constitute their social environment.

Positivists also emphasized the similarity between the sources that judges use for law and the rules some might make. about them (*fiats*, secondary rules, etc.). This directs our attention to the similarities between the social relations which affect judicial decisions.

But there is no more than *similarity* in these social relations, providing *similarity* in the way resources are viewed and *similarity* in the way they affect judicial decisions. The *actual* variation in them helps explain the differences, not only between judicial actions, but also between the rules of recognition or legal science *fiats* that different judges would construct if they tried. The far greater variation in the social relations affecting other legal officials helps explain the very different rules or *fiats* that they would generate (chapter 3.4).

However, the generation of rules that provide reasons for action is rarely itself governed by rules or *fiats*. In chapters 3 and 4 we saw reasons for avoiding such rules, and if we examine the social relations in which they are called on to generate rules, a rather different picture emerges. The situations officials respond to usually involve talk of rules, demands for new rules, and interpretations and enforcements of old ones (although the response of legal institutions is more likely to be a process so that what legal officials are dealing with is part of a chain of official response to that demand). In making these responses, officials and others involved develop 'skills' in the sense that they have experience in handling that situation and dealing with it in a relatively successful way. Their actions take on a familiar form, both in the ultimate response they make and in the way they lead up to it. Thereby they cause fewer surprises, arouse less hostility and are more likely to induce intended responses in others. The skill is threefold: (1) knowledge of the usual forms of behaviour of someone in their position, (2) ability to use those forms of behaviour to induce the desired response of another in the form of an action or decision, and (3) within those forms of behaviour, the ability to pursue the ends they set themselves (these are not necessarily selfish ends – they may be the ends of the client, improvements of efficiency, furtherance of an idea, or performance of what (s)he considers his/her official duties to be).

This skill element in law is touched on in different ways by different writers. Llewelyn emphasizes law as a 'craft' (1961, p. 364). Twining and Miers taught the skills under the evocative title *How to Do Things with Rules* (1982). Finnis refers to law as 'stylized and manageable drama' (1980, p. 283). The last provides an image of law involving a play in which there are fairly recognizable characters each with fairly recognizable patterns of behaviour (i.e. practices). It is perhaps like an 'experimental' play where there is no real script and the actors are given roles and told to respond as the person they are playing would do. This play is repeated over and over again with different performers playing the parts. Their interpretations of their roles may vary enormously, as do their reasons for playing them – their skill lies in achieving their ends while still behaving in the way broadly expected of that character. Hart himself starts with the fact that we know that we can find out what the law is on a point – we have the skill – it is just that we are not sure exactly what sort of thing it is we discover, and whether there are any basic principles that govern the discovery (1961, p. 2). We are like children who can do mathematics but are ignorant of its principles or whether there are any principles at all.

The most important skills for use in law involve the ability to formulate, use and argue about rules. They are skills involving verbal rather than physical manipulation – more like debating than carpentry.[1] The particular skills will vary considerably from solicitor to advocate, to judge, to legislator, to bureaucrat, to policeman. As Twining and Miers emphasize (1982), various officials and citizens do *different* things with rules depending on their social context, standpoint, etc. Legislators will need to argue the virtues of rules, policeman spot nonconforming actions by citizens, bureaucrats determine what personal action does conform, etc. But for many the most crucial skill is the ability to generate rules applicable to the case in hand for their own use as reasons for actions. Sometimes these are generated directly from the individual's own values, as in the case of legislators framing a law or bureaucrats exercising discretion (and perhaps, in rare cases, judges, where they realize there are no significant precedents to cover the case).

The positivists appreciated that the skill was more often that of deriving a rule from the action of another legal official or set of officials (the source). But even then it may be derived for different purposes – to provide reasons for oneself or for others who have sought advice, to predict how others will act or to persuade them how to act. Officials and citizens may create secondary rules for themselves to encapsulate the practice of their skills. On the other hand they may not think about it, merely exercising their skill in generating primary rules from the source.

But in all cases it is the source which predates the rule rather than *vice versa.* A new subordinate official takes up his/her post noting the fact that the predecessors were and are affected by the actions of the relevant superior officials. (S)he may consider it right, prudent or unavoidable to follow suit, in which case (s)he has a reason to consider the superiors as a source. If (s)he does formalize this into a personal secondary rule, it will postdate not only the existence of the superior officials who are the source, but also the existence of the power relationship, the practice of treating the officials as a source, and his/her practice of treating them as a source. At the very best the rule of recognition becomes a *part* of the subordinate official's *skill of generation* of rules from sources. That skill may include other rules, but like so many skills it is likely to be only partly based on, or expressible in, rules.

Positivists also emphasized the way judges and other lawyers generate rules for their own action from the actions of others (especially decisions written and statutes passed). This theory accounts for this as part of the way individuals view the social relations that constitute their social environment.

8.6   Towards a Theory of Law

So far we have been looking at the nature of social relationships found within what might be considered law. As we turn to the larger picture we are confronted by similar interrelated questions to those which sociological systems theories addressed. What are the effects of law, its impact on individuals and society, and how are they achieved?

When functionalist systems theories attempted to answer such questions, they had great difficulty for reasons that are worth recapitulating. The functions claimed were often *a priori* and the proposed institutional mechanisms were rarely plausible.

1   It is very difficult for an *institution* (let alone a set of them) to have an overall purpose or function because of the number of people, usually with differing values and perceptions, involved in it.

2   Even where the institution is founded by an individual or group with a distinct goal, new members may have quite different reasons for joining, including redirecting its activity towards different goals.

3   The assignment of a function or purpose is no more than the *selection* of certain of an institution's effects because of their significance to the assignor. That significance is based on the assignor's beliefs about what the institution's greatest effects *are* or what they *ought* to be.

However, in the theory outlined here, the questions and the answers come naturally. Law is seen as a massive web of social relations. Those social relations are defined in terms of the effects some actions have on others and the mechanisms by which those effects are achieved. In answering questions about the sum total of those relations the overall questions are addressed.

Within the massive and immensely complex web of social relations that constitute law there are smaller, tighter webs of legal institutions. These institutions take the form outlined in chapter 7.9.

Through this web of relations one person may affect the actions of many others both inside and outside legal institutions. (S)he achieves a far greater impact than ever (s)he could acting alone – by initiating multiple chains of interactions (s)he can mobilize the resources of many others. Yet those who are affected by these chains will usually be affected by other chains of interaction starting with the actions of other legal officials. Thus through the web of relations in law, one individual can affect many, and many may affect one individual. These effects are regarded as effects of *law* if (1) they are produced by the actions of a member of a legal institution, and (2) that action was itself affected by the action of at least one other member of a legal institution, i.e. they are part of a chain of interactions within law.

The impact of law on any individual is the sum total of the effects produced on that individual by all such relations. The sum of these effects on all individual members of a society is the overall impact of law on that society. The next two sections will consider those impacts in more detail.

Chapter 8.9 will consider the way that impact is achieved through the mêlée of institutions and relations. In doing so we shall get some idea of how the overall social mêlée affects legal institutions to produce a legal mêlée, how the legal mêlée reinforces the social mêlée, and how the chains of relations snake through this mêlée and ensure that social relations within law achieve their effects indirectly. Then, in chapter 8.10, we will consider the consequence this has for the kinds of effects that can be achieved through law.

8.7 Law's Impact on Individuals

Social relations in law are defined by the kinds of effects they have on those at either end of them. The overall impact of law on any individual is the sum of such effects. Naturally such effects vary enormously.

Sometimes an individual loses life, liberty or property. But most individuals experience law as imposing limitations and providing opportunities for the actions they take in everyday life. The limitations will sometimes take the form of barriers that make certain actions impossible. If discovered we just *cannot* use goods we have forcibly removed from another's possession, or live in a new house built less than ten feet from an Australian suburban street. But the limitations will usually be in the form of costs imposed on specific actions. Those costs may involve money and time or greater risk (as in the unenforceability of some contracts). Law may provide opportunities for citizens – tax concessions, social welfare, and ways of enforcing their wishes after death.

The effects of law on an individual go further. They affect the individual's environment by affecting the actions of others. Furthermore, by generally preventing or encouraging certain behaviour, law creates habits and, through them, ultimately attitudes (chapter 7.7). Above all, the law affects an individual's practical reasoning by making some things impossible and by providing reasons for and against action (when there are opportunities and limitations respectively). Of course, an individual may work on the practical reasons presented by the social relations of which (s)he is a part. The generalized normative feelings may be crystallized into rules. Those internally held rules may be seen as the individual's reaction to the social relations of which (s)he is a part. (S)he may give weight and priority to them according to the strength of the relation. (S)he may even try a 'rational reconstruction' of some of these rules, hence partially organizing his/her reaction to the social relations in order to facilitate his/her own action. Rules which, in the form they take in the individual's mind, appear to contradict each other, may be modified or rejected. In so doing, the individual may effectively alter the social relation. If a rule derived from manipulation, legitimate authority or a value-effect relation is rejected as inconsistent with a stronger value held, the social relation is extinguished. If a rule is derived from a relation of persuasion or competent authority and rejected, the relation will be weakened. However, if a rule is derived from a coercive or inducement relation, this kind of internal reflection cannot eliminate the threat/offer or the reason it provides and thus cannot eliminate the social relation (although the effectiveness of the relation and the reason derived from it may be weakened if the individual revises his or her values to make the threat less pressing and the inducement less attractive). If the rule is derived from a mixed relation of which coercion is a part, it strips away the noncoercive parts of the relation and may accordingly weaken the relation without completely eliminating it.

However, it must be emphasized that this ordering is partial, and both internal and unique to the individual. It will be unique to the individual for two reasons. First, the reasons (and hence his/her ends of the relations) organized are located in, and are uniquely a part of, his or her mind.

Secondly, the content of such rules will vary slightly and will vary more as the process of rational reconstruction puts them in an increasingly unique intellectual environment, and the location, context, activities and interests of that individual will lead him or her to reconstruct the reasons from a unique set of social relations. The organization will be partial because, as we saw in chapter 4, individuals will rarely have reason to take it far.

8.8   Law's Impact on Society

The sum of the effects on individuals is the overall impact of law on society. The functions and purposes that have been suggested for law provide a good shortlist of what some of the major effects on society may be. (The main problem with the functionalist account was not that these functions did not identify actual effects of law, but that they chose among the effects and defined law in terms of the chosen ones.) In chapter 5 the main effects discussed were: dispute resolution; 'reinforcement', 'reinstitutionalization' or 'reproduction' of existing practices; change (usually by reinforcement and reinstitutionalization of *new* practices); guidance; regulation; participation by the state in social and economic affairs (including the redistribution of resources); punishment or vengeance; maintaining social peace and preventing outbreaks of violence; legitimization; and the production and transmission of ideology.

These are some of the effects of law. Indeed, to some extent it is because institutions achieve, at least partly, one or more of these effects that we call them part of law. But it should not be forgotten that these overall effects are, where achieved, composed of multitudinous individual effects indirectly or directly imparted by members of legal institutions on individual citizens through social relations. Conversely, where these effects are only partially achieved, those relations are fewer and/or weaker, producing fewer or weaker individual effects. It should also be remembered that many of the effects of law are also the effects of other institutions. Thus if a particular effect is achieved, it is because the effects of a host of social relations, both within and without law, have achieved it. Cotterrell warns that law should not be reified and seen as something outside a society achieving some specified impact on it (1984, p. 70). There is no danger of that in this theory, which sees law as part of the interaction of members of society with each other. Indeed the theory outlined here can effectively redescribe the achievement of these effects. Any outcome that is achieved in society is the result of a large number of social relations affecting the individual and thereby furthering or inhibiting the achievement of that outcome.

1 *Dispute resolution* involves officials dealing with disputes by imposing orders by mixed authority relations on parties who come (or are brought) before them, and by the effect the anticipation of such orders has on others who settle for fear of losing in court (and sometimes even the costs of winning).

2 *Guidance* is achieved by many individuals taking on new values or strengthening existing ones through relations of legitimate and competent authority in which members of legal institutions are power-holders, by having their values strengthened by witnessing the imposition of force on noncompliers, and by perceiving the implied threat that the exercise of force has for them.

3 The effect of *punishment* is produced by legal officials exercising physical force.

4 The *maintenance of social peace* is produced by the many relations of inducement, coercion, force and anticipated reaction by legal officials that impose effective limitations on the use of force by individuals.

5 *Participation by the state* in areas of *social and economic life* involves opportunities and limitations for individuals in those areas of life engendered by the action of officials.

6 *The formation of practices* (in the sense used in chapter 7.7) is aided by law to the extent that social relations with legal officials (and hence the reasons derived from them) are fairly constant for the same person at different times (an individual's practice) or for similar persons at the same time (a group practice) or where different legal relations have, by chance, congruent effects.

7 *Reinforcement* and *change* involve the creation of new power relations using state resources that supplement those social relations already existing within society. This encompasses the functions of law described by Bohannen as the 'reinstitutionalization of practices or norms' existing in other institutions (1968, p. 73) and Collins in his 'metanormative' theory of law (1982, p. 90). The essence of these ideas is that there are practices in the community and that officials within the institutions of law, usually judges or legislators, make legal rules with more or less the same content. Collins points out that there will usually be a *choice* of *conflicting* practices and that it is this conflict which brings the matter to court. The theory outlined here maintains that practices in the community reflect the power and other relations to be found there, for instance the practices of employers and employees are largely the result of the exercise of various power relations by both groups. The parties attempt to extend or resist these exercises of power and change the practices involved. If the

dispute comes before it, the court creates a new power relation between employers and employees that operates via the institution of law. This will involve a chain of relations in which one citizen has a power of legitimate authority over some official in the institution of law and, through other relations internal to the institution of law, will end in a relation of some kind between another official and the other citizen. This new power relation will enshrine not the whole of the relationship between the parties but only a part, e.g. by *adding* to the power of the employer to remove employees from the premises, or adding to that of the employees by increasing the costs or difficulty of dismissal (by requiring redundancy payments or tribunals to hear claims of unfair dismissal). Thus the balance of the power relations between two classes of citizens can be changed, frequently also changing practices or the resources each can derive from them. Each side involved in the dispute will naturally attempt to persuade and pressure the court into reinforcing the areas of their relationship where they are strong. Such new power relations created by law play an important part in the process of social change discussed in chapter 7.12. Naturally, citizens may attempt to persuade or pressure a court (or a legislature or an official) into creating power relations that counteract power relations that another citizen has over him/her. However, in order to be successful this will normally require resources and other power relations in another area which can be brought to bear on the outcome. By this, law provides facilities for converting power in one area of activity into power in another.

The reinforcement or reinstitutionalization effects are seen by some Marxists in terms of the 'reproduction of relations'. The way this theory envisages this occurring, via the addition of power and other relations from or through legal institutions, helps to shift individuals who are subject to them into practices and then into relations with each other that are similar to relations that have occurred between similar persons before. However, the law plays only a part in this because it provides only some of the relations which generate these practices, and the variable impact of law on individuals and its associated effect of changing practices suggests that relations are 'produced' rather than reproduced and the degree of similarity in relations would help to indicate how similar the newly produced relations were to old ones.

8   The *generation and transmission of ideology*. Because law involves attempts to use persuasive interpretations of texts to justify the behaviour of, or claims by, litigants, many might see law as a prime 'site' (Hunt, 1985) for the generation of ideology. The power and other relations involved in the reporting of decisions and their use in other cases and in

legal advice given outside litigation might provide sites for transmission through relations of persuasion and legitimate authority. But lawyers' positivist detachment mutes the extent to which new justifications are sought and lawyers are just as likely to appeal to the 'ideologies' they think can be found in the judges' minds, so as sites for the generation of ideology they are limited.

Judges are not strong on self-justification. (Dworkin's Hercules is notable as a mythical exception.) They rely on technical interpretation of texts which are separated by positivist theory from value-judgments in their own minds and are separated by impenetrable prose from the value-judgments in the minds of citizens. As Hunt (1985) argues, law's effectivity as sites of transmission to the general public is greatly overrated.

However, the tendency of lawyers to avoid justification and to treat certain facts and rules as obvious and unavoidable might be seen as another ideological technique. The problems of effectivity of transmission arises here again and they are exacerbated by the trend Luhmann saw of an increasingly variable law as being contingent and noninevitable. The adversarial process, and the strong interests of at least one party in believing that the law should and could be different, militate against this too.

This view of ideology in law might be criticized for being too 'idealistic', insufficiently 'material' and insufficiently rooted in practice, and for treating ideas as too much of an independent variable from material reality. I would agree with Sumner that practices are 'ideological' in the sense that certain activities often appear to go with particular ideas and that participants in those activities are more likely to adopt those ideas. However, the actions and the ideological justifications and descriptions of them are still separate in that: (a) actions which the social observer cannot and would not in any case care to distinguish may be entered into without those justifications, (b) quite different justifications or explanations for those actions may be generated or adopted by participants, and (c) indeed actions may be stable while the ideological justification for them changes.

9   *Legitimation*. In a sense legitimation, the functionalist term, is narrower than the effects considered under ideology, encompassing merely the transmission of favourable value ideas to produce value-effect relations via relations of persuasion, manipulation, legitimate authority and to some extent competent authority. Law can help in this process but suffers from the same effectivity problems as ideology in general and is likely to generate opposite effects as well (see chapter 5.10).

8.9   Legal Institutions in the Social Mêlée

In the last section we saw how the action of legal officials can have significant effects on individuals throughout society. It is hardly surprising that individuals, groups and their mobilizing institutions attempt to influence that official action so that its effect upon them is favourable. They will attempt to exercise the full range of power relations over those officials. In so doing they may be aided by the officials' anticipation of unfavourable reaction and holding of values in which the group members are value-beneficiaries.

If there were only one powerful group involved and they could mobilize all their resources to the task, no legal official could resist. However there are many groups attempting to affect the actions of legal officials in different directions. Indeed such attempts occupy a central place in the social mêlée and, like other conflicts in that mêlée, they are frequently limited and inconclusive. The resources of the relevant groups can only be partially mobilized and the mobilizing institutions do not always direct those resources into the conflict (and would, in any case, have to decide into *which* conflicts to direct them). The other group is active in providing support for the legal official if (s)he resists the attempts to control his/her action, and active in resisting that action if (s)he succumbs. Targeted legal officials will themselves tend to resist attempts to control their actions as it is in their (usually perceived) institutional interests to maximize their range of choice (chapter 7.9).

The extent to which the outside group or institution can affect targeted officials depends not only on the resources that can be mobilized and brought to bear on them, but also on the intra-institutional social relations by which other members of the institution affect their behaviour, and on the officials themselves (they will have their own values which may either support or militate against the particular action sought).

The outcome of the external conflict will also be complicated and affected by conflict between and within the institutions of law. This is partly due to the usual causes of *inter-* and *intra*-institutional conflict – the constant struggle by officials within each institution to reduce the limits placed on them by officials in other institutions, and increase the opportunities for affecting officials in other institutions (i.e. to reduce the number and strength of social relations in which they are the power-subject, anticipator, etc., and increase the number and strength of those in which they are the power-holder, reactor, etc.). But the internal conflict is also partly stimulated by the external conflict itself – the different members being influenced by, or holding values supportive of, competing groups.

Legal history is replete with examples of conflict between the institutions of law: Crown versus courts then Crown versus Commons in the seventeenth century, Lords versus Commons and Congress versus Supreme Court in this century. These major conflicts were attempts to throw off or impose power relations that severely limited the actions of officials in one of the institutions. Usually the conflict is neither as dramatic nor as intense and involves a constant struggle of boundary-maintenance (which inevitably involves an attempt subtly to move those boundaries) as in Lord Denning's attempt to expand the role of the Court of Appeal by claiming the ability to ignore limitations imposed by House of Lords precedents (*Broome* v. *Cassell* [1971] 2 QB 354) and his more successful attempt to impose limitations on the actions of bureaucrats (e.g. *Congreve* v. *Home Office* [1976] 1 ALLER 697). Key bureaucrats have tried to resist the latter by influencing governments to push through legislation protecting their discretion from court-imposed limitations; and the struggle continues. Other examples are to be found in the attempts by courts to control police arrest and interrogation practices.

There is also ample evidence of *intra*-institutional conflict. Permanent internal conflict between and within party groupings is now regarded as central to the very nature of legislatures in western countries. Though less public, conflict within courts is endemic over both 'style' (Llewelyn, 1961) and substance (Schubert, 1968b). Bureaucracies, of course, are a by-word for intra-institutional conflict.

There is a danger that this internal conflict within law may divert our attention from the external conflict. Debates about the content of statutes and judgments, and clashes of personalities or interests within institutions, may be seen as the origins and determinants of conflicts rather than as a *part* of an overall conflict. The law is not above the conflict, nor unaffected by it. It is not 'autonomous'. But it is, in a sense, '*relatively* autonomous' (Poulantzas, 1975; cf. Hunt, 1985). This is because conflict over the action of legal officials must be fought on a particular battleground within legal institutions where the outcome is affected by the nature of those institutions and the officials and relations that comprise them. On that battleground some of the resources of conflicting groups are more useful than others, so that some outside groups may have success in some legal institutions disproportionate to their overall strength.

Law is also relatively autonomous in a further sense. Because the conflict over the action of legal officials is relatively inconclusive, it leaves certain officials with a relatively wide range of choice of actions that they can 'get away with'. Of course, there are many things these officials cannot do, either because they lack the resources or because they are subject to social relations that make performing the action either impossible or counter-productive (especially where the action mobilizes an overwhelming coalition of opposing groups and institutions, as the House of

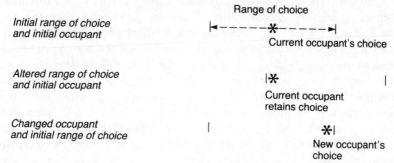

Figure 8.1   Affecting official action – changing the official and affecting his/her range of choice

Lords did in 1911, mobilizing against themselves the Commons, Crown and a plurality of the voting population). Where the official is left with a choice of action, other social relations, only some of them imposed by the conflicting groups, will provide reasons for choices within that range: power relations to which (s)he is subject and reactions (s)he anticipates will provide reasons whether because of sanctions or inducements they offer for various actions. The official's 'role' in the institution also has consequences for his or her choice of actions. This has two aspects (chapter 7.6): an internal matter of how (s)he values his/her place within the institution and what (s)he believes his/her action should be within it (role-orientation); and a relation of anticipatory reaction in the criticism (and worse) (s)he anticipates, should (s)he not fulfil what others perceive to be his/her role (role-expectations). There is usually a range of role-expectations (chapter 7.6). Consequently criticism will be limited and partly matched by counteracting praise if the action falls within that range.

Within institutions, officials' range of choice will vary. Those with the greatest range of choice are the key officials. They are power-holders, reactors and value-beneficiaries in relatively more relations and power-subjects, anticipators and value-holders in fewer ones. Consequently, outside groups attempt to affect not only the *action* of those in such key positions but *who* fills them as well. Indeed, changing the range of choice open to the holder of such a position (by altering the power relations affecting it) may have far less effect than changing the occupant. If the current occupant previously exercised his/her discretion within the middle of the range of possible options then, unless the range of options is changed so drastically as to exclude the old decision as a possibility, the occupant is unlikely to change the way (s)he acts (figure 8.1).

As in the conflict over official action, so the struggle over key official posts varies with the forms of power that the various groups can exercise over those who make the appointment. In the UK the cabinet determines most senior judicial and bureaucratic appointments. However, particular appointments are frequently affected by other incumbents and by specific interest groups (e.g. bar influence on judicial appointments). Appointment is often subject to power relations internal to the institution, and also subject to those factors that tend to produce a much higher proportion of uncontroversial candidates from some groups than others. This struggle is carried on simultaneously for all the key posts in legal institutions. But success, if it comes at all, will be preceded by long periods when struggle is inconclusive and each side must accept some appointments from other groups. Even when a group or class does succeed in dominating appointments within several institutions, such success is not simultaneous. Thus a group may find itself with the specific resources necessary for some appointments rather than others. A rising group may fill posts in the legislature first, the bureaucracy and judiciary next, and the police last of all (chapter 7.12). This differential rate of success in capturing institutions within the shifting social mêlée provides a prime source of the institutional conflict discussed above, through the different values and beliefs that appointees from different groups are likely to hold.

This conflict naturally helps explain why legal institutions do not harmoniously perform their functions (chapter 5.6). It helps explain why there is no simple or single hierarchy of sources (those sources being institutions in conflict with each other) and why the output of subordinate sources being affected by outside social phenomena does not fit into a pyramid of legal authority (chapter 3.5). It also helps explain the disorder of the textual output of legal institutions (chapter 4.4). That is a result of the historical struggles over official positions and the actions of their incumbents.

8.10 Indirect Achievement of Effects in Law

What enables key officials to have widespread effects on others is the large number of social relations in which they are power-holder, reactor and value-beneficiary, and the many chains of social interaction that their own actions can trigger. But the corollary of this is that the effects they have on individual citizens are achieved very indirectly. In the tax crackdown example in chapter 8.3, we saw how legislators can have very considerable effects on individual citizens. But those effects may be achieved only via a chain of interactions that pass through virtually every institution in law – at least one House of Parliament, cabinet, a ministry,

A Non-systematic Theory of Law and Society

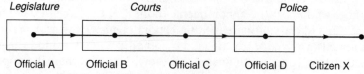

Figure 8.2   Simple chain of social interaction

the bar and a court. This is a major reason for including all those institutions in law. Unless they are considered a part of law, we must conclude that the effects of law are felt mostly through non-legal institutions. Rejecting such inclusions is possible but it tends to confine law to little more than a complicated rite, performed by a few high priests, with only indirect effects on society or ourselves. If the law is felt to be central to society and something with which we do have close and frequent contact, then this more inclusive approach to law will be preferred.

These institutions do not act as monolithic, impersonal machines through which effects are transmitted. Institutions are made up of chains of relations linking discrete individuals. These people have their own ideas and values, each will exist in his or her own (at least slightly) different environment and will have his or her own (frequently different) view of the relation through which (s)he receives and passes on the effect to those at the other ends of relations.

At each link in the chain of interactions, a separate action is required. In taking that action, each subsequent official actor will be affected by several social relations in which (s)he is involved – the social relation one step back in the chain is only one of these. Those other social relations may be completely external to law (especially power relations in which outside groups attempt to affect him/her). They may be parts of other chains of relations within legal institutions or may be mixtures of the two (e.g. when a court makes a decision favourable to suspects, civil liberties groups may attempt to coerce police to follow the ruling with a threat of adverse publicity). The conception of chains of relations should not be permitted to obscure the fact that they are part of the web of social relations and that these chains have been picked out because we are interested in how one person affects another via the effects (s)he has on the decisions of others. Rather than being a solitary chain as in figure 8.2, it is more like that in figure 8.3, with the dotted line being the chain picked out because of an interest in the ultimate effects that Official A has on Citizen X.

The range of choice of these subsequent official actors will vary. Those social relations, and the practices and values they generate, may limit it to

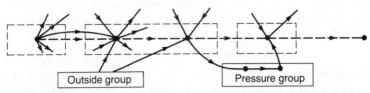

Outside group

Pressure group

Figure 8.3   Chain of interaction through the social mêlée

the extent that for all practical purposes there is only one action the actor can realistically expect to perform. Depending on what that action is, the chain of reactions will continue, stop dead or move off at a tangent. But many officials are not so constrained. Many are not tightly controlled or monitored, attempts to control them are via texts which have multiple interpretations, and many make a virtue of giving discretion and latitude to officials such as judges (not necessarily because they cannot control officials but in some cases because they do not want to). Foucault sees this decentralization of power as part of modern society (1980, p. 96), although in fact such decentralization of power is a necessary part of effective institutions (chapter 5.6). If, as a consequence of such factors, officials are left with a significant range of choice, they can intentionally or otherwise divert chains of interaction that pass through them from their intended path. Such officials are likely to include ministers and senior bureaucrats, policemen, prison officials and judges. It also includes those who have strong power relations over a small number of persons with few social relations which impose limitations on their action (including prison officers in inmates' cells, policemen in the 'deep peace' of the interrogation room, and the man who handles the punch cards).

The range of choice open even to key officials should not be exaggerated. Courts may twist legislation and, in some countries, rule it unconstitutional; but they could not interpret *all* legislation contrary to its initiator's intent or rule *all* legislation unconstitutional. Senior bureaucrats may frustrate their ministers but cannot do exactly as they please. So it is emphasized that it is only within the range of choice in the action they can take, dictated by the social relations in which they are involved, that they have discretion and an opportunity to deflect the chain of interaction of which they form a part.

Four aspects of law and society as depicted in the last two chapters enhance the significance of these intermediate steps in the chains of interactions, and the extent to which these chains of interactions are deflected to produce effects quite different from those expected by the initiator (or, for that matter, the social observer).

1   The variable success by different social groups and institutions in affecting the action of legal officials means that some officials in the chain will be influenced by some groups and some officials by others.

2   The variable success by those same outsiders over the filling of different official posts will likewise mean that different officials within the chain of interaction will want to deflect the chain in different ways. Where appointments to an institution are shared between conflicting groups, the direction of deflection will depend on *which* official the chain passes through.

3   The conflict between legal institutions weakens the links in the chain of social relations prior to that official's action, increasing the discretion of that official to do as he believes fit and again increasing the chance of deflection.

4   Some institutions have a disproportionate share in achieving some of the effects of law. Lower courts are more involved in punishment and the settlement of minor disputes, higher courts in the settlement of disputes and the choice of power relations that will be duplicated by law. Police are more involved in the maintenance of social peace, the legislature with guidance and the bureaucracy with the participation of the state in social and economic affairs. This disproportionate share may lead to practices and priorities that shift the effect that is finally produced on the citizen when a chain of effects passes through a member of a particular institution. For instance, the police may be delegated authority to bring evidence of offences before the court but their concentration, and consequent emphasis, on achieving the public order effects of law may lead them to see their role as one of obtaining convictions instead.

The indirect achievement of legal effects means that many of the effects finally achieved are not quite as intended. They may not even be intended at all (hence the high proportion of unintended effects in law). Nevertheless, the conflicting parties still consider the total effects achieved to be so great that even the intentional portion is worth fighting over.

8.11   Consequences for the Effects of Law

Because the effects of law on individuals and its overall impact on society have to be achieved through a mêlée of institutions and relations, those effects tend to be relatively crude, conflicting, incomplete and nonuniform. In explaining these characteristics we learn more about the nature of both law and the society of which it forms a part and also why functionalist systems failed, because they prevented legal institutions adequately achieving any prescribed effects, always producing contrary ones instead.

Crudity

The indirect achievement of legal effects and their consequent dilution, deflection and distortion leads to one of the great ironies of law. At the highest levels, the action of key officials is extremely precise. Acts of parliament can quite literally go to enormous lengths to define words and concepts and judges will spend pages of their judgments on finer points (though the number of judges involved often means that conflicting exercises in precision produce extremely imprecise results). Yet the effect on the public is far less precise, indeed it can only be called 'crude'. Law will affect an individual in one of three ways: (1) by the actual action of members of legal institutions towards him/her; (2) by his/her knowledge of the 'law', or of how members of legal institutions will act towards him/her, and any consequent modification of his/her actions; and (3) indirectly by the effects law has on other citizens thereby changing his/her environment. Only the first two will be considered in this section, it being fairly obvious that the indirect effects will be cruder still.

The interaction between members of legal institutions and citizens is certainly affected by the actions of legislators and superior-court judges through long chains of interaction leading ultimately to minor officials and citizens. However, despite all their efforts at precision and the clear specification of how those who have performed specific acts should be dealt with, the actions of the juries, police and bureaucrats who deal with individual citizens bear only a resemblance to that specification. This is again largely because of the number of intermediate relations through which the interaction must pass before it reaches the citizen, the causes of deflection and distortion inherent in such chains of interaction, the mixed and weak nature of the intermediate social relations, the many other relations that affect the intermediate actions, and the mutual hostility, institutional independence and varying ideological bents of the officials through whom the chains pass. (Indeed, a combination of these reasons may mean that actions of the legislator or judge come to nothing, many of the chains of interaction in law petering out long before they reach their mark). The problem is exacerbated because, along with a chain of intended effects, the initiator also initiates a chain of unforeseen effects which may reduce, or even cancel, the effects of the intended one. The problem is also partly a matter of discovery and proof. The legislator or judge may attempt to specify what is supposed to happen to someone who has performed a specific type of action (e.g. taken goods from another with criminal intent or set up a secret trust before death): but to find out whether the act has been done and then prove it is another matter. These are the weakest links in the chain of interactions between legislator and citizen. All the fine points of law come to nothing if you cannot even prove the basic ones. Indeed, the finer the points are, the more difficult it may be for JPs and juries to comprehend them and decide correctly whether they have been established. Finally, the crudeness of the overall effect is partly a simple matter of the difficulties involved in communication. However precise the message is initially, it is degraded at each translation each time another has to receive, absorb and put it into his or her own words or actions. The message is degraded even more rapidly if the receiver holds different perceptions of the communication from the communicator (i.e. if the relations are, as so often in law, asymmetrical).

By the time the message reaches the citizen it is a parody of its former legal exactitude. The citizen's knowledge of the law will be weak – gained, if at all, in a 'muddled and accidental fashion' (Hughes, 1960, p. 1011). Certainly (s)he does not know the finer points as spelt out in judgments or statutes. (S)he knows that depriving others of the goods in their possession is generally unlawful but (s)he might be surprised at some of the acts made criminal under the Theft Act 1968 (UK).

It might be objected that for an ordinary citizen the values (s)he holds and the other relations in which (s)he is involved provide an abundance of reasons not to steal. The law is unnecessary for that citizen so (s)he need not know its details. We should look instead for the effect law has on those for whom the balance of reasons is finer – those who contemplate or actually do steal and who are more likely to find out exactly what the law is. But even a thief's knowledge of the law will tend to be weak. (S)he has, perhaps, a fair idea that certain contemplated actions are against the law and that if discovered it will probably lead to gaol. If a lawyer later said the action was not covered by the law, (s)he would consider it a miraculous loophole, and the lawyer a clever twister of words. *Pace* Holmes (1897) the views of 'real' 'bad men' are not good guides to law.

Examples need not be taken from deliberate lawbreakers. A trader may hear of a new Fair Trading Act that has been passed. (S)he will vaguely appreciate some of the specific requirements (s)he must meet, and generally understand that standards of conduct must be raised. But the effect on the trade will be to encourage more care in business practices generally. (S)he may still may be breaking the law or his/her honesty may surpass the minimum required. The law has had an effect on the trade as it has had in deterring some from theft. But it does not operate as a fine navigational instrument charting the paths a citizen may and may not tread: it is rather an institutional bludgeon which many take as a warning to steer clear of whole areas of activity altogether.

Even when lawyers are consulted, the law does not operate as a finely honed tool. Lawyers have practices and documentary precedents which are designed not merely to skirt legal pitfalls, but to keep the citizen well away from them. They will advise clients to avoid many kinds of claims in their advertising so that there will be absolutely no danger of making statements for which they could be prosecuted. They will advise the use of two witnesses to a will rather than the use of any of the exceptions to this requirement, and they will even advise the use of the same pen by witness and testator to avoid any suggestion that the signatures were added later to validate an informal will. In doing so they are considering not so much what would ultimately happen in an appeal court if ever their client ended up there, but the difficulties the client could experience because of the doubts and the queries that could be raised by lower officials. They are offering advice on how to avoid possible time- and money-wasting encounters with lower officials, officials whose attempts to carry the effects of the appeal court's precise formulations of law to the public are fairly crude. This will be something of a self-fulfilling prophecy. Practices set up by lawyers will be presumed by many non-legally trained officials to be lawful, and legally trained officials will have practised or seen them practised and regarded them as normal. Similarly, when barristers advise and act for clients, they are not merely armed with the knowledge of what would happen on an appeal. They also consider processes involved in the lower courts in which they argue and how to handle the functionaries of such courts. Others who advise citizens on how to act in relation to the institutions of law are likewise concerned with the crude way in which the law ultimately operates. A Civil Liberties Union's advice on how to react to policemen will spend little time on the niceties of arrest law as expanded in courts, but will emphasize courtesy and civility when requesting rights while still under the physical control of the police. Again, a social worker's best advice to a client may be on how to deal with town hall, welfare and unemployment officials, rather than merely the criteria for welfare recipients. A citizen's contact with the law is almost exclusively through its lower officials; that is how the law affects the citizen; to a large extent that is what the law is for the citizen. The operation of the law through these officials is far cruder than in the judgments and statutes that prompt such official action. Lawyers who advise those citizens should ever be aware of that fact.

It might be objected that the use of texts in law is designed to solve these difficulties of communication and to make law precise in its meaning and effect. However, the interpretation of texts is variable according, *inter alia*, to varying standpoints, values, etc. Furthermore, as already seen, new texts are often created to explain older ones, adding further difficulties to effective communication. Although the creators of legal texts attempt to affect the behaviour of others by writing down rules they want citizens and officials to use as reasons for their action, those texts can get passed down a chain of relations being altered and reinterpreted and different rules may be taken out by the actors at each point in the chain. Each power-subject will be acting in his or her own context and interpreting the text in his or her own way from his or her own standpoint to produce rules or other reasons for his or her actions.

Law is not about solving problems or determining outcomes by author-itative texts with single interpretations and singular prescribed or pros-cribed activities. Law is about creating texts to affect outcomes because those texts are rhetorically interpreted by those involved in the 'problem' areas of interaction at which legal officials have directed their attention. The use made will vary with context, standpoint, etc. Individuals will 'do different things with the rule', or rather with the texts. In a sense, law can only 'throw texts at problems', only 'cast their texts upon the waters'. A good legislator should know this, and to an extent this has always been known. Certainly in areas of so-called private law, law is intended to operate on the motion of non-officials, legal texts being created with the intention that they be used by litigants and those planning their affairs.

The multiple and different uses of texts, like its institutional basis, are a source of both strength and weakness for law. Multiple uses mean that the texts are used more, thus increasing their total effect. But they also mean that the effects are less precise, more diffuse, and further from those intended by the drafters.

The phrases 'throwing texts at problems', and 'casting texts upon the waters' are used with two conscious connotations. First, the texts are not self-executing but operate only when used by others for their own pur-poses and are interpreted in accordance with their standpoints, values, interests, etc. Second, there is a tendency in modern western societies to throw texts at problems in the same way as they were, largely unjustly, accused of throwing money at problems. There has been a tendency to throw more and more texts at identified problems (like income tax avoi-dance) without really concentrating on how those texts are going to operate to deal with the problems. If one thousand pages of legislative texts do not solve the problem initially, it is highly unlikely that two thousand pages of texts will solve the problem either.

Conflict

The effects law has on a single person can, and frequently do, conflict and contradict each other (Hunt, 1985). They are the result of several chains of interaction culminating in the production of effects on that individual. These chains originate in the actions of different officials, often in different legal institutions. The effects the chain of relations is *intended* to have on that person or type of person (if any) will vary with: (1) the variety of actions possible for those officials given the social relations which affect their actions; (2) various institutional interests those officials share; and (3) their personal values (partly accidental and partly because of the differential ability of major outside groupings to influence those appointments). Thus the intended effects may conflict. Unintended effects are even more likely to conflict. Even if two chains of relations originate from the same official position, that position may be occupied at different times by persons with different values, or even one person with inconsistent or conflicting values (a prime minister wishing to promote both investment and pollution control may start many chains of relations, some of which end with officials seeking to encourage the same investment that other officials at the end of other relations set out to stop). Finally, different relations, though originating within the same institution or with the same official, may pass along different paths, through different chains of relations. These chains will pass through different institutions and hence through different individuals who have their *own* aims and values, and are affected by different social relations. Accordingly, their actions tend to deflect the chains of interaction in different directions. For instance, in a crack-down on violent crime a minister may force through legislation drastically increasing penalties and devote more resources to the police for the investigation of such crime. The police may bring more people before the courts, meaning that more suspects suffer the indignities of police custody. But the juries who decide cases, reacting against the heavy penalties consequent on a guilty verdict, might convict in fewer cases than before.

Incompleteness

The effects of law are *incomplete* in that only some areas of an individual's behaviour are affected. Law does not constitute a system of social control, but is felt by each individual as a set of discrete effects that impose limitations and provide opportunities in limited areas of life. The social observer's view of law will take the same form, merely adding effects that the individual does not notice – i.e. the effects of chains of relations ending in relations of manipulation, value-effect and unforeseen effects.

This incompleteness in the effects of law is largely due to the limited effectiveness of legal institutions. It will only very partially be due to the more usually offered explanation of limited desires to regulate social life – desires which should not carelessly be attributed to officials of legal institutions!

Non-uniformity

The vast number of individual effects of widely differing nature allows the many claims about the functions of law to be made. If only *some* of the effects are observed it will be easy to see law providing guidance, exacting vengeance, settling disputes, maintaining social peace or reinforcing existing practices. It allows many of these effects to be achieved simultaneously. But it also allows different sociological theorists, by focusing on *other* individual effects, to claim contradictory functions – the exacerbation of disputes, the aggravation of social tension and the promotion of social change by reinforcing new practices. The law can have a large number of unrelated or even contradictory effects on society because each of those effects involves summations of different sets of individual effects.

The various kinds of effects will not be distributed uniformly, some may fall predominantly upon certain social groups, the individual effects summed being mainly between legal officials and members of that group. Certain classes may be more affected by the law's vengeance than its ability to solve disputes (Hirst, 1979, p. 96), the actions by which legal officials maintain social peace may fall on some groups rather than others. Sometimes this will be because the chains of relations culminating in that effect will originate in different officials (e.g. laws controlling business may originate in Labour majorities and laws controlling unions may originate in Conservative ones). At other times it may be because chains of relations pass through different officials (e.g. legislation outlawing 'white collar' and 'ordinary' crime may be devised by the same Attorney General but are administered by a Corporate Affairs Commission and the police respectively. These bodies treat suspects very differently). Sometimes it will be because the officials through whom those chains pass have different attitudes to the different groups (i.e. different value-effect relations) resulting in different treatment of their members. Even a completely unprejudiced official may find it virtually impossible to act against members of some groups because of the power relations to which (s)he is subject or the reaction (s)he can anticipate if (s)he tries.

This differential effect of law on different groups may strongly colour the view of law held by their members. *Feeling* certain effects of law, they tend to see the achievement of those effects as the *function* law has in their society. They will also tend to generalize from the nature of the social relations they experience (i.e. the last social relations in the chains of such relations linking them to members of legal institutions). If, when seen from their end, these relations appear coercive or legitimate, then they will tend to believe all social relations in law to be similar.[2]

8.12 'The Law of ...'

The social impact of law is now seen as a set of discrete effects on citizens engendered where the chains of social relations in legal institutions finally emerge to touch them. The reinforces the possibility and importance of the compartmentalization of discrete areas of the law – wills, theft, contract, tax, etc. These areas of law comprise not merely compilations and rationalizations of what judges and legislatures have said and done, but also the effects those and other actions by key officials in legal institutions ultimately have on citizens via other officials. Law is not just a matter of 'what judges do about disputes'; that was always too narrow a formula. But it could be seen as 'what members of legal institutions ultimately do about citizens'.

Hence the answer to the question 'What is the law of theft?' is an answer to the question about what the members of the institutions of law do about protecting citizens from being involuntarily deprived of their possessions by anyone other than a legal official. This includes answers about what the legislature does in passing the Theft Act; what the police do about apprehending those they suspect are engaged in what they consider to be theft, and the difficulties and probability of discovery; what they do to those they arrest on theft charges; what barristers do in court; the difficulties and probabilities of convincing juries of guilt; what the courts do in sentencing and other courts do on appeal; what prison officials and guards do with convicted thieves sent to them; and the relations between all these actions. In short, the law of theft covers the type and probabilities of various actions being performed by various members of legal institutions in respect of those who do certain things to others' possessions, and about the interactions within a complex web of social relations that produce these effects.

Similarly, landlord and tenant law is a matter of how the various institutions of law affect the occupation of houses by one person with the permission of another.

Throughout these interactions, the text of the Theft Act or Landlord and Tenant Act usually plays a part, providing reasons for the actors. But what those actors do with the text, the rules and reasons they derive from it, and the importance of those rules and reasons in determining their own actions all vary considerably. The law of theft is not limited to the text of the Act. Neither is it limited to the reasons that a single academic, judge, legislator, policeman, etc., derives from it, nor even the reasons that all academics, judges, etc., derive from it.

This should not be taken as a denial of the value of specialized study of actions performed within one or two of the institutions – such as that by positivists on the way lawyers derive reasons and rules from the verbal actions of legislatures and courts. But from a social observer's point of view this is only a *part* of the law, a part of the chain of relations and institutions through which law operates – a fact which those who indulge in such specialized study should never forget. This requirement is even stronger for practitioners. Good advice to clients requires a knowledge of the likely action of officials who carry the final effect of those verbal actions through to the public, and with whom clients have to deal.

8.13   Legal Rights

This theory of legal disorder has a place for legal rights, certainly those rights conceived in the author's other writing (Sampford, 1975, 1986a, 1986b). Rights are there seen as 'four-dimensional' – an individual (A) has a right to do some specified action øing, if: (1) the state will not prevent A from øing (negative dimension), (2) the state will prevent others from interfering with A when øing (protective dimension), (3) A has the resources to øing, whether from the state or elsewhere (positive dimension), and (4) A regards øing as an acceptable action (psychological dimension).

The statement that A has a moral right is a value-statement that A ought to enjoy these four dimensions of rights. These moral rights may be stated at various levels of generality – as human rights where all human beings ought to enjoy these four dimensions, civil rights if all citizens should enjoy them, and as privilege, where they ought to be enjoyed by some citizens but not necessarily by others.

The extent to which A actually has a right to do ø can be expressed in terms of A's relationship to other legal officials and institutions. The negative dimension is fully realized only if there are no power relations that are used with the intended effect of preventing A from øing and no such anticipated reactions from legal officials. The protective dimension depends on power relations or anticipated reactions between legal officials and others who attempt to prevent A from øing. The positive dimension is provided to the extent that relations A has with others places sufficient resources at A's disposal to do ø. Legal institutions and officials may do this if they give those without the resources the legitimate authority to demand them of lesser officials. The psychological dimension is provided by the lack of manipulation and other power relations to produce value-effect relations in A not to do ø.

The belief that A has a legal right can be an important value held by individual officials, and may be an important influence on the activities of officials and thus important in determining whether A really has a right. It may be the reason for action that officials derive from their relations with other legal officials and institutions and from the texts that are a part of those relations (noting that many such texts are not worded in the form of a grant of legal rights). For example, officials may be power-subjects or value-holders in relations which require them to refrain from adversely affecting A when øing, or require them to prevent others from doing so, or require them to provide resources to A if A otherwise lacks them. However these value-beliefs are only a part of the achievement of rights by individuals, indeed only a part legal rights play in their achievement. Rights of citizens depend on, and exist in, their range of choice of action and whether it includes the right concerned. Like all other ranges of choice of action, it is dependent on the relations with other actors which can affect them and not solely upon the belief of those other actors howsoever derived.

8.14 Summary

The preceding sections have attempted to say something about law and provide at least a part of a description of the social phenomenon we experience and associate with the word 'law'. It is seen as a mass of social relations in all the varieties and mixtures found in the rest of society. These relations are formed into a massive interconnecting web in which each point is connected to many others rather than forming an ordered system of the types considered in chapters 3 to 5.

Within this web there exist some more intensively interconnecting constellations of relations that can be recognized as some of the familiar institutions of law. These relations concentrate resources in the hands of a small proportion of those individuals involved – the key *officials* of legal institutions. Thus, like society, law is partially organized into institutions but it does not have an overall structure, the shifting paths of the many chains of relations defying attempts to define one. These institutions are a part of the social mêlée. The institutions are in conflict with each other and with those outside. In the course of this conflict, key officials try to extend the range of choices open to them in the action they take, and to limit the range open to others. These institutions are also a *subject* of the social mêlée, with other institutions and groups attempting to control the action of key legal officials or at least to influence their appointment.

The effects of law on society are considerable. Many positions within the institutions of law offer scope for indirectly achieving such effects especially by the use of texts which are created for the purpose of providing reasons for the actions of others. However, the chain of relations of mixed nature and strength through which these effects must be channelled means that the effects achieved are often diluted, deflected or distorted versions of that which was intended, so that the effect, while strong, is a crude one. Overall, the effects of law on society are not structured into a system of functions but are the sum of many effects originating in many different parts of law, travelling via many paths, to emerge at many different points, to affect many individuals. As such, these effects are frequently conflicting, incomplete and nonuniform. But as their only common characteristic is that they originate within a complex disordered entity, it is unsurprising that these effects are themselves disordered.

8.15   The Quest for Order Revisited

It is hoped that this image of law, although different in total, is familiar in detail and fills the gap left by the rejected systematic pictures of law. It may also hope to answer further the question raised in chapter 6 – *why do so many people see law as systematically arranged*? Some answers have already been indicated – the comfort the belief engenders and the general fashion for systems theories (chapters 1.2, 6.3); the fact that judges sometimes strive to put some order into their decisions (chapters 3, 4); and the limited range of effects law has on different groups (chapter 8.11).

Another powerful impetus is a desire by jurisprudential theorists to unify the field they study, which may be linked to a view of what a theory should do for its subject. It is natural for theorists to consider that what attracts their interests is some *thing*, some *whole*, the unity of which they can demonstrate as a justification of their interest in it. Yet the subjects of academic study are affected more by institutional factors than by the attributes of the things studied (which in any case can be discovered only after the study has been going on for some time). Nowhere is this more true than in jurisprudence, which has naturally tended to ask questions of interest to students and teachers of law. These questions are largely about the activity of law graduates and the influences upon that activity, neither of which is likely to constitute a unity.

But there is no need for objects of jurisprudential interest to constitute a unity. That the questions are of interest is sufficient justification in itself. Indeed, the factor which most contributes to the disorder of law provides a *particular* justification for its study. Every aspect of society seems to have an influence on and be influenced by law. Everything we know about people and their interactions with others seems important to our understanding of law (cf. Kelsen, 1970). Law is not a neatly unified, systematized whole floating around in the calm backwater of society but exists at the vortex of the social mêlée where the strains show up most. It is a great drama, perhaps the greatest drama in which we are involved. Even if it does not have a plot, a start or a finish and even if the direction is appalling, like the quintessential Hollywood movie 'it has got everything'.

There is one further reason for the common belief that law forms a system – the fact that we can and do talk about law in such positive, even emphatic, terms. 'The law is . . .', 'There is a legal rule that . . .', 'There is a legal right to . . .'. How is this possible if law is so disordered?

But what is it that we can be so positive about?

1 Certain statements will be more or less endorsed by judicial officials and colleagues. These are the statements about what 'the law' is.
2 Certain actions are likely to be performed by certain officials.
3 After that action is performed, another person will be expected to act in a predictably narrow range of activities.

All these require actions (including speech acts) and the successful prediction of action does not require a system, merely that there is a reasonable regularity of behaviour – under similar circumstances similar actions are likely to occur. But under similar circumstances the social relations involved, and with them the actor's reasons for action, are also likely to be similar. Thus the similarity of outcome is unproblematic. And the real limitations on even the highest legal officials restrict them to a range of action within which it is very safe to predict they will act.

In any case, the predictability can be overrated. The statements most likely to be endorsed by colleagues and officials are those already made by judges. Repetition of these with their citation is quite safe as no one denies that the sayings of judges are a part of the law. The acceptability of new statements is less certain, but the closer they are to paraphrases of the above statements, the more confidence we have that they will elicit approving noises from judicial officials and colleagues. However, very little hangs on this. There are millions of such statements, and most of them will have multiple meanings among which the stater and endorser may well have taken different ones.

Prediction of what a judge will do is more difficult. It will involve an 'order' and often a statement of his/her own (Dworkin, 1986, p. 101) about what the law 'is' (which may be added to the millions there already are). We have no hope of predicting the exact words; we know merely that it will contain statements that are *similar* to *some* of the millions that are included in the above category and express some of the hundreds of sentiments that are expressed by them. (And all of this without even touching on judicial law-making!) The ideas (s)he picks out and the priority (s)he gives them are very difficult to predict and such prediction will require careful analysis of *his/her* personality, *his/her* social relationship and *his/her* value priorities as revealed in his/her other judgments and/or from other sources if available.

The order (s)he makes is related to his/her statements or, where there is no such statement, the statements of law made in front of him/her and those dredged from his/her memory that strike him/her as valuable. This statement, or statements, of law provides him/her with a reason for his/her action. But exactly *what* action it is a reason for will depend on the meaning of that statement to him/her, and how it meshes into the other processes within his/her practical reason. Consequently, we are not very good at predicting the orders that judges will give: something close to 50 per cent of barristers advising in civil cases get it wrong. It may be objected that *only* the uncertain cases get to court. But settlement of cases which do not go to court is not so much due to certainty (or even uncertainty) of what would happen in court as to certainty about the possible cost of finding out. The art of settlement involves the skilful mixture of the two.

The final kind of prediction that we can be positive about is the fact that one person's action is regularly followed by another. This does nothing to indicate system in law. It merely asserts the existence of a social relation, the very stuff of the nonsystematic social description adopted here.

In law, as in science, theories do not have to be systems, and systems theories are neither necessary nor sufficient for accurate prediction (see chapter 6.3).

8.16   Further Uses of the Theory of Legal Disorder

The last two chapters have provided the bare bones of a nonsystematic theory of society and law. This has been primarily directed to providing a description of law satisfactory to the social observer, both for its own sake and to reinforce the earlier rejection of systematic theories by providing an alternative.

However, there are many other 'problems' in social and legal theory that this theory can help to illuminate. It can do this by (1) using social relations as the basic unit of socio-legal description instead of social rules, norms or roles (all of which are seen either as phenomena of limited importance or as complex phenomena built from varying combinations of social relations) and (2) throwing off the constraints imposed by attempting to force these basic units into a system. Except where they bear on legal description, these problems have not so far been discussed. Space permits little more than a listing here.

1   *The relation between coercion and legitimacy in law* is largely described and accounted for in the way possession of one can often be used to gain the other.

2   *The nature of legal obedience* is seen to lie in the successful affecting of behaviour by members of legal institutions through the existence of all kinds of social relations in law.

3   *The relationship between legislature and judiciary* is simply analysed in terms of social relations between legislators and judges.

4   *The nature of judicial discretion* is seen in terms of the range of choice left open to judges by the social relations in which they are involved. Discretion appears broad only when some of the social relations that limit it are ignored.

5   *The limits to law* are established by the limited effectiveness of the social relations in law.

6   *The specification of official positions.* A useful way of specifying what a judge, barrister, policeman, etc., is can be provided by stating the set of social relations most commonly found involving such a person. Although this theory is constructed from the standpoint of the social observer it provides a small basis for theory-building and practical reasoning from other standpoints.

7   *The choice of legal activity.* An individual can do this by looking at the range of choice of action with which (s)he could be confronted in the variety of positions open to him/her and how those actions can affect others. (S)he can choose on the basis of which range of choice includes actions that achieve the fulfilment of the most values according to his or her own political theory. At the same time the individual can choose how to describe that activity and choose a role-orientation towards it.

8   *Theories of law from the standpoint of individual participants.* The parts of law with which individual legal actors come into contact and which are significant for the pursuit of their chosen activities were earlier taken to be law for those participants (chapter 1.3). Those parts are the social relations (and chains of such relations) in

law that provide opportunities for, and limitations on, that individual's pursuit of his/her activity. The theory of law for that individual will involve those social relations as seen from his or her end of the relation.

9 *Choice of action within a legal activity.* This is a conscious exercise of the kind of practical reasoning discussed in chapter 7.7. The legal actor's own political theory indicates which action to take from those that the nonsystematic theory tells us are open.

The next chapter will illustrate the last three uses of the theory for individual participants in the legal mêlée.

Notes

1 But skills of verbal and physical manipulation are similar in an important respect. There are many different ways of building a chair, producing things which look very different and which can be put to a variety of uses. There is no single 'correct' chair even though there is a skill and craft in making chairs. Some are better at their craft just as some lawyers are at theirs. But it is still a chair if it can support a human posterior and it is still a rule if it can support a legal argument.

2 This may account for much of the disagreement between those Marxists who emphasize repressive aspects of law and other theorists who emphasize dispute-settlement and the facilitation of private arrangements. The former consider the effects of law on the 'working class' and how the relations they have with members of legal institutions (mainly police and magistrates) appear to them. The latter may be thinking of the effects of law on the clients of lawyers, and how their relations with members of legal institutions (mainly lawyers and judges) appear to them. The shift of emphasis may be related as much to the increasing 'gentrification' of Marxists as to the change in methods by which capitalist states are sustained.

9

Legal Actors in the Legal Mêlée

9.1 Introduction

The criticism of systems theory has been from both the social observer standpoint and the standpoints chosen by the theorists concerned. The exposition of a theory of social and legal disorder has been solely from the social observer standpoint. For those whose sole interest in law is from that point of view (e.g. sociologists, historians, socio-legal theorists) this book could end here. However, as argued in chapter 2.4, jurisprudential audiences primarily comprise students, academics and the occasional reflective practitioner, enquiring citizen or enlightened judge. These current and prospective participants need a view of law from the social observer's point of view to understand the phenomena within which they interact with others and the nature of those interactions. However, such a view of law is, though necessary, not sufficient. It cannot tell a student which activity within law to choose, how it should be defined from his/her point of view and how to act within it. It will not be silent, it will provide reasons for those choices, but the choices will only be possible taking into account an individual's perceptions of his or her abilities and especially of his or her values. Given the interpersonal variation in values, even among those in similar positions and interacting with each other regularly, this addition takes on an even greater importance.

This chapter explores how that admixture of a theoretical understanding of the legal mêlée and of the actor's self and values can be worked through from individual points of view. The next few sections will discuss this in general terms. Individuals must first consider what activities are open to them and within each activity the range of choice of actions and the likely effects of those actions (chapter 9.2), then consider their values and political theory (chapter 9.3). Individual actors can then choose and define their activity and plan strategies and practices to accord with their political theory (chapter 9.4) and, if desired, create a theory of law from their point of view (chapter 9.5). In chapter 9.6 we see how this might work for judges, academics, barristers, solicitors, graduates and citizens. Finally, chapter 9.7 defends and emphasizes the individualism of this approach, arguing that if the variety of individuals was the rock on which systems theories are wrecked, it also provides the foundations for the nonsystematic theory.

9.2 Identifying and Understanding Potential Activities Within Law

Most individuals have at least some choice in the activities they pursue. The mêlée theory outlined in chapter 8 will indicate that alternative careers are like paths through the mêlée. Others may have trodden them and, if those with similar characteristics attempt to follow, they may well find the relevant social interactions similar. However, the relations and individuals involved will not be identical and the chances of success along any path will be variable.

The mêlée theory will also lead the potential travellers to identify those activities in a special way. They will not look to a system-derived role, function or duty. Rather they will look to the sets of social relationships of which barristers, judges, solicitors, etc., are a part. Then, taking into account the fact that these sets of relations are not identical, but vary with the individual occupants, they will look to the social relations in which they would be involved to consider the unique positions that they would hold if they followed those paths. In particular, they will look to the social relations with other individuals who are part of 'the law' and particularly at what participation in those relationships would mean from their 'end'.

Once those relations are identified for any potential activity, individuals can then consider those which provide resources and opportunities to affect others and those which impose limitations on those opportunities. Individuals can then consider the chains of relations and institutions of which those social relations are a part, the way this can extend the range and distance at which effects can be achieved, the probability of deflection and distortion of the effects intended by them, and the opportunities to do the same to the effects intended by others. Above all, they can consider the range of choice of action which those social relations will leave them. This range of choice that the nonsystematic theory of law leaves open to an office-holder is reasonably easily discoverable. This is in direct contrast to the difficulty of finding out the correct rule to be followed in a positivist system, the right answer in Dworkin's system, or an official's role in a sociological system. There is no necessity to create the impossible systems of rules, principles or roles – merely to identify the most significant opportunities for activity and the key restraints on them by seeing whom can be affected, who can limit that effect and in what way.

Thus the mêlée theory can help identify and describe the activities open to individuals. The choice of which activities to pursue and the actions to perform within them require the incorporation of values and political theory.

9.3 Values and Political Theory

Although some theories of law and society might still claim to generate values for individuals, this is not one of them. It holds uncompromisingly to a view of moral sovereignty. If an individual adheres to the proposition that killing human beings is wrong, it is valid for that individual because it is supported by his or her own values and those values provide its sole source. Of course a social theory might tell us that others hold similar beliefs and that they have influenced our own beliefs about killing. But these similarities and influences do not give those beliefs validity. Indeed, contrary beliefs would be valid to the individual moral sovereign, even if they were maintained against the views of the overwhelming majority. This directly analogizes to the *image* of an individual sovereign. Social theories might tell us that the sovereigns in Austin's time all had repressive laws and were influenced by economically powerful groups. But in Austin's view the sovereign was still the sole source of law and legal validity. Of course, Austin's theory suffered many problems because the legal sovereign was *not* a single individual and the subjects have such mixed reasons for the way they react to sovereign commands. But they are not problems for a theory of moral sovereignty.

The mêlée theory might not provide values itself, but it can provide reasons for moral sovereigns in the values they adopt. First, moral sovereigns cannot merely adopt society's or an institution's values because there are none. They must rely on their own values in order to choose. Secondly, it is unlikely that individuals will find (as opposed to claim) that all law is good or bad according to their values. The manner of its creation ensures that it will reflect conflicting values, some of which will cohere with the individual's own values and some of which will inevitably clash. Third, as society is analysed in terms of social relations by which some affect others, activities are evaluated in terms of the effects upon the reasoner and others which occur because the reasoner enters the relations which define the activity.

Political theories apply values to theories of law and society, telling us how they can and should be changed by individual and/or concerted action. As such it will include a much higher dosage of the individual's socio-legal theory. The simple strategies of preserving the institutions and values of society (conservative), seizing control of the centre (liberal/ reformer) or blowing it up (radical) are irreparably damaged by the mêlée theory. The institutions of society are in conflict and the values held and reflected within them are contradictory. Hence supporting any institution and value will damage others, making the fully conservative position impossible. The liberal/reformer approach is flawed because there is no core to control. The radical approach of blowing it up fails for three reasons: because society is already so disordered, because the source of evil within society cannot either be so easily identified or so easily removed, and because violent revolutions are no guarantors of progressive change (chapter 7.12).

The mêlée theory suggests that all political theories will find much to value and much to abhor in society. Accordingly, a political theory needs to be selective in the parts of society attacked, defended or targeted for reform. A political theory should identify effects which are in accord with its holder's values and those which are contrary to them. It then needs to identify the general strategies that will maximize the former and minimize the latter. Such strategies will involve action by many officials, whether co-ordinated or not, to exercise choice within the range available to maximize valued effects and minimize nonvalued ones.

The range of political theories that result from the interaction of this mêlée theory and the differing values is very wide. It is even possible that individuals may so value systems that their overriding political goal becomes the creation of one. However, the mêlée theory of law would tend to indicate the futility of such a goal in societies such as ours.

More plausible is the use of some ideal system as a model. Someone might describe what a perfect society which incorporated all the desired values would look like. This may be a new utopia or one of the social and/or legal systems that (s)he was disappointed to find did not yet exist. (S)he might then ask what effects (s)he could achieve to move society towards a closer resemblance to the model.

However, some theories may not place value on an ideal system but may value the mêlée itself. The disordered nature of law and society provides an enormous range of activities, institutions and social contexts and an even greater range of descriptions and perceptions of those activities. Such pluralism can be very attractive to both right and left. That the mêlée should appeal to both right and left should not surprise. The 'new right' seeks to throw off the constraints of traditional conservative values in the pursuit of individual gain. The left seeks either a better order or the freedom of an anarchist's disorder. The differences are more in terms of what should be done next – 'go all out for number one' or establish a more just and equal form of interaction – rather than of the present state of society whose unsystematic character is becoming increasingly clear to both sides of politics.

The mêlée theory should not be taken to suggest that intervention in the mêlée is impossible and that only market-based 'solutions' should be attempted. Some will argue against intervention because of the extent of unintended effects and because intended effects can so easily be distorted, deflected and diverted by officials placed strategically along the long chains of interactions by which the effects of official intervention must be achieved. However, this does not mean that effects cannot be achieved, especially if serious attempts are made to discover where distortion, deflection and diversion occurs. Of course, successful resistance to intervention is also possible, by identifying the same positions and exerting sufficient counter-influence.

Whether intervention and change or resistance to it is politically preferred, an understanding of the disordered 'mechanisms' by which each is achieved is necessary. During the struggle for control of institutions and their outputs, resources are never fully mobilized and the struggle is neither unified nor uniform but is carried on in a myriad of different contexts. In many of these, individual actors will see a chance to influence the result one way or the other by adding the effects of their own exercise of power to others' and tipping the scale for that struggle in that context.[1]

Whatever political theory is ultimately adopted, it will rarely exhaust the holder's values. Not all values concern the desired shape of society and the desirable means of attaining it, consciously or otherwise. Thus political theory must be blended with an individual's other values. That blending may be a formal affair in which hierarchies of values or even ethical content systems are established which provide defined places for direct self- and other-regarding values and to political values for the improvement or maintenance of society. More often there are less formal weightings in which some values tend to take precedence over others but in the manner of suppressory reasons discussed in chapter 7.7. However, as we have seen, the construction of such systems does not make the law any more systematic; in fact it tends to make law less so because of the different systems created by the diversity of moral sovereigns.

9.4 Choosing Activities

Once an individual has established the range of possible activities which are open, values and political theory can be applied to make a choice. It becomes purely a matter of determining the effects achievable (adjusted for their probability of achievement) within the various activities open and choosing the activity in which the effects achievable are most valued.

Once chosen, the activity may be redescribed or understood in a slightly different way. As the individual chooses an activity because of the valued effects hopefully attainable within it, the activity tends to be redefined in terms of the valued effects (e.g. a specialist solicitor's activity may be seen by them as essentially money-grubbing, crusading for causes or informing clients about their legal duties, etc.).

Once an activity is chosen and defined, practices and strategies within it must be decided. Again the criteria for choice lie in the maximization of valued effects. Again the mêlée theory can help to provide that necessary understanding. An intermediate step in most strategies will be the maximization of autonomy and power of the individual's position. This involves the maximization of the range of choice available to the occupant by a reassessment of the social relations of which (s)he is a part and an attempt to increase those to which (s)he is power-holder, reduce those in which (s)he is power-subject and diminish the number of unintended effects by the discovery of those effects.

Having seen the haphazard way in which many values are acquired (chapter 7.7), the legal actor would want to ensure that any internally felt constraints which support value-effect relations can be justified by the chosen political and ethical theory. An individual should not be constrained from pursuing considered aims by values picked up from practice, from the persuasion of others that (s)he now finds less convincing, or from some conception of his/her activity not related to his or her own political theory. (S)he must also check that these internal constraints are not limitations on action imposed by other social relations (e.g. the coercive power of others or their anticipated reactions) 'dressed up' as internal constraints to make the individual feel the more in control of his or her actions. In such cases, (s)he should reject the internal constraint and identify very clearly the precise extent of the limitation which the coercive authority or anticipated reaction places upon action. In this way (s)he avoids curtailing actions unnecessarily, or in ways his/her values do not require.

Strategies and practices for any individual activity will often be a unique and personal combination of values and political theories. However, the general mêlée theory can provide some assistance. As the ultimately intended effects can generally only be achieved through long chains of relations involving several other persons, and as reactions can be anticipated from others in a conservative profession to anyone who appears to do things differently, there is much to be said for putting actions in a form with which others are familiar and using the traditional legal skills to justify actions. As we have seen, these skills allow a legal actor to derive public reasons for action from the previous actions of other legal officials. These reasons are a superfluous addition to what should be the already sufficient reasons provided by the individual's own political theory, but they are valuable in preserving the effectiveness of the action they justify. Knowing of the disorder of law, individual legal actors can rest assured that, with the exercise of legal skills, the law will be a fertile field for the justification of even the most radical actions. They need not be discouraged by imagining law to be a uniform content system, set up and opposed to the values contained in theirs, or anyone else's, political theory. On the other hand, the ease of justifying any action their political theory leads them to take should not blind them to the very real limitations imposed on them by social relations involving others. Far more can be justified using these traditional skills than an individual legal actor could ever get away with.

9.5   A Legal Theory?

Part of such strategies and practices may include the creation of legal theories from the limited individual standpoints of particular activities. Such legal theories would generally include only a part of what is law to the social observer. It will include the parts of legal institutions that provide opportunities for, and limitations on, the pursuit of the individual's chosen activity – i.e. the social relations (s)he has with other people within legal institutions that make it possible to affect others and affect the way that (s)he does so.

The legal theory may be selective about the relations included. Where there are two social relations of similar scope and effect, it may be simpler and more convenient for the pursuit of the chosen activity and strategies to look at only one (e.g. where (s)he is subject to a pair of coercive and legitimate authority relations, (s)he may look only at the latter). More rarely, it may be convenient to treat one kind of relation as if it were another (e.g. treating a coercive authority relation as a legitimate authority relation because (s)he will have to pretend to regard it as such in publicly justifying chosen actions). If (s)he is a power-holder, there will be a tendency to overemphasize any element of legitimate authority and play down the others. But the comfort this tendency brings is overwhelmed by the disadvantages of not knowing the kind of power relations (s)he enjoys and hence their corresponding strengths and weaknesses. Likewise (s)he should attempt to discover the other social relations in which (s)he is reactor or value-beneficiary for by so doing (s)he effectively converts them into power relations.

The legal theory will include these relations (and the texts that provide the mechanism by which most of these relations are effective), but only as they appear from that individual's end. Where (s)he is a power-subject, social relations of legitimate authority appear as duties, coercive social relations as illegitimate impositions, and manipulations as values or factual limitations on action. Where (s)he is a power-holder, legitimate authority will appear as a 'power' or a 'right' in the sense usually used by lawyers. Where (s)he is engaged in manipulation it will appear as such to him/her but not to the power-subjects.

An individual's legal theory will see these relations in terms of the reasons (whether rules or not) they provide for action: that is the way that social relations of which legal actors are aware affect them. These reasons are the individual's conscious reaction to the texts, officials and institutions of law. (The unconscious and unknown effects cannot be included in an individual's theory of the law precisely because they are unconscious and unknown.) It is part of an individual's view of their role. It is part of the interaction between legal institutions and individuals, but it is the part that is contained within the individual's mind. Rules derived are not social rules but individual rules which are reactions to the social phenomena of law. They are social in their origin rather than in their nature. Coherence and consistency, and even system, may be attempted at this individual level. But system is more likely to be achieved in an individual's own values and ideals for law rather than in that individual's interpretation of the many and conflicting attempts of others to do the same thing.

Although an individual may thus create a theory of law, the social observer's theory which helped to define and choose that individual's activity cannot be permanently ignored. The social observers' theory will be needed:

1 so that (s)he can understand how others are reacting to his/her own actions,
2 to appreciate what parts of law (s)he affects and by what parts (s)he is affected in the activity (s)he has chosen and defined, and
3 whenever (s)he reconsiders participation in the activity and of the theory of law from its limited standpoint.

9.6 Some Consequences for Practice

This section will provide some indication of how various actors within legal institutions might apply the theory of legal and social order to defining and understanding their activities, setting goals and defining strategies and especially what it would mean for them in practice. Of course, a full account of these processes for any individual cannot be attempted as that is a long-term project and is as varied as the individuals who practise them.

Judges

To apply the mêlée theory judges would first analyse their position in terms of the relationships which provide limitations and opportunities for their actions. This allows judges to determine the extent of their range of choice, the room within which they have an opportunity to further their values (see chapter 8.2). Once having determined that range of choice there is no escaping the responsibility for making it (see Luhmann, chapter 5.7). It is no good saying that 'the text requires' or 'the law is' or 'the rule is'. Where there are multiple interpretations of the text and alternative versions of the law, when it is realized that the 'rule' is something created by the judge as a reason for him/herself and, (s)he hopes, others, such an approach seems naive, uninformed and unreflexive. It is not a question of whether the judge applies his or her values but what those values are to be and whether (s)he does it consciously or not. Where a choice exists yet is denied, a judge must be suspected of either concealing or being ignorant of what (s)he is doing. If the former is sometimes necessary, the latter is inexcusable.

This analysis of the judges' position suggests a new way of arguing for judges. They could seek to demonstrate that traditional techniques of legal interpretation produce conflicting answers and hence demonstrate the existence of the choice. Then they could state their reasons, in terms of values and political theory, for choosing the way they do. This is likely to deflect criticism that they are 'making the law up as they go along' or legislating for themselves. It argues that there is no alternative but to do so. Indeed it tends to shift criticism on to other judges. Demonstrating the need for a value-choice may make it appear that other judges are concealing or are ignorant of their motivations and unable to justify their actions.

Of course judges may not wish to be so frank. Their values may be well out of the mainstream and they may fear retaliation, loss of influence or even some kind of retaliation from the government if they declare them. However, that does not prevent judges applying their values to justify their choices; indeed they will need a political theory which can justify not only their reasons for action but also their reasons for concealing their reasons – few judges would in fact need the latter kind of theory in the West.

It should be emphasized that what is justified is the actions of the judges themselves, not the law as a whole. As argued in chapter 4, a law includes the actions of many judges. A single judge is responsible only for his/her own actions and should not take responsibility for the rest nor voluntarily subordinate his/her own considered values to the values which might be held by other judges. Each pursues their own values and political theories in generating rules for their own use and text for the use of others. The values used are not circumscribed by the mêlée theory except that some of the sources traditionally used for them are equivocal. An appeal to values embedded in society looks rather weak when society is so disordered and the law reflects those divisions and is itself a result of that conflict. The ascription of values to society, law (or parliament or government or a private club) is either a choice among the values actually held by individuals within those groups or some artificial construct. Both choice and construction will require the judges' values – it is just that their use and source will be less apparent to the judge and those who read them. As there is no escaping the necessity of judicial value-choice, it is surely better that those values be stated, criticized and defended. That way they are likely to be more fully considered than if left dormant in the judges' prejudices and unconscious motivations. Such a process would produce a range of conservative and moderate theories completely unrepresentative of the spectrum of political views and values in society and even among politicians. But that would lead those who appoint judges to consider not only an appointee's skill in providing alternative arguments for judicial action, but the values they will bring to that choice.

Legal Academics

When legal academics apply the mêlée theory of law they will find most of their opportunities provided by social relations of persuasion and competent authority. There are few limitations but they have to anticipate the reactions by editors and students if what is given is too different from what is expected.

Traditionally many legal academics have seen their activity as the exposition of a 'body of law' (in fact a set of texts) as a coherent body of rules, standards and principles. Indeed, according to Goodrich this kind of activity is almost exclusively confined to academia (1986).

The mêlée theory does not signal the end of exposition but suggests a new expanded role for it. Rather than presenting as coherent that which is not and whose manner of creation is unlikely to make it so, academics should attempt to highlight the inconsistencies. They should then look at the external conflicts which legal conflicts reflect, examine how those external conflicts were rephrased as legal conflicts (thus removing any mystery about how external conflicts are reflected in law – clients employ their lawyers to do that). It can then show the choices judges had to make (whether consciously or not), to try to analyse why they 'chose' the way they did, how the results of that legal conflict bear upon future, similar legal conflicts and the external conflict that generated it then and how to argue for themselves the merits of such causes.

By incorporating conflicting rules, principles and other legal propositions, this mode of exposition can actually cover and account for more material than traditional legal exposition. It is far more inclusive than a Dworkinian legal system. The latter declares many 'mistakes' and must exclude them from law (something which is very difficult for decisions which Hercules has no power to overturn). This kind of exposition includes both Dworkin's preferred decision and what he calls a mistake; it also attempts to explain why the conflict was generated and why it is likely to continue. In so doing it incorporates historical dimensions and social dimensions in the most natural way. It shows how it is impossible to discuss law without taking into account these dimensions but also how such an account will be impoverished and will necessarily fail to explain the material it seeks to cover.

Like most historical dimensions it easily allows a future dimension as well. We naturally ask ourselves whether the strength of the social forces, and hence the balance of social relations affecting judicial choice, will change. We will also ask who the judges will be and how they will exercise their choice within the range of choice left open to them.

A critical dimension is also easily accommodated. Legal academics can take sides in the conflict rather than suggesting that the law neutrally solves the problem or favours one side. They can be critical of the social forces and social relationships which shift judges' range of choice in specified directions. They can be critical of the appointment of benches, the values of whose members are unrepresentative of the range of views within the community. They can be critical of the way judges exercise their choice and hence enforce the responsibility for their own choices that is central to the judicial role. Academics can examine any judicial justifications of rules based on a claim that they will have certain desired consequences. Academics can discuss whether those effects really are achieved and criticize judges if they do not revise their chosen formulation of the rule when it is demonstrated that the consequences predicted by the judge do not arise.

The critical dimension includes the identificaton of the part that various officials and texts play in producing effects the academics criticize. Most importantly of all, it includes the identification of what has to be done to achieve desired effects or eliminate undesired effects by action in a variety of fields – judicial, parliamentary, social, economic and why action in some fields is insufficient (e.g. the failure of 1970s American activist lawyers significantly to improve the lot of the urban poor by litigation alone: Gordon, 1984).

Where some intended and desired effect is not being achieved it directs our attention to the point along the chain of relations where this occurs and indicates where new personnel need to be added or new relations created to ensure congruent activity by the valid official (e.g. if the tax crack-down in chapter 8.4 is failing, academics can identify judges who wilfully misinterpret the text of the Act, the existence of complex wording that is genuinely misunderstood, lax foreign-exchange control which allows income to leave the country without being taxed and so on).

Where broader objectives indicated by a political theory are sought, the mêlée theory can show how change requires actions at many different sites leading to realistic expectations of the degree of success achieved at any one of them. Academics should not expect any single change to achieve the desired effects but should appreciate it for what it is – a positive part of that broader change.

Practising Lawyers

When an advocate or barrister applies the mêlée theory (s)he finds relations of inducement between the client (through his/her solicitor) and him/herself of value-effect relations which may limit his conduct and relations of persuasion and sometimes manipulation between him/herself and the judge, jury or opposing lawyer. (S)he attempts a persuasive interpretation of the texts to influence the judge's action and persuasive interpretation of testimony to influence the jury and a persuasive prediction of both to influence the other lawyer to settle. In so doing (s)he becomes a part of the chain of relations between the text-creators and the citizens, but (s)he is classically one who is likely to bend or distort their effect – most of the time that is the very intention, and at least half the time that is what (s)he is paid for. For most barristers, the texts appear as a storehouse of debating points. Armed with the mêlée theory barristers will have renewed confidence that the debating points will be found. But they will also be reminded that the law will serve the same purpose for the other side and that many other relations (and through them other social forces) will affect the judge's/jury's decision.

The relation of persuasion is squarely directed at the individual to be persuaded. It does not involve some impersonal exposition of the law or the interpretation of the texts. That is how barristers achieve success. But few need to be told that. As Goodrich has forcefully pointed out, the view of law as a coherent body of texts is basically an academic fallacy. Persuasion can only affect a judge within a given range of choice that the judge is capable of exercising and a narrower range of decisions that the judge is actually likely to make. But barristers know that too – the only difference is that the basis of the range of choice is clearly seen as the social relations of which the judge is or has been a part.

A version of the exposition suggested for legal academics may be useful for barristers too and, if the judge has adopted it, essential. Where judges use more limited forms of legal argument, the barrister must follow suit, attempting to offer arguments that will move *that* judge in *that* social context who has *those* values. As such, the barrister who adopts the mêlée theory will have to substitute manipulation for persuasion.

For a solicitor or legal adviser outside litigation, the key relations providing opportunities and limitations are relations of inducement between solicitor and client and relations of anticipatory reactions between legal officials, other legally advised parties and the client. For solicitors the law is a disconnected series of actions that legal officials and others are likely to take because of the reasons for action they take from texts and from the existence of legal institutions. The job is very much to chart a path for the client through the legal mêlée. (S)he advises of effects that legal institutions might have on a client if the client engages in the client's preferred course of action, or what course of action is likely to result in, or avoid, specified effects.

A working theory of law from the standpoint of a solicitor's activity involves the social relations which affect him/her and the kinds of clients (s)he has, the institutions from which they emanate and the texts through which they partially operate.

The Law Graduate

On graduation the student of the mêlée will usually face a choice of activities within legal institutions. Those activities can be defined by considering the kinds of relations (s)he will enter and the kinds of effects that practice will have on clients, those the clients deal with, and sometimes the nature and effects of legal institutions. It is then very much a matter of that student's values and/or political theory as to which kind of activity, professional or otherwise, to enter, and what to do within it. There is not some single practice of law with any indispensable values or necessary legal point of view; instead there are a lot of positions to be filled and, for many, opportunities to fill them and to use them for valued ends.

Most kinds of practice involve assisting members of a class or group to strengthen their power and resources by litigation, avoidance of official action or mobilizing it in their cause. The choice of practice is hence dependent on which groups or classes of people the graduate's values tell the graduate to assist or, for those interested only in personal gain, from which groups most value can be extracted (these will generally be the most powerful groups within society, although lawyers have found that accident victims, whose financial assets increase very rapidly through insurance claims, have been a popular and lucrative source of revenue).

Some strategies involve undermining groups or institutions whose activities or resources threaten the achievement of desired goals. A more common strategy involves temporarily learning from the enemy in order more effectively to prosecute your values afterwards (e.g. lawyers in taxation departments often move to tax-avoidance law firms – unfortunately there is little movement in the other direction!).

The Citizen

When those who do not (or do not have the opportunity to) choose to enter a legal institution apply the mêlée theory, the law will be seen in terms of the limitations and/or opportunities it provides for their actions. Whatever path they seek to make through the social mêlée there will be legal institutions and officials and the texts they produce that will provide reasons for their actions. In most daily activities citizens will see that the power relations of legal officials bolster or undermine other social relations of which they are a part. Power relations and anticipated reactions of legal officials bolster managerial control over property that gives managers the resources to induce individual citizens and, to some extent, restrict citizens from securing resources by other means (e.g. bank robbery or fraud). In such cases, of course, the limitations imposed on the citizen provide the opportunities for another – the relative security that it gives the 'owners' and 'possessors' of property gives them opportunities to create power relations of inducement towards others.

Values in political theory will be mobilized to determine which of the possible paths through the social mêlée they should take and whether, and in what ways, they will attempt to affect legal institutions themselves (from voting Conservative to bombing police stations). Once a path is chosen then the law for that citizen will be what legal officials do about their own activity and a theory of law will highlight those effects which are most significant and which must be accepted, avoided or taken advantage of.

9.7   In Self-Defence

Some might criticize this approach as sceptical, nihilist, opportunist, cynical or even 'anti-social'.

As noted in chapter 4.7 'sceptical' is a word that is often thrown by those who believe in something strongly at those who do not. Because their belief is so strongly held, no amount of contrary argument or recalcitrant experience would suffice to shake that belief. So for them the only way to dislodge such a belief *would* be a thoroughgoing scepticism.

But this is rarely necessary for the opponents they brand as 'sceptics'. Nonbelievers may follow the Popperian or Quinean tradition and question the relevant belief, test it and find it wanting. As the systemness of law is not, for them, a firmly entrenched belief, nonbelievers can reject it after the numerous recalcitrant experiences provided by the failure of all attempted systems theories. That is hardly scepticism.

Nihilism, the loss of faith in, and rejection of, religious and moral principles, is an alleged vice for which critical legal scholars are often attacked by their more conservative colleagues (Carrington, 1984). Such attackers would almost certainly see this theory as another target. But the mêlée theory does not reject all moral principles but finds their locus in the individual mind and their source in an individual's moral sovereignty rather than in society.[2] It sees society as full of conflicting values. It sees those who assert general, communal or social values as merely insisting that their own values take precedence over others by denying the existence or legitimacy of the alternatives which are equally present within society.

Similar answers can be given to fears of those at the opposite end of the political spectrum. Horwitz sees the possibility that an awareness of law's complexity may lead us to a 'morally paralytic, cynical or professionally skeptical attitude' (1986, p. 393). Douglas says that those she calls the 'privileged powerless' see the meaning, categorization and interpretation of itself provided by the community as evil. Therefore, she argues, it becomes necessary for such people to deny the world. We need not be so paralysed. There are many interpretations, whether good or evil. Ours is one of many but because it is ours we find it hard to gainsay it. We should not be paralysed merely because ours lacks universality. We act on our values, not because they are society's, but because they are ours. These values are a vital part of ourselves and provide our purposes. As humans are purposive beings, the failure to follow them would be a denial of ourselves and of our humanity.

To some this may seem an anti-social assertion of an individual's moral sovereignty over the values of society. I admit that it is in the nature of moral sovereignty that, if that were the choice, an individual could not deny himself or herself by choosing the values of society, or even of a universal deity, over his or her own values. But no such terrible decision – between accepting or rejecting society's values – is forced upon us. Rather than declaring a one-person war against society's values, we can choose from the many values that have been pursued and have received expression in law and society as we have observed it. We dive straight into the social mêlée of competing values, choices and ends, the mêlée of competing groups and ideologies, and the mêlée of conflicting actions of those within competing and disordered institutions. We plunge into the struggle that has been raging within society since its inception, into the very struggle that is *society* and its law. In acting in pursuit of the political aims of our own political theory, we are quintessentially social in a society without order, and quintessentially legal in a law without order.[3]

Notes

1 It should be stressed that the mêlée described *is not 'the market'*. Theoretical markets are artificial mêlées in which only one form of power, inducement, is used. Outside the world of market theory, individuals will use the full range of their powers to achieve their ends, including, especially, manipulation (in advertising and PR) and coercion (in labour relations). Much 'market failure' can be explained in terms of these real-world additions to the power of inducement as well as unintended effects and value-effect relations which complicate the operation of real markets.

2 It even finds a social basis for values in that many values are actually held because of reasons derived from the actions of others – whether relations of persuasion, manipulation or legitimate authority.

3 This approach may be very liberating; it is also very daunting. One does not look to derive one's values or one's reasons for action in law or in any other field of action from a single source or system of sources. Likewise, the content of those reasons is not derived from a content system in society or its law with which disagreement would seem more difficult, especially if were some admixture of our own values in a complicated interpretative recipe like Dworkin's. Our role is not given by a functional system from which our withdrawal would by dysfunctional. The law could not be systematized on the basis of authority, content or effect. The key reason for each failure was the diversity of humanity that each system attempted to encompass. I would suggest that there is true irony here. The attempted systematizations of law reflect three admirable intellectual goals for any individual: a recognition of the source of moral authority, consistency and coherence in moral values and the maximal realization of those goals through related and supporting actions. It is not surprising that law was deemed to have the same goals (and sometimes even achievement). Such an approach is consistent with post-renaissance ideas which centred the state and temporal power on an individual human being and the ultimate moral authority on an individual god. What *is* surprising is the way law is still deemed to have these goals long after the demise of the individual monarch, and the rise of atheism and religious tolerance. Feurbach's great and lasting insight into religion was the way the virtues of individual humans were projected on to an imagined being external to them. Men (*sic*) created God in their own image but believed that God had created men in *His* image. This stunted their self-awareness and their capacity for moral development. There is, I suggest, a similar phenomenon with law. Individuals perceive the law as if it were the product of a single great mind rather than the inevitably disordered products of many minds (great or otherwise). In so doing, they reduce the

possibility of pursuing those perceived virtues for themselves. Neither the religious nor the legal phenomenon is surprising. The structure and virtues of an individual mind provide an experience with which any thinker will be familiar and to which others can relate without realizing that that they are recognizing is a part of themselves rather than a part of the more comprehensive social world which *includes* themselves.

If my perception of the ultimate source of the problem is Feurbachian, the suggested solution is rather Nietzschean. We should recognize as internal virtues and goals that which legal systems theories have claimed for law. We should recognize ourselves as having moral sovereignty, we should aim to make those moral values as consistent and as coherent as we can and we should order our actions as far as possible. In doing so we realize our potentials as individual human beings. That potential is not as free-willing (or free-wheeling) individuals but as individuals each with a unique set of experiences and resultant values with an internal capacity reflexively to reorder them and, in confronting one with another, remove those which do not fit the rest of our developed personality.

The responsibility of choosing the sources of our reasons, the content and the role we play in legal institutions may seem very daunting. It is even more daunting for those who seek personal systematizations of those phenomena as we realize that such systems must be constructed in, and be a part of, our minds rather than our minds being a part of the system. But such attempts are at least made at the right level, and with phenomena which are at least, in principle, systematizable. The wider phenomena of law and society are not systematizable – largely because of the variety of systems that others have attempted to impose on them. But, as we have seen, that heralds not the end of theory but the possibility of theories of disorder, the kind of theories which can cope with such phenomena as law and society.

References

Abercrombie, N. and B.S. Turner (1978), 'The Dominant Ideology Thesis', *British Journal of Sociology*, 29.

Ackoff, R.L. and F.E. Emery (1981), 'Structure, Function and Purpose', in Emery (1981).

Alexander, J.C. (1985), 'The Individualist Dilemma in Phenomenology and Interactionism', in Eisenstadt and Halle (1985).

Althusser, L. (1971), *Lenin and Philosophy and Other Essays*, New Left Books, London.

Angell, R.C. (1968), 'Social Integration', *International Encyclopedia of the Social Services*, 7.

Angyal, A. (1981), 'A Logic of Systems', in Emery (1981).

Archer, M.S. (1985), 'Structuration v. Morphogenesis', in Eisenstadt and Halle (1985).

Arnold, C. (1978), 'Institutional Aspects of Law', *Modern Law Review*, 51.

Austin, J. (1954), *The Province of Jurisprudence Determined*, Weidenfeld & Nicolson, London.

Avineri, S. (1968), *Social and Political Thought of Karl Marx*, Cambridge University Press, Cambridge.

Baldwin, J.M. (ed.) (1901), *Dictionary of Philosophy and Psychology*, Macmillan, New York.

Baum, L. (1980), 'Implementation of Judicial Decisions' in Evan (1980).

Beale, J.H. (1907), *Selected Essays in Anglo-American Legal History*, Cambridge University Press, Cambridge.

Beirne, P. and R. Quinney, (1982), *Marxism and Law*, Wiley, New York.

Benditt, T.M. (1974), 'Legal Theory and Rules of Law', *University of Western Ontario Law Review*, 13.

Bentham, J. (1970), *Of Laws in General*, ed. H.L.A. Hart, Athlone, London.

Beyleveld, D. and R. Brownsword (1982), 'Critical Legal Studies', *Modern Law Review*, 47.

Biles, D. (ed.) (1977), *Crime and Justice in Australia*, Australian Institute of Criminology and Sun Books, Melbourne.

Blackstone, W. (1979), *Commentaries* [1765], University of Chicago Press.

Blau, P.M. (1964), *Exchange and Power in Social Life*, Wiley, New York.

—— (1968), 'Social Exchange', *International Encyclopedia of the Social Sciences*, 7.

—— (ed.) (1976), *Approaches to the Study of Social Structure*, Open Books, London.

Bloor, D. (1983), *Wittgenstein: A Social Theory of Knowledge*, Macmillan, London.

Bodenheimer, E. (1977), 'Hart, Dworkin and the Problem of Judicial Law Making Discretion', *Georgia Law Review*, 11.

Bohannen, P. (1968), 'Law and Legal Institutions', *International Encyclopedia of the Social Sciences*, 9.

Boyle, P. (1984), *Stanford Law Review*, 'CLS: A Young Person's Guide', unpublished paper, conference on Critical Legal Studies, 1984.

Braybrooke, E.K. (1976), *Ignorance is No Excuse*, Cheshire, Melbourne.

Bredemeier, H.C. (1962), 'Law as an Integrative Mechanism', in Evan (1962).

Brilmayer, R.L. (1977), 'The Institutional and Empirical Basis of the Rights Thesis', *Georgia Law Review*, 11.

Brittan, A. (1981), 'The Symbolic Dimension of Law and Social Control', in Podgorecki and Whelan (1981).

Buckley, W. (1967), *Sociology and Modern Systems Theory*, Prentice-Hall, Englewood Cliffs, NJ.

Cain, M. and A. Hunt (eds) (1979), *Marx and Engels on Law*, Academic Press, London.

Carracciolo, R.A. (1979), 'Contradictions in the Legal System', *Archiv für Rechts und Sozialphilosophie*, 65.

Carrington, P.D. (1984), 'Of Law and the River', *Journal of Legal Education*, 34.

Chambliss, W.J. and H. Siedman, (1971), *Law, Order and Power*, Addison–Wesley, Reading, Mass.

—— (1983), *Law, Order and Power* (2nd edn), Addison-Wesley, Reading, Mass.

Clark, P.B. (ed.) (1972), *Compliance and the Law*, Sage, Beverley Hills.

Cohen, G.A. (1978), *Karl Marx's Theory of History: A Defence*, Oxford University Press, Oxford.

Collins, H. (1982), *Marxism and Law*, Oxford University Press, Oxford.

Coser, L.A. (1956), *The Functions of Social Conflict*, Routledge and Kegan Paul, London.

—— and B. Rosenberg (eds), (1982), *Sociological Theory*, Macmillan, New York.

Cotterrell, R. (1984), *The Sociology of Law: An Introduction*, Butterworths, London.

Cousins, M. and A. Houssein (1986), *Michel Foucault*, Macmillan, London.

Craib, I. (1984), *Modern Social Theory*, Wheatsheaf, London.

Crozier, M. (1964), *The Bureaucratic Phenomenon*, Tavistock, London.

Dahl, R. (1963), *Pluralist Democracy in the United States: Conflict and Consent*, Rand McNally, Chicago.

Dahrendorf, R. (1958), 'Towards a Theory of Social Conflict', *Journal of Conflict Resolution*, 170.

—— (1985), *Law and Order*, Stevens, London.

D'Amato, A. (1975), 'Towards a Reconciliation of Positivism and Naturalism: A

Cybernetic Approach to a Problem of Jurisprudence', *University of Western Ontario Law Review*, 14.

Delphy, C. (1984), *Close to Home*, Hutchinson, London.

De Michiel, Y. (1983), 'The Subjected Body', *Australian Journal of Law and Society*, 1.

Dewey, W. (1901), 'System', in Baldwin (1901).

Dworkin, R.M. (1967), 'The Model of Rules', *University of Chicago Law Review*, 35.

—— (1975), 'Hard Cases', *Harvard Law Review*, 88.

—— (1977), *Taking Rights Seriously*, New Impression with Reply to Critics, Duckworth, London.

—— (1978), 'No Right Answer', *New York University Law Review*, 53.

—— (1980), 'Law as Interpretation', *Texas Law Review*, 60.

—— (1981), Draft of *Law's Empire* circulated to graduate students, Oxford University.

—— (1986), *Law's Empire*, Beknap, Cambridge, Mass.

Edelman, B. (1979), *Ownership of the Image*, Routledge and Kegan Paul, London.

Ehrlich, E. (1936), *Fundamental Principles of the Sociology of Law*; trans. W.L. Moll, Harvard University Press.

Eisenstadt, S.N. (1968), 'Social Institutions', *International Encyclopedia of the Social Sciences*, 14.

—— (1985), 'Macro-Societal Analysis: Background Development and Indications', in Eisenstadt and Halle (1985).

—— and H. Halle (1985), *Macrosociological Theory*, Sage, London.

Elliott, P. (1980), 'The Organization as a System', in Salaman and Thompson (1980).

Emery, F.E. (ed.) (1981), *Systems Thinking*, Penguin, Harmondsworth.

—— and E.L. Trist, (1981), 'Socio-Technical Systems', in Emery (1981).

Engels, F. (1975), See Marx and Engels (1975).

Etzioni, A. (1971), *A Comparative Analysis of Complex Organizations*, Free Press, New York.

Evan, W.M. (ed.) (1962), *Law and Sociology*, Free Press, New York.

—— (ed.) (1980), *Sociology of Law: A Socio-Structural Approach*, Free Press, New York.

Farago, J.M. (1980), 'Judicial Cybernetics: The Effects of Self-Reference in Dworkin's Rights Thesis', *Valparaiso University Law Review*, 14.

Ferguson, R. (1984), 'Commercial Expectations and the Guarantee of the Law: Sales Transactions in the nineteenth century England', in Rubin and Sugarman (1984).

Feuer, L. (ed.) (1969), *Marx and Engels: Basic Writings on Politics and Philosophy*, Fontana, London.

Feiblemann, J. and J.W. Friend (1981), 'The Structure and Function of Organization', in Emery (1981).

Fine, B. (ed.) (1979) *Capitalism and the Rule of Law*, Hutchinson, London.

Finnis, J.M. (1980), *Natural Law and Natural Rights*, Oxford University Press, Oxford.

Fish, S. (1982), 'Working on the Chain Gang: Interpretation in Law and Literature', *Texas Law Review*, 60.

Fitzgerald, P. (1975), 'Laws and Systems', *Western Ontario Law Review*, 14.

Fitzpatrick, P. (1983), 'Marxism and Legal Pluralism' *Australian Journal of Law and Society*, 1.

—— and Hunt, A. (eds) (1987), *Critical Legal Studies*, Basil Blackwell, Oxford.

Foucault, M. (1980), *Power and Knowledge*, Harvester Press, Brighton.

Fowles, J. (1971), *The Collector*, Jonathan Cape, London.

Frank, J. (1949), *Law and the Modern Mind*, Stevens, London.

Fraser, A. (1986), 'The Political Architecture of Federalism', *Bulletin of the Australian Society of Legal Philosophy*, 10.

Friedenberg, A. (1971), 'The Side Effects of the Legal Process', in Wolff (1971).

Friedrich, C.J. (1963), *Men and Government*, McGraw-Hill, New York.

—— (1966), *Revolution*, Atherton, New York.

Froman, L.A. (1980), 'Organization Theory and the Explanation of Important Characteristics of Congress', in Evan (1980).

Fuller, L. (1969), *The Morality of Law*, Yale University Press, Newhaven, Conn.

Gadamer, H.G. (1975), *Truth and Method*, Sheed and Ward, London.

Galanter, M. (1974), 'Why the Haves' Come Out Ahead', *Law and Society Review*, 9.

—— (1981), 'Justice in Many Rooms', *Journal of Legal Pluralism*, 19.

Galligan, B. (1987), *The Politics of the High Court*, University of Queensland Press, Brisbane.

Gasking, D. (1960), 'Clusters', *Australian Journal of Philosophy*, 38.

Giddens, A. (1971), *Capitalism and Modern Social Theory*, Cambridge University Press, Cambridge.

—— (1984), *The Constitution of Society*, Polity, Cambridge.

Goodrich, P. (1986), *Reading the Law*, Blackwell, Oxford.

Gordon, R.W. (1984), 'Critical Legal Histories', *Stanford Law Review*, 36.

Gottlieb, G. (1982), 'Relationism: Legal Theory for a Relational Society', *University of Chicago Law Review*, 50.

Gouldner, A.W. (1960), 'The Norm of Reciprocity: A Preliminary Statement', *American Sociological Review*, 25.

—— and H.P. Gouldner (1963), *Modern Sociology*, Hart-Davis, London.

Gramsci, A. (1971), *Selections from the Prison Notebooks*, Lawrence & Wishant, London.

Greenawalt, K. (1977), 'Policy, Rights and Judicial Decision', *Georgia Law Review*, 11.

Habermas, J. (1979), *Communication and the Evolution of Society*, Heinemann, London.

Hacker, P. (1977), 'Hart's Philosophy of Law', in Hacker and Raz (1977).

—— and J. Raz (eds) (1977), *Law, Morality and Society: Essays in Honour of H.L.A. Hart*, Oxford University Press, Oxford.

Hamerow, T.S. (1958), *Restoration, Revolution, Reaction*, Princeton University Press, Princeton, N.J.

Harris, J.W. (1979), *Law and Legal Science*, Oxford University Press, Oxford.

—— (1980), *Legal Philosophies*, Butterworths, London.

Hart, H.L.A. (1954), 'Definition and Theory of Jurisprudence', *Law Quarterly Review*, 70.
—— (1961), *The Concept of Law*, Oxford University Press, Oxford.
—— (1977), 'American Jurisprudence Through English Eyes: The Nightmare and the Noble Dream', *Georgia Law Review*, 11.
Hay, D. (1975), *Albion's Fatal Tree*, Pantheon, New York.
Helmer, J. (1974), *The Deadly Simple Mechanics of Modern Society*, Seabury Press, New York.
Hindess, B. (1987), *Politics and Class Analysis*, Blackwell, Oxford.
Hirst, P. (1979), *On Law and Ideology*, Macmillan, London.
Hobbes, T. (1929), *Leviathan*, Oxford University Press, Oxford.
Hobsbawm, E.J. (1969), *Industry and Empire*, Pelican, Harmondsworth.
Hodson, J.D. (1976), 'Hart on the Internal Aspect of Legal Rules', *Archiv für Rechts und Sozialphilosophie*, 62.
Holland, R. (1977), *Self and Social Context*, Macmillan, London.
Holmes, O.W. (1897), 'The Path of the Law', *Harvard Law Review*, 10.
Honoré, A.M. (1975), 'What is a Group?', *Archiv für Rechts und Sozialphilosophie*, 61.
—— (1977), 'Real Law', in Hacker and Raz (1977).
Horwitz, M. (1986), 'Are Law Schools Fifty Years Out of Date?', *UMKC Law Review*, 54.
Hough, J.F. and M. Fainsod (1979), *How the Soviet Union is Governed*, Harvard University Press, Cambridge, Mass.
Hubbard, F.P. (1976), 'One Man's Theory', *Maryland Law Review*, 36.
Hughes, G.B.J. (1960), 'The Existence of a Legal System', *New York University Law Review*, 35.
Hunt, A. (1985), 'The Ideology of Law', *Law and Society Review*, 19.
—— (1987), 'The Critique of Law: What is 'critical' about Critical Legal Theory?', in Fitzpatrick and Hunt (1987).
Jenkins, I. (1980), *Social Order and the Limits of Law*, Princeton University Press, Princeton, NJ.
Johnson, A.C. (1966), *Revolutionary Change*, Little Brown, Boston.
Jordan, N. (1981), 'Some Thinking About "System"', in Emery (1981).
Kairys, D. (1982), *The Politics of Law*, Pantheon, New York.
—— (1984), 'Law and Politics', *George Washington Law Review*, 52.
Kamenka, E. (1966), 'The Concept of a Revolution', in Friedrich (1966).
Katz, M.F. (1986), 'After the Deconstruction: Law in the Age of Post-Structuralism', *University of Western Ontario Law Review*, 26.
Kelsen, H. (1970), *Pure Theory of Law*, University of California Press, Berkeley.
—— (1980), 'The Marx-Engels Theory of Law in Evan (1980).
Kennedy, D. (1982), 'Legal Education as Training for Hierarchy', in Kairys (1982).
—— and P. Gabel (1984), 'Rollover Beethoven', *Stanford Law Review*, 36.
King, B.E. (1963), 'The Basic Concept of Hart's Jurisprudence: The Norm out of the Bottle', *Cambridge Law Journal*, 1963.
Kinsey, R. (1978), 'Marxism and the Law: Preliminary Analyses', *British Journal of Law and Society*, 5.

290 *References*

Krislov, S. (1972), 'The Perimeters of Power', in Clark (1972).

La Nauze, J.A. (1972), *The Making of the Australian Constitution*, Melbourne University Press, Melbourne.

Larrain, J. (1979), *The Concept of Ideology*, Hutchinson, London.

Lasswell, H. and M. McDougal (1970), 'Criteria for a Theory About Law', *Southern California Law Review*, 44.

—— (1975), 'The Relation of Law to Social Process: Trends in Theories about Law', *University of Pittsburg Law Review*, 37.

—— and W.M. Reisman (1967), 'The World Constitutive Process of Authoritative Decision', *Journal of Legal Education*, 19.

Laszlo, E. (1972), *Introduction to Systems Philosophy*, Gordon & Breach, London.

Law, J. (1986), *Power, Action and Belief*, Routledge and Kegan Paul, London.

Lenin, V.I. (1976), *The State and Revolution*, Foreign Language Press, Peking.

Llewelyn, K. (1961), *The Common Law Tradition*, Little Brown, Boston.

—— (1962), *Jurisprudence*, University of Chicago Press.

—— and E.A. Hoebel (1941), *The Cheyenne Way*, University of Oklohoma Press.

Lloyd, D. (1973), *Idea of Law*, Penguin, Harmondsworth.

Lukes, S. (1974), *Power: A Radical View*, Macmillan, London.

—— (1977), 'The Phenomenon of Law', in Hacker and Raz (1977).

Luhmann, N. (1985), *A Sociological Theory of Law* 1972, Trans. E. King and M. Albrow, Routledge and Kegan Paul, London.

Macauley, S. (1963), 'Non-Contractual Relations in Business: A Preliminary Study', *American Sociological Review*, 28.

MacCormick, N. (1977), 'Challenging Sociological Definitions', *British Journal of Law and Sociology*, 4.

—— (1978), 'Dworkin as PreBenthamite', *Philosophical Review*, 87.

—— (1979), *Legal Reasoning and Legal Theory*, Oxford University Press, Oxford.

—— (1981), *H.L.A. Hart*, Edward Arnold, London.

—— (1983), 'Contemporary Legal Philosophy and The Rediscovery of Practical Reason', *Journal of Law and Society*, 10.

—— and O. Weinberger (1986), *An Institutional Theory of Law*, de Reidel, Dordrecht.

Mann, M. (1970), 'The Social Cohesion of Liberal Democracy', *American Sociological Review*, 35.

Marsh, T.G. (1975), '*Hedley Byrne & Co v Heller & Partners* Diagrammed', *University of Western Ontario Law Review*, 14.

Marx, K. (1909) *Capital* vol. 3, Charles Kerr, Chicago.

—— (1975), *Collected Works*, Lawrence & Washart, London.

—— and F. Engels (1970), *Selected Works*, Progress, Moscow.

Merton, R.K. (1938), 'Social Structure and Anomie', *American Sociological Review*, 3.

—— (1957), *Social Theory and Social Structure*, Free Press, New York.

Moore, J.N. (1968), 'Prolegomenon to the Jurisprudence of McDougal and Lasswell', *Virginia Law Review*, 54.

Moore, S.F. (1978), *Law as Process*, Routledge and Kegan Paul, London.

Munzer, S.R. (1977), 'Right Answers, Pre-existing Rights, and Fairness', *Georgia Law Review*, 11.

Nagel, S.S. (1965), 'Predicting Court Cases Quantitatively', *Michigan Law Review*, 63.

—— (1979), *Decision Theory and the Legal Process*, Lexington Books, Lexington, Mass.

—— and M.G. Neef, (1977), *The Legal Process: Modelling the System*, Sage, Beverley Hills.

Norris, C.G. (1985), *The Contest of the Faculties*, Methuen, London.

Oberdiek, H. (1976), 'The Role of Sanctions and Coercion in Understanding Law and Legal Systems', *American Journal of Jurisprudence*, 21.

O'Donoghue, N.D. (1973), 'The Law Beyond the Law', *American Journal of Jurisprudence*, 18.

Olivecrona, K. (1971), *Law as Fact* (2nd edn), Stevens, London.

Olsen, M. (1971), *The Logic of Collective Action*, Schocken Books, New York.

Opalek, K. (1971), 'Law as a Social Phenomenon', *Archiv für Rechts und Sozialphilosophie*, 57.

Oppenheim, F.E. (1961), *Dimensions of Freedom*, St Martin's, New York.

Parsons, C.T. (1949), *The Structure of Social Action*, Free Press, New York.

—— and E. Schils, (1982), 'The Basic Structure of the Interactive Relationship', in Coser and Rosenberg (1982).

Pashukanis, E.B. (1978), *Law and Marxism*, Ink Links, London.

Paterson, A. (1982), *The Law Lords*, Macmillan, London.

Payne, M. (1976), 'Hart's Concept of a Legal System', *William and Mary Law Review*, 18.

Pirenne, H. (1936), *Economic and Social History of Medieval Europe*, (transl. I.E. Clegg), Routledge and Kegan Paul, London.

Podgorecki, A. and C. Whelan (eds), (1981), *Sociological Approaches to Law*, Croom Helm, London.

Posner, R.A. (1972), *Economic Analysis of Law*, Little Brown, Boston.

Poulantzas, N. (1975), *Classes in Contemporary Capitalism*, New Left Books, London.

—— (1982), 'Law', in Beirne and Quinney (1982).

Pound, R. (1954), *Philosophy of Law*, Yale University Press, New Haven, Conn.

Prothro, J.W. and C.W. Grigg, (1960), 'Fundamental Principles of Democracy: Bases of Agreement and Disagreement', *Journal of Politics*, 22.

Quine, W.V.O. and J.S. Ullian, (1970), *The Web of Belief*, Random House, New York.

Quinney, R. (1973), *Critique of Legal Order*, Little Brown, Boston.

Raz, J. (1970), *Concept of a Legal System*, Oxford University Press, Oxford.

—— (1975), *Practical Reason and Norms*, Hutchinson, London.

—— (1979), *Authority of Law*, Oxford University Press, Oxford.

Riesman, D. (1951), *The Lonely Crowd*, Yale University Press, Newhaven, Conn.

Roach, J.L. and L. Gross, (1972), 'A Systematic Reconstruction of Parsons' Social System', *Archiv für Rechts und Sozialphilosophie*, 58.

Roberts, S. (1976), 'Social Control in Small Scale Societies', *Modern Law Review*, 39.

—— (1979), *Order and Dispute*, Penguin, Harmondsworth.

Ross, A. (1958), *On Law and Justice*, Stevens, London.

Roy, D.F. (1973), 'Banana Time, Job Satisfaction and Informal Interaction', in Salaman and Thompson (1973).

Rubin, G.R. and D. Sugarman, (1984), *Law, Economy and Society*, Professional Books, Abingdon, Oxon.

Ryan, A. (1987), *The Philosophy of John Stuart Mill*, Macmillan, London.

Salaman, G. and K. Thompson, (eds) (1973), *People and Organisations*, Longman, Harlow, Essex.

—— (eds) (1980), *Control and Ideology in Organisations*, Open University Press, Milton Keynes.

Sampford, C. (1975), *John Rawls' Theory of Justice*, unpublished thesis, Melbourne.

—— (1980), 'Some Limitations on Constitutional Change', *Melbourne University Law Review*, 12.

—— (1984a), *Law Without Order*, first draft of chapters 7 and 8 of *The Disorder of Law*. Selectively circulated, Oxford.

—— (1984b), 'Legal Systems and Legal Theory', in D. Galligan, (ed.) (1984) *Essays in Legal Theory*, Melbourne University Press, Melbourne.

—— (1986a), 'The Dimensions of Rights and their Statutory Protection', in Sampford and Galligan (1986).

—— (1986b), 'The Dimensions of Liberty and their Protection by Courts', *Law in Context*, 4.

—— (1987a), 'The Codification of Constitutional Conventions', *Public Law*, 19.

—— (1987b), 'Recognize and Declare', *Oxford Journal of Legal Studies*, 7.

—— (1987c), 'Asymmetry in Legal and Social Relations', *Archiv für Rechts und Sozialphilosophie*, 28.

—— (1988), 'Theoretical Dimensions of Legal Education: A Response to the Pearce Report', *Australian Law Journal*, 62.

—— and D. Galligan (eds) (1986), *Law, Rights and the Welfare State*, Croom Helm, London.

Savigny, F.C.V. (1975), *On the Vocation of our Age for Legislation and Jurisprudence* (1831), (transl. A. Hayward) Arno Press, New York.

Sawer, G. (1965), *Law in Society*, Oxford University Press, Oxford.

Schubert, G. (1968a), 'Judicial Behaviour', *International Encyclopedia of the Social Sciences*, 8.

—— (1968b), 'Political Ideology in the High Court', *Politics*, 3.

Schur, E.M. (1968), *Law and Society: A Sociological View*, Random House, New York.

Selznick, P. (1980), *Law, Society and Industrial Justice*, Transaction Books, New Brunswick, N J.

—— (1981), 'Foundations of the Theory of Organizations', in Emery (1981).

Shaw, W.E.H. (1976), *Marx's Theory of History*, Hutchinson, London.

Shiff, D.N. (1976), 'Sociological Theory: Social Structure of Law', *Modern Law Review*, 39.

Simpson, A.B. (ed.) (1973), *Oxford Essays in Jurisprudence (Second Series)*, Oxford University Press, Oxford.

Singh, C. (1986), *Law: From Anarchy to Utopia*, Oxford University Press, New Delhi.

Snyder, P.F. (1981), 'Anthropology, Dispute Processes and Law', *British Journal of Law and Society*, 8.

Stone, J. (1966), *Social Dimensions of Law and Justice*, Maitland, Sydney.

—— (1968), *Legal System and Lawyers' Reasoning*, Maitland, Sydney.

Sugarman, D. (1983), *Legality, Ideology and the State*, Academic Press, London.

Summers, R.S. (1977) 'Naive Instrumentalism and the Law', in Hacker and Raz (1977).

—— (1981), 'Pragmatic Instrumentalism', *Cornell Law Review*, 66.

Sumner, C. (1979), *Law and Ideology*, Academic Books, London.

—— (1983), 'Law, Legitimation and the Advanced Capitalist State', in Sugarman (1983).

Sutherland, E.M. and D.R. Cressy, (1974), *Criminology*, Lippincott, Philadelphia.

Tapper, C.F.H. (1971), 'A Note on Principles', *Modern Law Review*, 34.

—— (1982), *Computer Law*, Longman, Harlow, Essex.

Thompson, E.P. (1975), *Whigs and Hunters: The Origin of the Black Act*, Allen Lane, London.

Tigar, M.E. and M.R. Levy, (1977), *Law and the Rise of Capitalism*, Monthly Review Press, New York.

Trubek, D.H. (1977), 'Complexity and Contradiction in the Legal Order', *Law and Society Review*, 11.

Turk, A. (1980), 'Law as a Weapon in Social Conflict', in Evan (1980).

Tushnet, M. (1984), 'Perspectives on Critical Legal Studies', *George Washington Law Review*, 52.

—— (1986), 'Critical Legal Studies: An Introduction to its Origins and Underpinnings', *Journal of Legal Education*, 36.

Twining, W. (1973), 'The Bad Man Revisited', *Cornell Law Review*, 58.

—— and D. Miers, (1982), *How to Do Things with Rules*, Weidenfeld & Nicolson, London.

Ulmer, S.S. (1965), 'Towards a Theory of Subgroup Formation in the United States Supreme Court', *Journal of Politics*, 27.

Unger, R.M. (1976), *Law in Modern Society*, Free Press, New York.

—— (1982), 'Critical Legal Studies', *Harvard Law Review*, 96.

Vago, S. (1981), *Law and Society*, Prentice-Hall, Englewood Cliffs, NJ.

Veblen, T.B. (1925), *The Theory of the Leisure Class: An Economic Study of Institutions*, Allen & Unwin, London.

Verdun-Jones, S.N. (1976), 'The Jurisprudence of Karl Llewelyn', *Dalhousie Law Journal*, 1.

von Bertallanfy, L. (1972), 'The Quest for Systems Philosophy', *Metaphilosophy*, 3.

von Jhering, R. (1924), *Law as a Means to an End*, trans. I. Husik, Macmillan, New York.

Wallace, J. (1978), 'Current Problems in Legal Theory', *Monash Law Review*, 4.

Weber, M. (1978), *Economy and Society*, University of California Press, Berkeley.

—— (1982), 'Social Action and Interaction', in Coser and Rosenberg (1982).

White, A.M. (ed.) (1968), *Philosophy of Action*, Oxford University Press, Oxford.

Wilkinson, (1981), 'The Potential of Functionalism for the Sociological Analysis of Law', in Podgorecki and Whelan (1981).

Winch, P. (1958), *The Idea of a Social Science*, Routledge & Kegan Paul, London.

Wittgenstein, L. (1958), *Philosophical Investigations*, Blackwell, Oxford.

Wolff, R.P. (1971), *The Rule of Law*, Simon and Schuster, New York.

Woozley, A.D. (1979), 'No Right Answer', *Philosophical Quarterly*, 29.

Wrong, D.H. (1961), 'The Oversocialized View of Man in Western Sociology', *American Sociological Review*, 26.

—— (1979), *Power: Its Forms, Bases and Uses*, Blackwell, Oxford.

Young, J. (1979), 'Left Idealism, Reformism and Beyond', in Fine (1979).

Index

Index by Fiona Barr